EDGAR CAYCE ON

Religion,
Spirituality,
and Psychic
Experience

EDGAR CAYCE ON

Religion, Spirituality, and Psychic Experience

by Harmon Bro, Ph.D.

ARE
PRESS

ASSOCIATION FOR
RESEARCH AND
ENLIGHTENMENT

A.R.E. Press • Virginia Beach • Virginia

A.R.E. Press
215 67th Street
Virginia Beach, VA 23451-2061

ISBN 978-0-87604-545-9

Cover design by Richard Boyle

To my Duluth sponsors—
who saw the need for this book
and made possible the research behind it.

Table of Contents

Preface

Harmon Hartzell Bro, Ph.D. (1919–1997) was a psychotherapist, an educator, a writer, an ordained minister and an inspirational lecturer. As a young man, for more than a year, he lived and worked in the Cayce home and witnessed several hundred readings. That experience enabled him to come to know Edgar Cayce better than most individuals who have written about the Cayce legacy. Eventually, Harmon wrote his doctoral dissertation on Cayce's life and work, as well as several books about the Cayce information, including this one, *Edgar Cayce on Religion, Spirituality, and Psychic Experience.*

Harmon first came to Virginia Beach in 1943 as a young minister, just graduated from the University of Chicago Divinity School. He came to meet Cayce first-hand, as he was troubled that his mother, Margueritte Harmon Bro, had become involved with some "psychic or miracle worker" named Edgar Cayce. Harmon's mother had served as a missionary from China, where Harmon was born, and the idea that she had become involved with some kind of psychic caused him some measure of concern. However, what Harmon witnessed in Virginia Beach was very different from anything he might have imagined. An October 1943 letter to his wife, June Avis Bro, expressed his enthusiasm for a work that would transform his own life. That letter stated, in part:

Thin tubercular women, crippled boys, cancerous workmen, arthritic grandmothers knotted in pain – they all find healing. But that's only the beginning – what really happens to them is what has happened to Mr. and Mrs. Cayce, Gladys Davis [Cayce's secretary] and some others – they find that "there is a river" of God's love flowing about us all, only waiting to be tapped by humble minds. The real miracles at Virginia Beach are the radiant, transformed lives, the people who go away realizing that they can actually find God and know Jesus and live like it. They say, "I am my brother's keeper" and their lives show it. They say, "There is only one God" and all their friends feel it. Buddhist, Muslim, Jew, Catholic, Mennonite, Christian Scientist, Humanist, Presbyterian – it goes on like the "Ballad for Americans" – they all find what they are searching for in the work of the readings and Mr. Cayce.

Don't think this is all sober business. I've laughed till I've ached during these last few days. These people who live so very sincerely seem just as near to the bubbling fountain of humor as they do to the well of eternal life. Mr. Cayce is just as much fun in his readings as he is out of them.

I could go on darling. But it gets me too excited…

Harmon and June Bro moved to Virginia Beach and became close friends with the Cayce family and worked as members of the Cayce office staff. At the time, there was a tremendous increase in requests for Cayce's readings as a result of the publication of Cayce's biography, *There Is a River*, by Thomas Sugrue, which was followed by Margueritte Harmon Bro's own article in *Coronet Magazine* entitled "Miracle Man of Virginia Beach." Harmon and June listened to hundreds of readings. They had access to all correspondence, and they had the opportunity to repeatedly see how people's lives where changed by the Cayce work. Edgar Cayce died in 1945.

Harmon became interested in psychology and decided to continue graduate work. He went on to Harvard and then to the University of Chicago where he did a doctoral dissertation based on a study of the Edgar Cayce readings. For this dissertation, he coined the following phrase for Edgar Cayce: "a seer in a seerless culture."

From that time forward, Harmon had a wide experience in investigating psychics and psychic phenomena. His work in psychotherapy, coupled with his background as a minister, provided excellent additional material, insights and background information for this book. Rather than dealing with the Edgar Cayce readings on Bible passages, history or characters, Harmon has turned to the mental and spiritual readings that Edgar Cayce gave, and to a series of some several hundred readings on spiritual laws that Cayce gave on soul growth and personal transformation. In each section of this book, Harmon discusses Edgar Cayce on a specific spiritual law and then relates this to the field of physical research concerned with parallel types of psychic phenomena.

This book should be challenging to any person interested in psychic phenomena and spirituality. Highlighted against basic religious and spiritual principles, the varieties of psychic phenomena that are discussed come into much clearer perspective. Edgar Cayce saw psychic experiences as being related to the spiritual and soul nature of humankind. Religious professionals of all faiths should find this information helpful, as should individuals interested in their spiritual growth, as well as anyone exploring the possibilities of personal psychic experiences.

For some, this may be the first introduction to Edgar Cayce. "Who was he?"

It depends on through whose eyes you look at him. A goodly number of his contemporaries knew the "waking" Edgar Cayce as a gifted profession photographer. Another group admired him as a warm and friendly Sunday school teacher. His own family knew him as a wonderful husband and father.

The "sleeping" Edgar Cayce was an entirely different figure – a psychic known to thousands of people in all walks of life, who had cause to be grateful for his help. Indeed, many of them believed that he alone had either saved or changed their lives when all seemed lost. The sleeping Edgar Cayce was a medical diagnostician, a clairvoyant, the founder of holistic medicine, the most documented psychic of all time, and a devoted proponent of biblical lore.

Even as a child, on a farm near Hopkinsville, Kentucky, where he was born on March 18, 1877, Edgar Cayce displayed powers of perception which seemed to extend beyond the normal range of the five senses. At the age of six of seven, he told his parents that he was able to see and talk to "visions," sometimes of relatives who had recently died. His parents attributed this to the overactive imagination of a lonely child who had been influenced by the dramatic language of revival meetings popular in that section of the country. Later, by sleeping with his head on his schoolbooks, he developed some form of photographic memory that helped him advance rapidly in the country school. This gift faded, however, and Edgar was able only to complete his seventh grade before he had to seek his own place in the world.

By the age of twenty-one he had become the salesman for a wholesale stationery company. At this time he developed a gradual paralysis of the throat muscles, which threatened the loss of his voice. When doctors were unable to find a physical cause for this condition, hypnosis was tried but failed to have any permanent effect. As a last resort, Edgar asked a friend to help him reenter the same kind of hypnotic sleep that had enabled him to memorize his schoolbooks as a child. His friend gave him the necessary suggestion, and once he was in a self-induced trance, Edgar came to grips with his own problem. He recommended medication and manipulative therapy that successfully restored his voice and repaired his system.

A group of physicians from Hopkinsville and Bowling Green, Kentucky, took advantage of his unique talent to diagnose their own patients. They soon discovered that Cayce needed only to be given the name and address of an individual to be able to tune in telepathically on that person's mind and body, as easily as if Cayce and the other individual were both in the same room. He needed, and was given, no other information regarding any patient.

One of the young M.D.'s, Dr. Wesley Ketchum, submitted a report on this unorthodox procedure to a clinical research society in Boston. The story was picked up on October 9, 1910, by *The New York Times*, which carried two pages of headlines and pictures. From that day forward, people from all over the country came seeking help for every imaginable problem.

When Edgar Cayce died on January 3, 1945, in Virginia Beach, Virginia, he left well over 14,000 readings—documented stenographic records of the telepathic-clairvoyant statements he had given for thousands of people over a period of forty-three years. In 1931, Cayce founded the Association for Research and Enlightenment (A.R.E.) to research, document and disseminate his psychic information.

The readings constitute one of the largest and most impressive records of psychic perception ever to emanate from a single individual. Together with their relevant records, correspondence and reports, they have been cross-indexed under thousands of subject headings and placed at the disposal of psychologists, students, writers and investigators from around the world.

Today, Edgar Cayce's A.R.E. offers membership benefits and services, a bimonthly magazine, newsletters, publications, conferences, international tours, an impressive volunteer network, the Cayce/Reilly® School of Massotherapy, the A.R.E. Health Center and Spa, a retreat-type camp for children and adults, prison and prayer outreach programs, and A.R.E. contacts around the world. A.R.E. also maintains an affiliation with Atlantic University.

For additional information about the Edgar Cayce work, contact A.R.E., 215 67th Street, Virginia Beach, VA 23451-2061; call (800) 333-4499; or visit the Web site EdgarCayce.org.

~ ONE ~
The Puzzle of Psychic Experiences

Edgar Cayce looked at the waitress and grinned.

He had been through a hard day, handling part of the thousands of recent letters from all over the world that asked his clairvoyant aid on problems as varied as terminal cancer, early baldness, mental illness, a lost ring, unjust imprisonment, a missing soldier, whom to marry, and whether to begin a career in law. As usual, he had managed to answer personally only a small number of letters, explaining what he tried to do for people in his twice-daily unconscious trances, and why he gave priority to serious medical or psychological needs. To the rest of the letter writers he had been able to send only a form letter and a descriptive leaflet about his puzzling abilities, now the subject of investigation by a small research society that inquirers were welcome to join, if they wished to try his assistance. His secretary had made certain that all money other than membership fees enclosed in the letters opened that day had been sent back. Now it was time for him to relax.

His wife had just ordered clam chowder. They sat at a window table in one of the few restaurants operating in the winter along the ocean-front at Virginia Beach, Virginia, not far from his home. He was about to order the chowder, too, as were the present writer and his wife. Then Edgar Cayce caught an impression about the neatly uniformed young waitress, standing there with pencil and pad in hand. Perhaps because he was in high spirits after the day's work and enjoying the evening out (he always enjoyed good food, restaurants, and new places), he did something rare for him in his later years. In mischievous solemnity he said to the waitress, "You shouldn't marry him."

The startled waitress turned to stare at Cayce. "Do I know you?"

"Nope," he replied. "But you know I'm right. You shouldn't marry him. You've had two husbands already, young as you are, and you're about to make the same mistake on the third as you did on the last two."

Flustered, she murmured something polite and hurried to get the clam chowder. Returning with the soup, she looked hard at Edgar Cayce, who again smiled broadly at her, and she decided to trust him. "Look here," she offered, "I don't know who you are or why you said that, but I think you might be right. Do you know something that I don't know?"

"Maybe," he answered. "Why don't you sit down for a bit?"

She sat, while her other customers continued their leisurely winter dinners. "The part about the two husbands already was right," she began, "but I haven't made up my mind completely about the man I'm going with."

Everyone at the table laughed. Cayce had no business knowing about her two past husbands. The whole situation was ridiculous. But being around Cayce meant bumping into the impossible.

He told the waitress he had just felt an impression about her, and thought she might want to hear it. After a bit of bantering that she enjoyed, he began to speak seriously to her, pointing out that all three men were too old for her. She was being drawn to them, he explained, to get them to take the place of her father, who she felt had deserted her by divorcing her mother.

Her face grave, she nodded. "Right on the ages, though I never connected that with my father—especially because at times I have really hated him. Suppose you're right; how do I get over my father, anyway?"

Cayce was not flip. He spoke briefly about how hard it was to forgive and "turn loose of those who hurt us—hurt any of us," he added with a gesture that took in himself and the whole table. "But we all have to do it sooner or later, don't we?" His manner was gentle, playful, yet direct.

Customers were signaling her, and she rose slowly. "Can I talk with you sometime?"

"Sure," he responded. "You might want to visit our Tuesday night Bible class." It was unlike him to invite a stranger to the group that way. But he acted as he felt.

Visit she did, after getting the details when the check was paid.

She came only a couple of times, joining the dozen who had gathered weekly for several years in the library of Cayce's office, which adjoined his home, and who had now gotten to Matthew after starting in Genesis. But one of those Tuesdays she stayed to talk with Cayce in his little study crowded with souvenirs. When she left, her face was glowing.

"She's made it," he commented quietly as she left. He relaxed with a cigarette, and soon he was into the story of an earlier experience when he had also volunteered something to a stranger. The place had been the main street of a city in the Southwest, back in the days when he was using his abilities there to locate oil and raise money for the hospital he wanted to build, for those who sought his medical counsel. Standing on the street in front of a store, he had greeted by name a complete stranger who passed him. The man had nodded absently and then turned back to question Cayce, who admitted he had guessed the name through a psychic hunch. The stranger, a local bank official, took Cayce to lunch, and in the midst of the meal dared Cayce to write out the combination of the bank vault. Cayce scribbled it on a napkin and passed it over to him, electrifying his host and incidentally beginning a warm friendship that lasted for decades.

Can anyone read the life of a stranger as he would scan the contents of a book? Had Cayce made lucky guesses?

Was it also a lucky guess the writer observed nearly twenty years later when he sat in a crowded New York airport restaurant with a European psychic who asked the airport waitress, "How are your two grandchildren in England?" "Fine," was her answer as she started towards the kitchen. Then she did a double take as broad as classic farce. "Why did you ask about my grandchildren? Do you know them?" The psychic didn't. But when she produced from her purse in a nearby locker a photograph of the youngsters, he fell to chatting with her about the personal characteristics of each child, delighted with each new hit he made. He did so well, as the writer observed on other occasions, that the waitress actually forgot for a moment he was only a psychic. She was caught up in celebrating the youngsters with someone who so well appreciated and understood them – until she stopped in real bewilderment. "This is impossible," she objected. "Are you some sort of a relative?"

He wasn't.

Had it been a lucky or unlucky guess that led the third-grade schoolteacher in a Wisconsin town to phone the chief of police, shortly after a county-wide hunt for a murder suspect had been announced, and to report his name? She was a quiet, loving spinster, the soul of propriety in the town where only a few close friends knew she could "see" things. She counted the chief of police among these friends, as she did the present writer, and did not hesitate to tell the lawman that the wanted man was the father of one of her schoolchildren. She "saw" the story when she looked at the child that morning, even though the boy did not yet know of his father's crime. And she felt she had to call, for the safety of the child, because she was sure the father was dangerously ill of mind, though a respected citizen in the community and an absurd choice as a murderer.

She proved quite right. "Of course," she commented when the writer reviewed the case with her; her mind was obviously on the boy and not on a psychic feat.

Does this sort of thing go on in the human family? How long has it gone on?

Did Nathan act on a prompting of this sort when he challenged David for taking Bathsheba and having her husband killed? Were Paul's friends guessing when, "filled with the Spirit," they warned him not to proceed to Jerusalem and certain arrest, despite his Roman citizenship? What had Jesus seen about one woman's husband when he asked her for water at a Samaritan well?

Did Swedenborg "watch" a fire hundreds of miles away as it threatened his home, in the events recounted by that cautious philosopher, Kant, after he personally investigated them? Did that nineteenth-century one-man ecumenical movement, the Hindu Ramakrishna, really keep track of his disciples "physically" while they were on their travels? In modern times, did that buoyant and devout Catholic socialite and crystal-gazer, Jeanne Dixon, actually foresee the assassination of President Kennedy and try to warn him through friends, as she had personally warned Roosevelt of imminent death before him?

Edgar Cayce Sharpens the Puzzle

The frustrating puzzle of such events, the subject matter of parapsychology, would be easier to ignore were it not for the modern figure of Edgar Cayce.

What Cayce did not was not done in a corner.

He did not publicize his abilities nor make extravagant claims for them. But during his lifetime he was several times the subject of extensive newspaper investigation, as well as of a sensitive biography. His work led to the building of a small but accredited hospital and a modest liberal arts university, though both expired with the Depression. He became the center of a pioneering but knowledgeable national research society of hundreds of lay persons and a few professional people.

He kept records of everything he did, after the halfway point of his career, so that at his death he had a fireproof vault almost as large as his study, jammed with filing cabinets for fourteen thousand transcripts of his trance discourses, medical reports, engineering and geological reports, records of historical digs, and results of psychological studies of his abilities.

He made his records, his person, his work, his finances, his family, and his friends and relatives open to investigators who came from Harvard, Duke and elsewhere—just as the present writer came for study, midway in a graduate program at Harvard and the University of Chicago.

Cayce did not claim to explain his abilities, though he had theories by the end of his life. He did his work, and he tried to increase its helpfulness by following it up with letters, personal friendships, a few study groups, and an informal "Congress" of people he had helped, held every June.

He broke every stereotype used to discredit psychics.

Not other-worldly, he based none of his work on communication with the dead, though he was sure from his personal experience that the dead were not dead. Not worldly, he never went beyond making a good living as a photographer who built up several studios, and never managed more than a modest and irregular income from the research society that sponsored his work for the last twenty years of his life.

Not a showman, he turned down all offers from theaters, circuses, the lecture circuit, bureaus, moviemakers, and radio (the writer watched him

refuse a lucrative radio spot for a cereal company, not long after reject-
ing a trip to Hollywood pressed upon him by a star he admired). Not
a recluse, he took his ability straight to the countryside of gushers and
derricks when he tried to raise money for his hospital by locating oil in
Texas; he also went twice to the White House and traveled to nearly every
major city in the U.S. in a long lifetime of trying to discover how best to
use his abilities. Not a saint, he had a temper and moods that sometimes
strained, though they did not break, the mutual bonds of his family and
many relatives. Not a religious fanatic, he taught Sunday school all of
his life because he enjoyed it and was good at getting people to think
fresh thoughts about the Bible. Not a simple man, he was an inventor,
a prize-winning photographer, a storyteller, a green-thumb gardener, a
memorable though rambling lecturer, an organizer of regional church
activities, and an articulate letter-writer.

And through most of his life he was a walking museum of psychic
abilities.

When he once needed a label for the door to the room where he gave
free trances in early manhood, he called himself a "psychic diagnostician."
Yet it was clear to the observer at the end of his life that he did not think
of himself primarily as a chapter in the history of psychical research.

He knew psychics great and small, and once exchanged trance readings with the gifted medium Eileen Garrett, in which each described
from an unconscious state what each saw the other doing. He knew
the jargon of psychic circles well, from *apport* to *yellow aura*, and had a
personal experience to tell about each classic phenomenon from Ouija
boards to levitation. He met or was studied by investigators of many
kinds. And he encouraged his son to put on a New York radio program
on telepathy, as well as to submit materials from his records for study
projects at two universities.

But in his own mind and memoirs Edgar Cayce was no more a psychic
wonder than he was a hypnotic freak—and he probably spent as much
time in hypnotic trance as a busy corporation executive spends on the
telephone. He thought himself, as his dreams and diaries showed, a man
with a job to do—like others with other talents.

He knew he had a talent and that it was at its best a remarkably
good one. But he also knew it had missed a few times when he was

under heavy strain, and that he was using it on medical matters where a mistake could cost a life, however much he warned his trances were only "experiments" completely subject to medical interpretation and counsel.

He learned that his talent functioned best when he stuck close to his own religious norms. After reading the Bible or praying or teaching a class that discussed forgiveness, he was more fun to be with, more sure in his judgments about using his outrageous abilities, and more accurate and detailed in his next trance session. He saw his talent as operating lawfully, and that while learning the laws he had better try to help others more than himself, and to stick as close as he could to "the Giver of all good and perfect gifts."

What were the psychic dimensions of Cayce's talent?

The question sounds redundant. If Edgar Cayce was a psychic, how does one speak of the psychic dimensions of his talent?

He was a psychic. But it must remain an open question whether his chief talent, even in trances, was extrasensory. For anyone who heard a number of his unconscious sessions, Cayce's work was as much poetry as prediction, as much renewing as reporting. He dealt in lives. Facts were instruments, precise and important for him to retrieve. But the word *readings* only betrays how barren is American speech on this kind of phenomenon. Cayce's twice-daily trances had the character of encounters. They were speech between individuals, which made all parties liable to think hard about life or even God, at any point in the exchange, though the readings be on colonies or colonialism or colleges.

There was a danger in his work that the visitor did not always see. His family and staff well knew that there had been times when it had been impossible to waken Cayce from his trance state, when none of the hypnotic suggestions worked and when the passing hours were marked by his flagging respiration and pulse, until they ended up quite simply on their knees, asking for his life. Little was said of these occasions, and good spirits prevailed at the entry of Cayce's "reading room" twice each day. But something more than a performance, a feat, was undertaken, as they saw it; the man's life was on the line, each time. This meant that his trances were to them not only phenomena, however practical and concrete, but events that involved them all at their core. Not surprisingly, they distinguished carefully between what was said by the waking Cayce and what was said by "the Information," as they called the unknown source or sources of his trances, which they viewed as inclusive of Cayce, yet independent, intelligent, impersonal, and in keeping with biblical faith.

Still, Cayce was a psychic. Whatever else he might be remained a worse puzzle than his psychic ability. Perhaps his trances were wisest in the term they habitually used for him—a *channel* or *this channel*; it was precisely the term used in the same trances to describe everyone, as each fulfilled a vocation.

What were the dimensions of Cayce's psychic ability, the amplitudes and modes of his being a psychic channel?

He appeared to the careful observer to be psychic in three different states of consciousness: while he was awake, while he was asleep and sometimes dreaming, and while he was in a self-imposed trance—also sometimes dreaming.

In each of these states his ability could be observed to operate in three levels that shaded into each other: (a) a *natural* or relaxed level, (b) an *enhanced* or focused level, and (c) an *elevated* or visionary level. Observation gave little cause to expect flawless performance at any of these levels, but the impression grew on the observer that the chances of accuracy and helpfulness were better as Cayce entered the elevated level. Paradoxically, it was this level where evidential material was lowest, though breathtaking when it occurred, for Cayce seemed in this level to be primarily concerned with the life situation of a person or a group as they stood before God and their own souls.

Cayce Awake

Awake, Edgar Cayce had a flow of psychic experiences sufficient for an exceptional lifetime without trances. He had to work to keep down the waking flow of impressions, he said, so he could enjoy normal relationships without seeing too much. He invented card games, including a noisy one called "Pit" or "Corner the Market," which became an American staple for a generation, so that he could play cards, which he thoroughly enjoyed, without reading the minds of opponents who concentrated as they did in bridge. He told stories to strangers, more often than he engaged in real exchanges with them, partly because story-telling kept him from getting too close to them psychically. He kept his family and secretary and good friends and relatives close at hand, to be ready buffers between him and the problems of others, and to allow him to relax without stumbling onto unwanted material.

At the natural or spontaneous waking level of PSI, or psychic ability, he seemed daily to pick up moods and thoughts of those around him, both in direct impressions and in casual glimpses of auras. Because of this, Cayce was not easy to live with, as the writer can testify; one could never be sure of privacy of thoughts, or whether Cayce might react to someone's ugly mood that nobody else had noticed. He seemed to have swift effects on the moods of others, even of those who were quite used to him, as though he were broadcasting depression or love or joy to those about him. Working with him was like working in a tank of fluid where everybody's movement carried promptly to Cayce and might come bouncing back with doubled force or a special twist. Just policing one's thoughts and emotions became a daily task for those who, like the writer, attended the twice-daily trance sessions, because experience showed that the quality and helpfulness of his productions would vary, though in narrow compass, with Cayce's sense of the buoyancy and peace of mind of those around him.

It was not unlike the man awake to mention someone he thought would telephone soon or to observe that a certain letter or visitor was coming—and be correct. When several times he told his wife and the writer that he would never again see his two sons in the service, he refused to be consoled by encouragement—and his own death bore out his prediction.

Surprisingly, he showed relatively little natural ability to affect objects or induce healing, although these abilities of mind over matter (which researchers call *psychokinesis*, or *PK*) were thought to run in his family.

A few moments of earnest concentration could lift his waking ability to an enhanced level. Holding a letter in his hand as he dictated, he would pause to tell a secretary what the sender looked like, of whether there was hope for the case. Dictating to the writer's secretary when his own was overloaded, he stopped to tell the girl she was pregnant, and to mention the sex of the coming child; he startled her, for while she had just been to the doctor and confirmed the pregnancy, she had not yet told her husband. Cayce had found years ago that he could send for others to come to him by concentrating on them, but had also decided not to play around with his ability. Probably some part of his enhanced waking ability further showed in deft probing and equally deft listening when friends and relatives came to him for informal waking counsel, approaching him not as a psychic but as a good man whom they admired and loved. Not infrequently they reported, "He helped me make my own decision and it worked out right." A similarly unspectacular ability might be suspected as he sorted out and responded to serious seekers among those in his Bible class, where he would illustrate a point in imagery familiar to the questioner, or amplify a thought in an observer's own phraseology. In another kind of psychic event where only friendly interest appeared at work, he reported to the writer seeing a dead husband present in the room where he conversed with a widow.

What might be called *elevated PSI* came to Cayce more rarely while awake. But there were visions, such as that of a chariot in the sky and a man beside him in full armor, when he looked up from gardening; these sights he associated with the devastations of World War II, and they shook him severely. Like other earnest Christians before him, he cherished a few times when he thought he saw and spoke with his Master, recording these experiences in his diary notes. Less dramatic instances of possible PSI at an elevated level may have appeared when he prayed with great simplicity and sincerity until there was such deep peace in the room that nobody wished to leave, and one could see tears glistening in eyes across the room. Something like a current or field of goodness and promise seemed built up around him at such times, and not by eloquence.

Cayce Asleep

Even when Cayce went to sleep at night, he had his share of psychic happenings. Early in life, as the writer verified with townspeople from his boyhood home, he had discovered that he could pray over a schoolbook, touch down to an inward "promise" he had once received in a vision, and go to sleep with the book under his pillow. When he awakened, he would find a photographic image of the desired pages in his mind. It was not studying, but it was a help on tests. His classmates resented his unusual ability, enough to recall the feeling for the writer many decades later. Once in early manhood Cayce had done his sleep–learning so well, with the catalog of a book firm from whom he wanted a job, that at the end of his life he could still recite from it. Perhaps a similar process worked for him in his daily Bible reading, combined with lifelong teaching of the Bible, to help him to "know by heart" practically all of the New Testament and much of the Old Testament, as the writer repeatedly verified.

By concentrating and praying, Edgar Cayce seemed to have been able to affect his recovery from illness during his sleep, speeding up the re-cuperative process. However, during an illness of some six weeks, which the writer witnessed, he did not succeed in doing it, and his own trance given on the subject told him that taking a sulfa pill had slowed down recovery more than usual for him.

Dreaming at night, Cayce seemed to be as naturally psychic as awake. He dreamed of stock market quotations, of people he should see to increase his income, of greed among associates, of trips he would take—right alongside dreams, which a psychologist would recognize as normal accompaniments to daily living. But there were also enhanced levels of dreaming, in which he previewed step by step the development and loss of his hospital, or building up of study groups. Far more than most people, although still only a few times a year, he dreamed of detailed scenes and events from ancient times: Egypt, Greece, Israel. It had become his conviction that such dreams were accurate recollections from his own past lives, but of course such supposed retrocognition was impossible to verify. He had dreams of meeting on another plane some cherished relatives and friends who had died; to him, these experiences were real encounters, and the kind of psychic dream experience that many could have if they chose. Once he dreamed of his own death, with a physiol-ogy not unlike that of his final illness, and followed by his wife's early death—which proved accurate.

Elevated psychic experiences may have been present in a few dreams of his being summoned to another plane and charged with a work to do; but this too eludes verification. Real to him were a few dreams of meeting Christ – the more real because not pompous but built around themes of eating, talking, walking with "the Master."

Cayce in Trance

His trance activity also seemed to an observer to operate at different levels of psychic acuity. He had dreams during some of his trances, while busy exploring faraway scenes and talking in an unconscious state with some other part of his psyche; these were likely to be enhanced dreams, better focused than were many nighttime dreams—teaching him a lesson about laws of growth, or helping him understand the person for whom he was giving a reading, or taking him back to a vivid scene from another time in history, or showing him his own stages of consciousness while he was active in a trance state. But there were other dreams from the trance periods that had a visionary and elevated character, introducing him to the figure of Death, or reminding him of Christ.

In Cayce's trance speech itself, the level that appeared most like that of natural psychic pickup in daily life showed primarily in little asides, made before the start of the formal discourse of the trance. On medical or business or other practical readings Cayce was directed by his wife to locate the person in question, and after locating the state, the city, the street and address, he often astonished his listeners in Virginia Beach by commenting on the weather where "he" was, in Florida or Alaska, or by describing a sweeping view down an avenue in Denver, or by mentioning whether his subject were asleep or reading or talking, or feeding a pet. These observations proved so incredibly accurate and detailed, as they were investigated over the years, that they became one of the least controversial aspects of Cayce's clairvoyance. They were matched by equally brief asides as he gave "life readings," or vocational and character counsel, when he might mention items from the place and date of the person's birth—such as a dangerous storm that morning, or for whom the new baby was named, or how many boys were born in the U.S. that day, or whether there had ever been suicides in that county. In the same undertone he also went back through the years of his subject's life, starting from the present and running back to birth, mentioning times of severe stress, or noting, for example, that as a girl the subject had been "a very good little flirt," or pointing out just when the decision to become a teacher had been made. To the listeners these comments suggested eerily that everyone leaves somewhere in creation an impression of all he has been and done, which may be recaptured and reviewed by another intelligence, sometime, somehow.

Besides these comments, however, his readings contained occasional answers that seemed to originate from a natural level of ability—especially when he seemed impatient with a questioner's manipulative attitude. At such times the listener had the feeling that much of the waking Cayce was near the surface—as when he told one man asking about organizational activities to do some thinking for himself, lest he begin asking whether to blow his nose with his right hand or left.

In stately and rhythmic language, the content of most of Cayce's readings and trance experiences seemed congruent with enhanced psychic perception while awake or dreaming. In this formal vein the trance speech never failed to identify an individual for whom counsel had been given before, though the person might have sought aid decades earlier and have been forgotten by the waking Cayce and his secretary. In the same measured prose the unconscious source continued by describing where in the U.S. to find the best physician for surgery of nasal passages, or how to combine certain drugs that pharmacists claimed would not combine, or which colleges a given teenager ought to consider, or the face of a woman to be met some years hence and best chosen as a counselee's wife, or how a given subject remarked that one should "Work hard, play hard," or the tide and winds that would make the best day of the month to dive for a sunken treasure, or how to study the camber of airplane wings, or the form of government of ancient Inca civilization, or when World War II would end. The rhythmic-breathing Edgar Cayce touched upon these matters instantaneously, as though some cosmic file or computer were open to him on any subject where he was directed by an individual's need.

The trance source seemed simultaneously aware of how much could be effectively communicated to the listener. Repeatedly the trances began with the warning that only as much would be given as could be helpful to the person listening; not surprisingly, specialists got more technical subjects than lay persons, and conscientious listeners more encouragement and information than dabblers. While some kind of swift intelligence seemed to be moving through space and history and realms of present knowledge, not to mention commenting on happenings on planes beyond death, another part of whatever consciousness was at work in the sleeping Cayce was watching and correcting his secretary's spelling across the room, or answering typed questions before they could be read, or responding to unvoiced inquiries of a listener, or insisting on giving a reading for a seeker whose letter of application had not yet arrived.

The enhanced abilities of Edgar Cayce would have been striking if they had been separate bits, strung out as long lists of targets for him to shoot at. When, however, he produced an intricate medical diagnosis of every organ system of a body, or a picture of the layers in the character structure of a busy human being, or a comprehensive sketch of ancient Judaic schools of the prophets, or a discourse on the warring financial interests that precipitated the Depression, or a report on the fault lines that underlay a series of earthquakes, or the history of tensions in a marriage, or a review of real estate prospects in a resort town—the probability of each little hit was compounded by its linkage with the others in meaningful wholes, and the reflective observer could only gasp.

There were a few times when personalities identified themselves as speaking through Cayce as though he were a medium, usually at the end of a trance session; here, too, enhanced abilities seemed to be at work, but not of a "direct voice" type so much as mediated through the personality and vocabulary of Cayce—similar to the process which the writer eventually observed at work in the medium Arthur Ford. Generally, however, Cayce and his associates were convinced that discarnate personalities were not giving his readings.

There were also times when the language of the trances changed to a statelier and more urgent style, woven swiftly around biblical quotes and paraphrases. When this elevated level appeared in trance material, it was likely to be the freest of all in time and space. There might be comments on the details of a biblical incident, such as the walk to Emmaus, or predictions of the fate of nations, such as racial bloodshed in the U.S. or observations on cosmic events, such as the coming of Christ. But these factual items seemed incidental, noted as one might pick jewels from the wall of a cave one was hewing for safety, when jewels mattered little. For the elevated material had the strong note of urgency, which the scholar Rudolph Otto had noted years before about moments when one felt oneself close to "the Holy." Typically this elevated material came in the midst or at the end of readings, and once Cayce had moved into the heightened state, he was not likely to return to the more detached discourse in which most readings took place. What raised Cayce to the elevated level was not predictable; usually it was something very beautiful or very serious in the person for whom the trance was being given, but sometimes it could be a need in someone else in the room, or a note that had great meaning to Cayce the man. On very rare occasions the elevated material came in a style of severe warning and call to righteousness, as stern as from some archangel of old. Even more rarely, the voice of the sleeping Cayce fell to a hush, and he said, "the Master passes by," or spoke his encouragement "as from the Master;" yet this material was handled with great care to claim no special authorization but only that which every Christian may have as he prepares and attunes himself with the Lord.

In one trance session that the writer heard, a group of Cayce's associates and board members of his little psychical research organization were asked, "What will ye do with this man?" It was a question they found hard to answer, and in less than a year Cayce was dead, largely through self-imposed overwork of trying to give six, seven or even eight readings at a session where he formerly gave but one—hoping to catch up on the backlog of misery that thousands of letters brought him each week. The same reading warned that what Cayce did and said was nothing new and should never be made the subject of a "cult, schism, or ism." His listeners were not being asked to glorify Cayce, which his trances had uniformly refused to do (reserving for Cayce the most curt readings given, though also patient and with helpful encouragement). And his listeners were not being asked to promote an organization or movement, the historic response to an unusual phenomenon with spiritual dimensions. They were being asked instead what they would do with their own lives, with their own abilities; they were being asked to understand and use the laws they were seeing at work in Cayce, seeming to produce goodness and health and joy in people's lives.

What were those laws? Neither parapsychology nor any other psychology is in a position to explain what Cayce did for so many years. But parapsychology is at a point in its history when it is ready anew to consider theories, ready to consider even unusual programs for developing psychic ability, so long as they work. Perhaps it is time to see how the Cayce source explained the workings of psychic ability at various levels, and how it coached a group of determined lay persons for fourteen years in developing productive forms of such ability through personal development and spiritual growth in a series of tasks later written up as *A Search for God*.

~ TWO ~
The Cayce View of Psychic Experiences

In the view of the Cayce trance source, both psychic perception and psychokinesis were advanced forms of creativity.

Psychic activity was not a phylogenetic remnant from an earlier state in animal evolution. To be sure, humankind had once found psychic ability more readily available to him than now. But in that dim prehistory a human being was not at first an early anthropoid. A being was, according to Cayce's view, at first that part of creation called a "soul," given freedom to roam the universe and create playfully with the rest of the cosmos.

Some souls went their way, glorifying God by fashioning, through psychic energies, realms of beauty and form that had only to be intensely thought to be objectified. Other souls came upon the earth, tumbling its way through the heavens in its own plan of evolution through "kingdoms" of inanimate matter; these particular souls used their native force to interrupt and toy with earth's evolution, fashioning such beings as they wished out of animal forms and entering into those forms to enjoy the play of earth's energies. Earth's energies and beings were good, as Genesis says, and fashioned by God for earth's own becomings. But the exploring souls, like wayward children, used their great psychic energies to divert genetic streams, forming their own mutants and monsters, as well as sexual playthings. Eventually these particular souls—millions on millions of them – trapped themselves in the kingdoms of earth, until they forgot their full destiny to become co-creators with God, and sought rather to identify altogether with animal instinct and life cycles.

To enable the self-snared souls to discover the goodness of earth as God's creation without hopelessly distorting themselves and earthly evolution, they were given their own revolutionary process. They were programmed to reincarnate in successive human forms, interspersing human lifetimes with periods in other planes of specialized conscious-ness that built intelligence or beauty or kindness or courage or purity. In living as human forms, souls would find their great psychic energies more difficult to tap, available only under stiff requirements, so that they could do less damage than before. But their original energies were still there, awaiting human development to a level of shared goodwill where souls might again be trusted with so much power.

In this picture, the state of the soul in between-life planes of "death" was nearer to its true nature, and accompanied by more free psychic abil-ity, than the state of the soul in a human body, except when that human body was—as in the devout of God—bent wholly in service of its fellows. From this perspective the usual question of psychical research – "Does one survive death in some form that uses psychic powers for communi-cation and manifestation?"—was inverted to become "Does one survive birth—and with what measure of his true psychic powers?"

This cosmic mural from the Cayce source had elements to offend the common sense of the modern individual. The hard-won scientific truths of animal evolution would seem threatened by affirmation of a separate order of souls. The Church's long battle to affirm the goodness of life here and now would seem lost in a view that might lead to escapism from earthly reality. And the claim of great psychic powers as the birthright of souls would seem an infantile wish to think the individual as a god, despite the evidence of finitude that crowds upon human life.

Yet the Cayce source picture was not that souls had ever possessed all knowledge or all creative power in some psychic superstate. They had available to them as lasting knowledge and power that which came from use; whatever they tried to build in the universe became permanently theirs. They could draw upon an infinite set of patterns and energies that the Cayce source called "the Creative Forces" (and which others may have at times called archetypes); what they used responsibly became a permanent resource to them. He who truly and unselfishly loved became increasingly capable of psychic awareness of the needs and states of those he loved, as well as increasingly capable of giving healing energies and refreshment to those whom he sought to love. What a man did, he had. He who built unselfish beauty had ESP to find the materials of beauty, and PK to bring people and things into actual relationships of beauty.

The source of all human becoming, whether psychic or any other, was the Creative Forces—those pattern-giving and energy-releasing designs or fields that danced forth from the One, affecting two other orders that also proceeded from the One: mind and matter. Creation on earth was a blend of matter with mind (however primitive, mind was there in the tropisms and reactions of microorganisms, and in the polarities and valences of chemicals); but the driving, evolving Force was superordinate to either matter or mind alone and expressed itself through these.

The soul was a microcosm of the One, containing as potential in itself all the Creative Forces that God Himself had so far seen fit to call into being in creation. Each individual soul was made in the beginning with all other souls, and bore the character and drive of the Creator so faithfully as to be "in His image." Each soul was destined to be a full companion with God, creating and sustaining untold galaxies and planes of reality with Him, using its resources by free choice in harmony with the purposes of God, and relinquishing its wayward self-indulgence while remembering all it had been and done. As the Cayce information so often described the destiny of the soul, it was "to have the estate with Him which was in the beginning, and be conscious of same." In such a view the long journey of discovery and becoming of the soul was eternal gain not only to the soul but to God Himself, Who delighted in free and conscious companionship of souls. Yet God did not allow souls to turn from His ways forever, for after untold opportunities some who continued to reject His ways would be returned to their original estate with Him—without consciousness of what they had been and done, won and lost.

In this cosmic history-beyond-history, psychic ability was the birthright of every soul, part of its native creativity, ready to find and affect whatever the soul needed for its unselfish work in the universe. Psychic capacity was as native to the soul as were love, inventiveness, patience, integrity, wisdom; it came into play to serve these.

Psychic ability was not, from this perspective, a special prerogative for souls in planes generally called "after death," though disembodied "entities" might use telepathy to communicate, and PSI to precipitate invisible or visible forms by concentrated thought. A soul who had lived a miserable life or series of lives would find at death little to draw upon in his treasure house of activated psychic ability; he might be a psychic cripple on other planes as he had been but partly alive on earth. Quoting Jesus, the Cayce source often reminded, "As the tree falls, so shall it lie." The popular view of jumping out of bodies into a heaven of freedom of awareness and productivity had little support in this picture of psychic abilities of the living and the dead.

Nor was psychic ability a strange, occult force to be mastered by alignment with stars, by the aid of aliens, or by the invoking of principalities or demons or powers. Seeking along these lines might so concentrate the consciousness of a living person as to awaken for better or worse some realm of the soul's developed treasure of psychic capacities. But enduring growth in spirituality, growth in grace, growth in that Godly love that preferred others, growth in psychic ability on whatever plane of life or death was growth in high creativity with God.

A given level of psychic ability in a human being could not, then, be used as a measure of his present spirituality; for he might be presently misusing this resource as he might misuse any of his talents. To be sure, a high level of ability was an indication that somewhere, somehow, the soul had chosen and used the psychic resource for good—exactly as high levels of musical or mathematical ability indicated. But the proper spiritual question for anyone to ask was not "What have I got, in which I may take my pleasure?" but "What am I doing with what I have?" The latter question alone was the question of spirituality.

There was no point in seeking psychic development as a shortcut to revelations, a shortcut to potency with one's fellows, a shortcut to supposed higher realms. It was fruitful to seek "the higher gifts" of psychic abilities insofar as they emerged for each as potentials from the One Spirit who "divideth to every man as he wills," but such gifts should be sought and used in "faith, hope and love" or they would either disappear or actively harm the soul who sought them—even through mental or physical illness. The effort to force psychic manifestations by dissociation or trance would bring some results for almost anyone who tried these methods assiduously, for every soul had some psychic inheritance both built up and native. But the last state of those who forced psychic ability by these or any other methods might be worse than the first, if complexes from the unconscious were to rush into the void made by abdicating consciousness, or if unwanted discarnates took over the vacated personality.

Viewed against this life–and–death backdrop, what were the sources of psychic ability in everyday life?

Three Levels of Psychic Experience

According to the Cayce information, every soul in a human body had some measure of psychic ability as its birthright from creation, helping the person to protect his existence and enhance his daily function. This was a level of natural psychic experiences, awake and in dreams, which operated to warn an individual of threats to himself and his loved ones, as well as to alert him for opportunities he was constructively seeking and to guide him into better relations with other souls. Hunches, apparitions, premonitions, glimpses of auras, moments of healing energy and radiance, delicate outreach to affect other persons and things—all of these would stream into consciousness, through the unconscious; or stream out from the person, in greater or lesser degree depending on his awareness and use of them. These were the natural psychic happenings available to every soul whose life was not so cluttered with defenses and guilts as to block off the flow of such energies in the same way that he or she blocked off impulses to love, to play, to learn, to build.

In addition, each soul had ever available to it an avenue of psychic awareness and action that far transcended its own native inheritance. The soul might, when fears were laid aside and purpose and practice quickened it, reach beyond its natural endowment to the unspeakable riches of God, which flowed into consciousness to match the soul's resources. There were no necessary limits to psychic experience here, when need and opportunity joined with intent; as Jesus promised, "Greater things than I do, shall ye do," and "I will send you the Holy Spirit, to make known to you all the things from all times." Yet this overall process of joining the native resources of the soul to the resources of the "Universal Forces" was not capricious or magical, but lawful and developmental in its general outlines, however freely the laws might be transcended on occasion by divine mercy.

A soul might expect its natural psychic ability to be enhanced by Universal Forces, along lines of its past endeavors and application of talents. One who had served at healing of any kind, not just healing by prayer, might expect readier hunches on medications for a sick child. One who had been an explorer of new lands might expect clearer impressions of buried mineral deposits to appear in his psyche—more readily than one whose preoccupation had been with sculpture. One who had sought to awaken and coach talents in others might expect to find rising in him the energy to psychically affect others by direct action, more quickly than one whose gaze had been upon interpreting languages. In such a process the natural psychic endowment of the soul was enriched by the overlay of specially developed psychic talents; enhanced abilities followed naturally upon concentration, or preceded shock, either to widen the aperture of the soul's native abilities or to join the soul to the larger resources of the divine, or both.

These were the usual lawful forms of psychic ability. Yet under pressure of great need and great love, souls might at any time slip into harmony with the One so that treasures not yet fully earned might be poured into consciousness either as knowledge and insight or as force and outreach. In these elevated states, not only useful facts but the very bones of the universe, the pulse of creation might come into reach—as they did for Job of old when the vision from Yahweh broke upon him. Psychic ability then became not simply a useful tool for day-to-day operations, but an unforced awareness of "the way things are," and an invitation to work with the grain of life. Rightly seen, psychic ability was ultimately not a phenomenon of unusual perception, but part of the everlasting quickening and guidance called *faith*; it was not as a mysterious esoteric power but part of the overflowing goodness with humans called *love*. It was part of the eyesight of the soul into creation, part of the muscle of the soul to build and to give.

When and how was the soul given access to the largest psychic awareness? This was not for the soul to dictate, though it might build its readiness by use of chosen gifts and interests. What the soul could attempt, however, was to respond to a force like itself, loose in the universe, which "ever seeks its own." That force the Cayce source called "the Christ Spirit," or the "Christ Consciousness," originally given to everyone. Souls who had tangled themselves in the web of instincts and energies, in the panics of animal creation, might have great difficulty in finding their way out, great difficulty "in even beginning to think and love aright." But they would find as part of their natural psychic inheritance that they had an ability they need never lose; it was an ability to turn toward the Christ Spirit, which would awaken answering chords within themselves. This Christ Spirit was not a vague ideal or idea but a vital, living reality—a shaft of Light ever shining in a particular way, "the Light that lighteth" everyone if choosen. The key to the highest psychic ability, then, was the effort to attune the deep springs of personhood to the Christ Spirit, whose life and being served to reflect God to humankind, focusing the One to become believable and bearable for the confused consciousness. Over and over the Cayce source spoke of the "other Force," the "Christ Force," ready to "bear witness with the soul," to meet and strengthen and guide the natural divine energies welling up in an individual. This Christ Spirit did not take one over, nor make one an automaton, for that would frustrate the plan of creation for each soul to reach its own powers, its own full consciousness. And no soul's becoming was a matter of indifference to the Christ nor to the Father, for, according to the Cayce source, each soul was created at the beginning with its own unique inherent design, as original and delightful as each snowflake, and capable of glorifying God as could no other design. The primal energy and dream of each soul held the qualities of goodness and inventiveness and purity ascribed to the Godhead; but buried within this glowing field of forces was the soul's own seed of unique becoming—a seed that might predispose a soul to one kind of psychic gift or another, at various times in its journey.

The Process in Psychic Experience

But how did actual psychic experience come about in the consciousness of a human being? How did the events occur?

The imagery of the Cayce source was one of fields—fields exemplified by the dance of atoms in a bar of steel, or the play of energies in a thought, or the radiant presence of an angel. In this view, everything had its fields, and all fields had complex patterns of "vibration" of the One Force. When fields of the human psyche were set into phase with a given field "out there," then psychic perception or psychokinesis could take place, in greater or less degree—sometimes even by accident, or without conscious intent, as the phenomena of poltergeists suggested, or the phenomena of medieval saints having to be restrained from levitation, or the accurate perception of a future event in which the percipient was only marginally involved. As a rule, however, active desire and focus were needed along with attunement of fields to bring about psychic events. Accordingly, the Cayce source added to the word *attunement* a companion term, *service*, as the other necessary pole for effective psychic happenings: What one sought to use in service to enhance happenings. What one sought to use in service to enhance human life, and had trained the psyche to employ creatively, would meet the innate possibilities given by attunement and yield what are called psychic phenomena.

A wide range of variables might affect one's attunement with other event-fields. Important among these variables was the capacity to conceive what might be going on "out there"—whether in another person's mind, or in an event of geological importance. Psychic ability could operate most readily to validate or shape the actual flow of impressions from memory and the unconscious, or the natural flow of energies through habits and the unconscious into events, by way of psychokinesis. If the flow were barren, through disuse or inexpertness, then the heightening push of psychic force had trouble proffering itself. Accordingly, experience, application, cultivation of talents were essential to enlarge the range of options upon which creative psychic impulses might assert themselves. Service created the tunes for attunement; there was no magical way to attunement.

Yet psychic attunement to desired persons and events, or to object fields, had its methods and procedures, yielding greater or lesser effect in a given situation.

Essentially, these procedures were what the Cayce source described as "turning within," or "seeking the still small voice," or "asking God's help."

But in specific physiological terms, the Cayce source spelled out a chain of states in the fields that made up a human being, activated for effective ESP or PK. There was first of all an invisible force-field that surrounded and interpenetrated each cell of the organism; it was called "the real physical body" and guided the maturation of the body, as well as its healing. Psychic activity first of all took place in the real physical body, through seven vortices in this invisible but important field—vortices that Hindu tradition called *wheels* or *centers*. Each was associated with an underlying endocrine gland in the physiological body, which it affected in delicate ways, stirring the discharges which in turn stimulated the flow of sensory imagery into the central nervous system—yielding ESP impressions—or stirring a flow of vital energy which poured out through the vortices as PK. These responses in the physiological body to the invisible "field body" were not random but occurred in chains of interaction affecting the endocrine glands and both the autonomic and central nervous systems. The optimum interaction patterns within the body were those that the Cayce information called the Hindu term *kundalini*—a welling up of creative energy and focus in the person, a raptness that was also productive. Active in study, in work, in play, in loving, in suffering, in worship, this kundalini circuit was called into play in the best and safest psychic experience, and kept in alignment by the deep purposes or ideals of the person, as expressed in the choices made, insights reached, productive service rendered, and prayer and meditation undertaken. The channel for the best psychic activity was therefore kept clear and effective by all forms of creativity, not by isolated acts of incantation and concentration. Yet each individual had his own memories, symbols, hopes, and intentions placed that aided his best flow of kundalini.

The physiological side of psychic experiences, according to this view, was affected by whatever affected the endocrine gland function, or the function of the body's two great nervous systems. Injuries might cause sudden activation of unwanted and uncontrolled psychic abilities (as the history of psychic research well illustrated), while changes in endocrine secretion or medication might quickly affect or shut off an ability (as the history of the field again showed). Variations of rest, balance, anxiety, tension, and even diet might be traced in their effects upon psychic ability. And in the actual moment of a psychic flash, or psychic impulse sent outward, particular processes of breathing, posture, and even the invisible action of the force-fields of gems upon the body might be traced.

Over and over the Cayce material stressed the lawfulness of psychic happenings. Yet the total picture developed was not a mechanical one. The body, including its delicate chemistry and nervous impulses, was in the last analysis a servant of the mind. What the mind chose and held before itself either quickened the body as one tunes a musical instrument or let it go slack to psychic impulses. If the mind and will were turned toward shared creativity, whether of loving or of fashioned forms, then resources would be drawn from the soul to yield helpful psychic impulses for these tasks. If, in addition, that creativity were carrying on creativity built in some earlier lifetime in the soul's journey, then the psychic capacities could be expected to flow yet more freely. And if the person achieved purity of heart and enduring love toward his fellows, he could expect to find, as well, those times when the psychic stream overflowed its usual channels and to find himself supplied with whatever was needful for the situation, from the Giver of all good and perfect gifts. These were the basic variations in psychic performance, psychic gifts, psychic phenomena, according to this source.

Psychic Experience as Creativity

Ultimately, there was only one category that affected the development and safe use of psychic ability: creativity. This was not creativity in the narrow sense of novelty, nor self-expression, nor cleverness, but creativity in the sense of God Himself described as Creator. In this sense, creativity was the soul's entering into events in such ways that the consequences were other events, each working to fulfill the promise of shared human existence. Some creativity built persons—as when a parent held the hand of a fearful child, yet released it when the youngster was ready to venture on his own. Other creativity built forms—as when an artist painted a portrait, yet did not substitute a portrait for fully perceiving a human face, but gained sensitivity from the portrait for the next encounter with a real person. Creativity might be as little as not forgetting to water a garden, or as great as laying the foundations for a country in its constitution or its music. But in the real, shared work of giving and building, man could find his destiny, so like that of the One whose unseen image he bore. And reaching ever fuller stature in the long journey of the soul, each individual might increasingly expect to see, by what could be called psychic ability, "face to Face" instead of "darkly," and each might expect to bless and refresh and heal and renew another, through adding to the other's natural energy an energy that might be called psychic ability but was more often called "love."

The question of the conditions for effective psychic ability then became the question of the conditions of any creativity. What were, indeed, the essential conditions of humanity's creativity with one another and with the unseen co-Creator, the Father of all? In the view of the Cayce source, these conditions were what humankind has sought to understand and practice through the intricate forms and traditions of religion. Myths, symbols, dogmas were employed, however clumsily at times, to increase the attunement that individuals sought with the Source and to increase the service of others for whom that Source ever waited and whispered and reached. Likewise, rituals, initiations, processions, sacraments, codes and commandments were all developed to focus and train each individual's energies into alignment with the One, in a flow of new and abundant creations. This was the ultimate function of faiths, of traditions, of religious communities and covenants, according to the Cayce source.

Yet each individual had freedom of will, and godlike powers in his or her creativity. Each might choose, and often did choose, to dally, to become bemused, to squeeze for self instead of sharing with others the fruits of creation—whether in the primal Garden or in the ghetto. And each could use religious forms and modes to justify turning aside, to still doubts, to cover sins. So the quest for creativity, for the effective conditions of creativity must be made over and over again, in each generation, by each people, and at one time or another by each soul. For the altar that was supposed to reflect the glint of the One Light might easily be turned to reflect the face of the self-seeker.

Those who would develop safe and useful psychic ability, then, had no choice but to work upon religious understanding and practices, whether these were overt in theological propositions and duties, or covert in personal codes of honor and generosity. Each individual must sooner or later ask about her or his relation to the ultimate Source of good in life and in the lives of others, if that person was not to coast on the achievements of a past life, or to slide into narcissism, or to develop cruelty that seeks to force from others the secrets of life buried by personal concerns for power or possession or position or passion.

A group of Edgar Cayce's friends from Norfolk and Virginia Beach, who had together been attending various religious lectures and study groups, asked him one day in September 1931 whether he could give them lessons in spiritual development through his readings. They were especially interested in developing some measure of the astonishingly helpful psychic ability that each of them had experienced through Edgar Cayce's trances—whether that aid had been medical or vocational or financial or marital, or something as elusive as peace of mind and soul. Cayce agreed to try, and together they sought lessons from his source. Promptly they learned that the lessons would be given them only slowly, under the requirement that they live out and talk through and practice each lesson in turn. There was no pressing ahead for secret wisdom; it would not be given them. They learned that the life of each one would come under examination of his or her own conscience, and under the loving concern of others in the group, stimulated by terse but firm encouragement and coaching from the trance source. And they learned that they had to undertake daily disciplines of prayer and meditation at times they agreed upon, as well as less scheduled but equally important disciplines of guarding their tongues and thoughts, or sorting out their ideals, or training themselves to see the best in one another, in spouses, in strangers.

They did not secure lessons in breathing exercises, or in concentration, or in astrological charts, or in crystal balls, or in dream prognostication, or in visualizing, or in laying on of hands—although all of these were mentioned and some treated at length, while a few processes such as healing became the subject of yet another group and project. What they received were lessons in the major conditions of creativity, one by one. There were twenty-four such lessons, later published in two little volumes, which they wrote up together under the title of *A Search for God*, and a twenty-fifth lesson, which was to have been the start of another series interrupted by Cayce's death. They were required to develop their own insights on the themes suggested in the trances, and to write these up in their own words, not parroting Cayce. Likewise, they were to work out their own illustrations from daily experiences of growth, not simply quoting from the Bible or from biographies.

Their task was long, and some of the personnel of the group changed. But over the years the members each grew. And they developed a startling variety of psychic experiences, of each major type, and at each level of intensity—some awake, some in dream, and some in vision or in rapt state of prayer or meditation. They developed helpful energies for healing and blessing those who needed their aid.

They did not become great psychics. None became an Edgar Cayce. Yet the development of their own limited talents to full flower was for them a greater source of satisfaction than the showcasing of genius.

For they were seeing and working out for themselves the conditions of creativity, step by step, together. And they were finding rewards of joyful, productive lives that far exceeded the novelty of psychic manifestations alone.

In struggling to grasp the mystery of psychic experience posed for them by the work of Edgar Cayce, they opened in their studies the way to a yet greater mystery—the mystery of each soul's full partnership with God. This, rather than blinding revelations or marvelous signs, became for them the spiritual significance of psychic experience. The unknown opened into the known, the hidden into the near at hand, and the mysteries of phenomena into the mysteries of the gracious love of God meeting each man on his way.

What was the path they took towards a creativity that was psychic and more than psychic? Exactly how did they find phenomena linked with fulfillment, happenings linked with habits, impressions linked with intentions, PSI linked with the soul, service linked with the Servant?

∽ THREE ∽
Communication with the Dead

It was Sunday morning. Edgar Cayce stood before his adult Bible class in the white-steepled colonial brick Presbyterian Church at Virginia Beach. Some thirty men and women had gathered from neighborhood homes and from homes an hour's drive away. They were in good spirits, ready to think, to chuckle, to pray, to discuss, until time for the stately Presbyterians' worship at eleven o'clock.

Cayce had read aloud the Old Testament passage describing Elijah's contest with the priests of Baal, where each sought to prove whose divinity was real by bringing down fire upon piled wood. Though the events were extravagant, Cayce had read the account thoughtfully, without flourish, as one might reread a well-worn letter from a battlefield, touching upon familiar but prized details. When he put the Bible down and began to speak, it was to characterize Elijah's stubbornness and fierceness; he began with the man, not the phenomena of fire from the sky.

Picking up one detail after another from Elijah's life, Cayce sketched a portrait of a devout man, an extremist, a reformer. He made the brooding intensity of Elijah seem almost a presence in the room, until his listeners were responding, nodding. Those who knew Cayce well may have recalled the portrait of a bearded old prophet that hung over the filing cabinet in Cayce's study—a photograph that had won him a prize, though his subject was a weary derelict whom he had pulled off the street to pose for him at his studio in Selma, Alabama.

Elijah's faith was the subject; Elijah's extraordinary gifts and experiences were only workings of that faith. It was a perspective that Cayce always developed when treating the miraculous in the Bible, and one that appealed to his listeners; it suggested that God could still do mighty works in their lives, though the mighty works might be as unheralded as continuing to live with a drunken husband, or handling the shuffling walk of multiple sclerosis, or building an enviable reputation for integrity as a sales executive. Though Cayce did not refer to his own abilities as he taught the Bible, his own presence before his class was a quiet reminder that wonders were not yet over; he did not need to labor to evoke a biblical world where man and God were not strangers.

Midway in the period, Cayce paused to look intently at one side of the room; he pursed his lips and waited briefly. Then, as he continued, he spoke with a bit more emphasis, and a flash of a smile. His imagery sharpened, and none in the room had difficulty imagining the smoke from Elijah's fire, while the priests of Baal stared sullenly at their flameless logs.

The period drew to a close, the members greeted one another heartily, singling out the few visitors (such as the present writer) for welcoming handclasps, as well. The room held no sense of hidden secrets, no psychic mysteries; here Edgar Cayce had simply shared again a talent he had used every Sunday since boyhood: teaching church school. The class members had become part of a throng of hundreds in his home churches of Kentucky, Alabama, Ohio, and Virginia, and at stations of missionaries around the world; they were never gathered except in Cayce's imagination, yet were his own "people" and flock for half a century of service.

What had interrupted Cayce that morning? At Sunday dinner in his home, after his wife had served a tasty Southern meal, he told the writer and others present that he had seen a number of discarnates, "dead" people gathering from another plane to share in the class. They had seemed to him to file in and take the empty chairs at one side of the room, although a few had stayed in the back. The sight had not been new for him, because he felt he often saw these unseen visitors at his classes and at public lectures such as those he had given on alternate Sunday afternoons back in the days of the Cayce Hospital. They were similar to the unseen visitors he occasionally glimpsed in prayer moments just before giving his daily readings, as others sometimes reported seeing them in the room—entities that his trance source confirmed were often there, listening and sometimes hoping to speak or be noticed in some other way by the living.

What had caught Cayce's attention that morning was a feature of his visitors that he had seen a few times before: they were primarily Jewish, some wearing skull caps and shawls. He did not see their presence as a special tribute to him, for he felt that the dead often gathered where devout people studied and prayed together, to learn and grow as did the living. Rather he spoke of the visitors' sincerity and seeking, and noted the love of the Bible, of the Law, which often marked Jewish faith more deeply than the life of Christians. To Cayce, awake or in trance, Old Testament faith was not a story outdated by the New Testament; he made no gratuitous comparison between supposed Christian "love" and Jewish "legalism." Instead he viewed the entire flow of biblical history as a stream of men and women living on a high plane with their God—on a plane where the closeness of God made the differences of traditions, however genuine and important, seem less important than in the usual Sunday school homilies. Not church or synagogue but the promises of God to the people who covenanted with Him were the heart of the drama—perhaps a note more real to Cayce because he felt his own life and work intelligible only in terms of a promise given him when he was thirteen and often renewed in his quiet times since.

Some at the dinner table asked why the dead should wish to learn of the living. Did not they have their own places of study and worship? Were they not freer to seek and instantly attune to centers of spiritual teaching than when on earth? Responding along the same lines as his trance readings, Cayce commented that sometimes the dead needed the prayer-energy of the living to find their way; they often needed, he said, to be prayed for by the living who remembered them, as well as welcomed in the inward thoughts of worshippers in churches and temples. But also, it seemed to him, there were lessons that the living faced and grasped, because of their freedom of will and choice, in a different way than could the dead; the discarnates or entities could catch the force of these lessons by being present at times of spiritual searching, as a music-lover might learn of the structure and phrasing of a symphony by seating himself in the rear of an auditorium where an orchestra rehearsed.

Cayce's view of the dead learning from the living was the same as that independently developed by the Swiss psychiatrist Carl Jung, who did not, however, allow his observations to be published until after his own death.

How did Cayce feel about seeming to see the dead? He made no great fuss about it, for such glimpses had been a part of his life since boyhood. Yet he was interested in each experience and often prompted to tell a story. On this occasion it was his wife and secretary who told the writer their own story. They had heard Cayce go to the door one night and seem to greet somebody; the conversation they heard from their rooms upstairs had lasted well into an hour. Mrs. Cayce had even called downstairs when the visitor left, to inquire who had been there—receiving the incredible reply that it was a young woman they had known in another city who had since died, calling on Cayce to discover what had happened to her and what she should do next. The story was strange enough to bring forth humor at the dinner table, and yet nobody was prepared to say it was impossible. The writer in particular recalled it when one day later he and Mrs. Cayce both heard footsteps on the walk and the door opening to the library where Cayce sat. Yet inspection showed nobody there, only Cayce laconically remarking as he smoked a cigarette, that he had received a "visitor" whom others ought to be able to see if they looked a little harder on such occasions.

He had his store of experiences of the dead, both awake and asleep. There had been that night back in Selma when he and his wife had once tried a Ouija board—and decided never to do it again. Messages had poured through, including one that helped to locate the body of a drowned child. There were those visionary experiences that came shortly after he went unconscious for his trance, when he seemed to see himself following a thread of light through plane after plane of beings, whom he took to be souls who had died and were in various states of development or growth, from earthbound states to states of light and song. He had even noticed waxy shells, which his trance readings told him were lifeless remnants left behind to disintegrate, as souls on other planes went on their way.

More than once his dreams had seemed to put him in touch with his dead mother, who had greeted him warmly, and had even assured him that she would soon be reborn as the child of a loved relative. In a similar mood were those times when his mother or a treasured family doctor had seemed to break through at the end of his trances with a stream of happy exchanges and encouragement, as well as messages to other members of the living family; on at least one occasion those in the reading room heard such an exchange as one might overhear one side of a phone conversation, while Cayce himself recalled it all as a dream on awakening.

One man who secured hundreds of readings from Cayce over a pe-riod of six years was especially interested in life beyond death, which he called, after Ouspensky, "fourth dimensional" existence. In his read-ings, more than in any other collection in the thousands of Cayce trance sessions, there were perhaps a dozen times when particular entities whom he sought to reach—and felt he did reach in his own dreams and prayers—seemed to speak through the entranced Cayce. These entities were mostly his father and his mother–in–law, but also two business-men with whom he sought to work closely in earning money to found a hospital and university, as well as supposed philosophers and on two occasions characters from New Testament history. How much of all this was real, the waking Cayce, who remembered nothing of the content of his trances, could not specify. But the general sense of the closeness of the dead, in his trances as when he was awake, was a living part of Cayce's daily experience—even in that peculiar phenomenon, which he could not explain, of sometimes knowing instantly as he passed a cemetery the names and dates of those buried there, as he had often verified in detail. Asked about apports, or objects materialized for the living by the dead, he showed the writer a silver dollar that he kept in his dresser as a memento of a time at a campfire in the Southwest, when it had been given him as from his mother.

How typical of the world of psychic phenomena were Edgar Cayce's experiences of the dead?

They were similar to claims that stretched back to antiquity, enshrined in stories like that of Saul and the Witch of Endor calling up the ghost of Samuel and perhaps having a variant in accounts of the post–death appearances of Jesus. They had features in common with anthropological accounts of the shamans of Eskimo and Tibetan tribes consulting the spirits of the dead. They had parallels in China, in Africa, in Sweden; for whether self-delusion or reality, reports of communication with the dead have been as old and wide as humanity. But which of these reports bears up under modern scientific scrutiny?

Today's empirical study of the possibility of surviving death and communicating with the dead began with the earliest investigations of the Society for Psychical Research in England in the nineteenth century and continues with the present-day inquiry of American research centers into what is today called IPA, "incorporeal personal agency." An early investigation was a census of hallucinations, conducted among thousands of people in England and later repeated in both England and America, attempting to discover how people think they see the dead. Dr. Louisa Rhine's monumental file of spontaneous psychic cases, compiled at Duke University, also contains similar material, carefully organized as to whether the perception of the dead occurred awake or asleep, at the moment of death or later, with details of demise or not, and whether visually or in some other sense of presence and identity. The British inventor of research equipment, Tyrrell, completed a study of apparitions in the 1950's, at the same time the American sociologist Hornell Hart was reviewing the experiences of the living in seeming to leave their bodies in full consciousness—presumably as the dead might do. An American researcher, J. G. Pratt, devised a method for evaluating verbal material that might be presented from a supposed discarnate, by breaking it into items that could be scrambled and offered to various subjects for claiming, to determine the percentages of hits and probabilities. Karlis Osis of the Parapsychology Foundation in New York set about investigating what may lie beyond death by studying the deathbed reports of the dying, while Carl Jung, and more recently others working with LSD and terminal cancer, have studied the dreams of the dying, to learn how the unconscious represents the state and event of death. In his book, *Venture Inward*, Hugh Lynn Cayce reported on his study of cases of mental illness developing out of the attempt to contact the dead.

But by far the largest body of research on communication with the dead has been on the work of professional or amateur *mediums*, individuals who feel they have developed the capacity to contact the dead at will, whether in mental mediumship (receiving messages through impressions) or direct-voice mediumship (seeming to have their vocal apparatus taken over by other personalities) or writing mediumship (having their hands produce scripts while the medium is in a trance) or physical mediumship (seeming to materialize parts of bodies, produce unexplained objects, or manipulate instruments or temperature, or levitate the medium's body). The names of researchers on such phenomena vary from literate amateurs such as Hamlin Garland (who found mysterious buried crosses) to careful modern psychologists such as Gardner Murphy (who discussed the obscure poems of classical literature produced independently by a number of mediums whose combined messages added up to *cross correspondences*, an intelligent literary whole seemingly devised by one entity of the next plane). It was William James at Harvard who was so impressed by the mediumship of Mrs. Piper that he arranged for her to be sent to England for further study; it was the American investigator, Dr. Prince, who did the first thorough study of the St. Louis author, Pearl Curran, who claimed to be producing scripts in out-dated English by a discarnate named Patience Worth. Then that careful British worker, Carington, studied the controls of a number of able mediums in experiments, which suggested that these controls may have been complexes of the medium, showing the obverse of the waking or conscious personality. The controversial Bishop Pike reported his seeming contact with his dead son through American medium Arthur Ford, whom the present writer studied in repeated tape-recorded sessions.

Out of this immense total of man hours no agreed-upon conclusions have been reached. It would be safe to assert that all the investigators agree that some mediums, especially the famed Palladino, have at times produced obvious frauds, whether by conscious design or by the too-willing action of an entranced unconscious, and that such deception will remain a hazard so long as the research rests upon talented individuals, rather than upon processes demonstrable with a wide variety of subjects. There would also be considerable agreement that definitive experiments about survival of consciousness beyond death will have to wait until more is known about the modes and range of ESP; at present, every fact needed to document the reality of a discarnate can also be treated as a target for the medium's telepathy and clairvoyance, so the ESP and PK today account for too much, as raw effects, to allow the discrimination of perceptions and actions of discarnates from all other psychic happenings. Finally, there would be considerable agreement among investigators that ordinary people have experiences enough like those of mediums to suggest that communication with the dead, if it is ever convincingly established, will prove to be a widespread human phenomenon, and not one of professionals or of religious spokesmen alone.

While in a state of trance or altered consciousness, Edgar Cayce had much to say to many seekers on the subject of communication with the dead. His information insisted that anyone could learn to recognize signals or impressions from departed loved ones, although his information also developed a theory of post–death planes of growth where discarnates would be less and less easy to reach, in a full theory of reincarnation consistently maintained by this source as by such other modern psychics in trance as Arthur Ford and Eileen Garrett. Like many another source, Cayce's insisted that some entities slept for long periods upon dying, while others hung about the earth in bewildered attempts to carry on as always. Part of this source described how discarnates sought to aid the living in problems of health, vocation, business affairs, developing a philosophy of life, learning how to love in families, childbirth, and childcare; much of such guidance from discarnates came, it was suggested, in dreams and prayer periods.

However, the Cayce readings were slower than most psychic sources to encourage systematic mediumship with the dead. Partly this hesitance arose from the insistence that the dead did not know a great deal more than they did while living, for the subconscious of the living, it was claimed, became the functioning mind or unconsciousness when one died. But also there were warnings that dependence on the dead was as unwholesome as dependence on a living person, detrimental to both parties. One who clung to a discarnate loved one could hold back that soul from its proper development. Besides, the effort to compile experiences of the dead that could convince skeptics was hopeless; the state of death was so unlike that of earth consciousness that it would only be understood briefly by humans when they entered a "raised" state of consciousness and saw and understood things that words and analogies could not adequately convey. It was emphasized that one should not expect general revelations from discarnates, for the path of communication between the living and dead lay along the line of love, not wisdom. Finally, the Cayce readings never wearied of urging those who sought psychic development to make their attunement with Christ, not with the dead; in such attunement they would be brought spontaneously and safely to such experiences of the dead as they could handle in their own growth, without becoming inflated or distracted from the business of living. Moreover, in the spirit of Christ, the living would find themselves prompted to pray for the dead.

Both during Cayce's lifetime and afterwards, many individuals interested in the Cayce-source views of death and the possibility of communication past death have kept records of their experiences and have shared these in study groups and special seminars. Their preliminary findings have been varied, but with points of agreement. When unwanted interference occurred, as though from invasion or obsession by entities, there were typically several elements found together: hormone imbalance created by illness or injury affecting the circulation to endocrine areas, conscious or unconscious desire to solve life problems by shortcuts instead of sustained growth and service, conscious efforts at dissociation or intense concentration, and underlying currents of sexuality and hostility such as are commonly found in neuroses. On the other hand, seeming contact with the dead that did no harm to the living appeared most often in dream material, or in times of prayer and meditation, or in flashes of subjective light associated with meditative states, or in experiences where the healing of guilt and regret seemed as appropriate as in forgiveness among the living. Over and over the Cayce counsel seemed borne out, that the purpose in entering relationships governed their helpfulness in meeting the dead, as in meeting living; whether one sought a belonging of childish dependency or of mutual maturity before God was a critical element.

Belonging in Creativity

In the view of the Cayce information, the first religious question for those who sought to grow in any form of talent or creative activity together, including psychic activity, was the question of belonging. The kind of relationships one sought with others, and the outcome sought from such relationships, would influence every aspect of one's growth and daily life—from child rearing to business acumen, from constriction of blood vessels to romantic love, from the making of music to the character and scope of contact with the dead. The first chapter of the little training manual, *A Search for God*, was entitled "Cooperation." Its emphasis on creative ways of belonging to one another would not surprise a psychologist investigating the conditions of effective psychic experience, including possible communication with the dead.

Those who seek to find and share with the dead as a means of enhancing their own importance, by identification with supposed super-beings, might well make the same mistake as those who seek self-fulfillment among the living by identification with the famed, the glamorous, the powerful. Not fulfillment but emptying of personality results from such projection, Erich Fromm has so bitingly shown in his description of symbiosis, a relationship in which two needy individuals use each other but never really meet as human beings. If the psyche works to balance itself in encounters with the dead as with the living, then surely it would limit such uncreative encounters, or distort them in such a way as to bring the perceiver into mischief with himself so that he would have to grow up. Interestingly enough, this appears to be the path of many a journey through exercises to break the barrier of death: the seeker comes upon just enough evidential material to keep him going, but just enough sick material to put him into a jam with his associates and force him to insight. In his love affair with the dead he finds much the same outcome as the teenager with a crush on an older teacher: growth through pain of self-discovery.

Research might well bear out the contention of the Cayce source that the nature of belonging affects all psychic activity and all other creative activity. How far might the flow of helpful psychic impressions on business affairs be impeded by the desire to take advantage of others, even those in the same firm? How freely could the flow of healing energies occur if the concern were to impress or captivate the sick person rather than to set him free? And would not the issue of true and false, rich and shallow belonging affect the originality of the artist, the faithfulness of the priest, the independence of the adolescent among his peers, the security of the scholar, the judgment of the over-promoted consumer? How far was the Cayce source, stressing belonging as the beginning of creativity, anticipating the emphasis on group therapy in modern psychiatry, so sharply espoused by theorists such as Mowrer, writing on the effectiveness of Alcoholics Anonymous?

What the Cayce readings set forth in their insistence on cooperation appeared to be one of the oldest religious questions: the theological issue of covenanting. What does it mean to be a church, a Chosen People, a Buddhist Sangha, a Jewish kibbutz? How does religious covenanting differ, if at all, from joining a gang, identifying with the firm in one's gray flannel suit, merely absorbing the values of the establishment in politics and art and sex?

In the Cayce view, mere joining and membership, even enthusiastic identification with religious institutions and leaders and causes, availed man of nothing in itself, except to get man moving, and might be dangerous. Cooperation was rescued from conformity or escape to group identity only when it was covenanting with God. Over and over, the Cayce readings referred people to Exodus 19:5, where there appeared a saying used in many variations in the Old Testament: "If you will be my people, I will be your God, and will make you a peculiar treasure unto myself." The cooperation in a family, a store, a football team, a nation or a union of nations, had to be essentially of this order, however unverbalized the pledge.

Knowledge quickened in such covenanting could be trusted; seasoned in the community of the faithful, it might even be called revelation. But private visions pursued for their own sake, not bent to the service of others, would destroy a man's sanity and usefulness. "Knowledge not lived is sin" was a frequent refrain of the Cayce readings. The right order, then, was living relationships that produced workable truth, whether by psychic means or by reason or science, rather than truths that called for promotion by religious bands and societies. "Christ ye serve, and not a church," people were warned, while at the same time they were as strongly encouraged to join situations that were, in their living fulfillment of cooperation, "the nearest shadow of the heavenly home."

Might one count on psychic quickening to arise from group fields where there was a genuine cooperation before God? The answer offered was the biblical reminder "Where two or three are gathered in my name, I am in the midst of them"—to encourage, to disclose, to heal, to bless. By the real force of an extrapersonal energy and intelligence whom men called Christ, and whom they approached when they put on the loving "mind of Christ," natural psychic ability was quickened into enhanced and even elevated psychic ability. Paraphrasing Paul, the readings insisted in literally hundreds of passages that "His Spirit is ever ready to bear witness with our spirits"; something quite literal was meant, including psychic quickenings and confirmations as well as heightenings of psychokinetic energy, rather than a vague goodwill that made men feel glad they were well behaved.

But what was the nature of cooperation that might be called covenanting with God, whether in the home or marketplace or playground or lovers' hideaway? According to the Cayce readings, such belonging would involve man's keeping the two great commandments, which these readings never wearied of rehearsing: service and attunement.

Cooperation embodied service when it was infused with the right answer to the question so often repeated in these readings, "Am I my brother's keeper?" That right answer lay in the boldest possible assertion that though God was not exhausted by the human soul, He was Himself in and of the nature of the human soul. As one served his brother and blessed him, then, he did so to God Himself, not symbolically but literally. The Cayce readings often made this point by quoting Jesus, "Inasmuch as ye did it to one of the least of these my brethren, ye did it unto me." And they went on to add a stringent injunction, "Until you can see in each soul that you meet, though in error he may be, that which you would worship in your Master, you have not begun to live aright." The firmness of these assertions by the Cayce source was often a shock to the listener who had accepted such teachings as poetic injunctions, not as statements about the real divinity in his brother; listeners realized that if Cayce were here speaking the truth, then a radical form of loving others, even the enemy and, as these readings put it, "those who reject His way," would be demanded.

Yet the commandment of service was no call to sentimentality or indulgence, in cooperative belonging. One's responsibility was to meet each person where he was and then build him, lift him, strengthen him—

whether by prosaically bandaging his foot or by beseeching the help of angels from heaven for his stubborn temper. And cooperation could involve struggle, indeed would involve struggle if one took seriously the Christ way; each person who sought to learn cooperation would have to learn to "so live that you can look any man in the eye and tell him where to go." And each would have to develop that sturdy identity before God, which the readings meant when they said, "Every tub must sit on its own bottom." The ultimate goal in cooperation was the little phrase so central to the Cayce readings that it appeared in scores of prayers suggested for people to put in their own words and use many times a day: "to be a channel of blessings for others." The blessings were of course God's blessings. They would be what each could best give out of his resources, without depleting the giver to his damage; yet they would be fully creative events or happenings of a given moment, not stereo-typed blessings of giving away tracts or Bibles or holy sayings. Being a channel was not a matter of setting prim and self-righteous examples for others. "Don't just be good; be good for something," was the refrain of the readings in their continuous insistence on real creativity in every dimension of man's life—money, dance, governing, carpentry, lovemak-ing, ballgames, temple rituals. And who was the brother to be served? As might be expected, the Cayce readings defined this brother as the next one needing aid, needing respect, needing an opportunity, needing an opponent to fight him for his best self; the brother could not be defined by ties of kinship or nationality or religious bonds, although all of these ties involved promises and duties that must in their place be kept.

Yet service without attunement might be vastly ineffective, a mere do-goodism or even an unconscious using of others. For cooperation really to succeed, the persons involved needed to work together with the wis-dom known by the parts and cells of the body producing a whole out of millions of cells; they would need to work together as do the heavens in "unity, order, harmony." That kind of cooperation could require a know-ing that transcended the mind of man, though man must use his every wit to understand his brother. So there must be the effort to bring hu-man consciousness into alignment with an over-arching Consciousness greater than its own, that of the Father. As the Cayce readings used the phrase beginning "Inasmuch" with which to tag the basis for service, so they used a quotation from Jesus to establish what was meant by attunement: "I go to prepare a place for you"—in consciousness, said the Cayce source—"that where I am ye may be also." As man turned his deepest desire in the direction of Christ, and paused for definite acts of attunement, he could hope to best guide his efforts at service and to enrich his energies with energies beyond his own, from a source as high as God and as immediate as his own soul. Without such attunement, any soul could expect to slip into "selfish aggrandizement," the precise Cayce definition of sin. His supposed service could become seeking power for his own ends, rather than building for the greater good, and this was the root of evil in man, the perversion of his incredible capacities. However, attunement in cooperation did not mean shutting oneself away, any more than it meant pursuing a spiritual athleticism of self-development; one could seek guidance in the midst of a busy life of building and loving and serving. Indeed, without these active expressions, the channels for attunement in belonging would become clogged.

There was in the Cayce readings a remarkable absence of assurance that one could make it to a full human stature simply by belonging, by identifying, with the right groupings or traditions. To be sure, neither insight and truth nor love and productivity could be reached without full covenanting in groups—whether in the family or work groups or play groups or political parties. Yet there was no group or combination of groups that would allow the seeker to sit down and take his pleasure, not needing a living, provoking God. These readings offered no salvation by identification, and certainly not by inviting Cayce-ites. Nothing short of a living, daily process of "self-bewilderment in Him" could be trusted.

How might the right kind of belonging be cultivated, so that it might bear fruit in psychic experience and other creativity as well? The answer of the Information was painfully prosaic, beginning with "look to the little things." Helpful speech and deeds, kind thoughts, overlooking failures as far as possible—these were the basic disciplines of that belonging, which was covenanting with God. One had to learn to be mindful of attitudes in each situation, often by specific exercises, such as trying to go one day without a harsh word. Yet not negative controls but positive, outgoing attitudes were the prize; over and over this source insisted: "magnify the agreements," or "see that which is good in the other fellow," or "know that each is trying to build with his life what he sees of God," or "be interested in the other fellow if you expect him to be interested in you."

Training for full cooperation required more than hygiene of attitudes; it also required active commitments. This source urged individuals to join in groups of like-minded seekers, for Bible study, for sharing personal experiences and insights, for tasks of service to others, for intercession, for meditation. And such groups should not rely overmuch on the stimulus of meetings, for cooperation must be built daily. They should keep a regime, which each group worked out together, including daily prayer and meditation, as well as exercises of growing in cooperation, and should keep records of their growth as shown in dream and vision. Prayer, including prayer at the same times of day by the whole group, wherever they might be, and prayer by each group member for other members as well as for strangers, was constantly stressed, with the admonition that one dare not ask God to do for himself what he would not himself be willing to do for his brother. Out of such shared disciplines a group might slowly come to be "of one mind," and that mind the mind of Christ in some measure, so that cooperation could produce a group field for protection of the members, as well as for drawing in the "answering Spirit of Christ" to meet the needs of others.

Could cooperation be worked out in small groups alone? The Cayce source was insistent that cooperation, the right kind of belonging before God, must first be learned and practiced in small groupings. But it was equally insistent that the same spirit had to come in time to pervade the affairs of nations. Cayce's readings honored the idealism of communism, though not its expression in either Russia or materialism, and prophesied that in the long, long run new leadership for humankind would come out of Russia and China. At the same time, the readings set a high value on the American dream of freedom and just opportunity, promising that if more and more cooperation in economic and business and racial affairs took the place of selfish exploitation or defensiveness, America could continue to offer genuine world leadership. God was seen as a God of nations and peoples as well as of individuals. Yet the key to changes in the life of nations might often be found in the disciplined, determined growth of individuals in small covenanting groupings. The final outcome of the work of a few was potentially more than most people imagine, for the prayers of but a few who were in accord and lived as they prayed might—as with Abraham of old—save a city, or even a people.

Communication with the Dead and Belonging

The Cayce readings offered cooperation as the fully creative mode of belonging, which was the starting point for development of all gifts, even for building of people and cultures. Might cooperation actually produce enhanced communication with the dead?

A long-time associate of Edgar Cayce's married after his death and shared with her husband, an attorney, a rich pilgrimage of inward growth and outward service to fellow seekers. When her husband died, in his sixties, she was inconsolable, despite her studies of the Cayce ideas of life beyond death and her lifelong church work. Yet she continued in her occupation of librarian, guiding others to the volumes they needed; her manner remained cooperative, though the light was gone from her face.

On her first birthday after her husband's death, she awakened early and was keyed up, her mind once more on death because of the demise of a friend. She had dreaded her birthday, because her husband had always celebrated it in some imaginative way, with a gift and a trip together. Yet on this day she felt her apprehension lifting, and a sense of quickening that helped her morning chores and prayers. Later in the morning she found that a much-needed book was not in its proper place and was dismayed, for she needed it for a reader. Then a quiet and happy kind of closure occurred within her, as she was prompted to look in another section of the library, under a different though similar number. She found the book at once. A short time later another needed book was missing; promptly again came the sense of what number to look under. There she found it—and found something else, as well. She found an inward assurance, filling her with joy, that her husband, dead but a few months, had reached her through the barrier of death on her birthday and joined her in this helpful prompting—an act of service for others. His formless yet real presence seemed to make it known to her, in the recesses of her thought, that he was following through on the intent he had often voiced when living, especially during the helpless days of his last illness, when he repeated that he would like to aid her in her work.

From that moment in the library her spirits lifted, and she never again tasted the deep loneliness and depression that grief had brought her. She did not seek to make her husband her errand-boy in the library, as she had not while he was alive. This was not the way in which they belonged to one another, not the nature of their covenant. Yet she knew, in a certainty that she found difficult to describe to the writer, that the cord of love joined them through death as it had in life, and that each could give assurance and aid and loving energy to the other as it was needed. She prayed for him afterwards as naturally as she used to do before she got up to fix his breakfast. And she understood—she felt some portion of why the act of sharing and giving, in breaking bread together, had opened the eyes of two disciples after they had walked the Emmaus road with their unseen Master.

～ FOUR ～
Hunches and Impressions

Edgar Cayce shook his head. "I don't sleep on books any more," he told the writer. "I don't have to." He was enjoying the puzzled looks of those standing about him in his library, as he spoke of his boyhood knack for securing almost photographic impressions by sleeping on books—an ability featured in his recently published biography.

"Here," Cayce said, reaching for a book in the writer's hand. The volume was still in its mailing jacket, unopened, having just been received for review in the little Bulletin sent out regularly to members of the Association for Research and Enlightenment. The writer was to read the book and perhaps review it.

Holding the book in his hand, Cayce stood there thoughtfully. He did not attempt to read the mailing jacket or stare at the book. Then he said, "It's about a death, of a young woman and her husband, together. The father saw them, had a psychic experience of them at their funeral, and this book is about what he saw and what it meant to him." Then he handed the book back to the writer and walked off into the other room, completely sure of himself and as pleased with his brief, spontaneous performance as if he had hit a beautiful golf stroke.

The plot of the book, entitled *Lighted Passage*, turned out to be exactly what he had described. A young woman and her husband had been in an auto accident on their honeymoon. Her father, a Presbyterian minister and the author of the book, had seen what seemed to be her spirit leaving her body in the last moments of her life in the hospital, and her mother had seen the same, independently. Later, at the funeral, the father had seen both bride and groom in the back of the church, glowing in the responses of relatives and friends who had come to share the memory of the two young lives. Still later he had received impressions—some of which he described to the writer when he later came to Virginia Beach to visit Edgar Cayce—of the work of helping souls on planes after death, in which he believed his daughter and son-in-law were now engaged.

The flow of hunches and impressions seemed as normal to Edgar Cayce as the flow of incidental memories in the minds of others going about their daily work and play. He seemed to sense which cases most needed his help as he glanced over letters, and he quietly added certain appointments to his crowded schedule of readings, while he put off other applicants for months. Strange, however, were his experiences of scheduling readings in such a way that unusual diseases turned up in runs of a day or two. Was it Cayce's impressions about the seekers? Or had his unconscious somehow drawn to him four cases of polio at once, or six leukemia all in a couple of days, without another case of polio or leukemia for several months? While the cause of such baffling synchronizing might presumably have been that Cayce was giving the same medical information to each indiscriminately, medical follow-up reports made this explanation unbelievable, and the puzzle had to be left like so many puzzles about Edgar Cayce's abilities—unanswered.

His family and associates became accustomed to little events that betrayed Cayce's access to hunches and impressions: his hurrying home from a drive to meet a stranger whose visit had not been announced, his predicting a furnace breakdown, his "seeing" an opponent's hand of cards in a game, his encouraging a teenager to believe that his parents would forgive him, his detecting the marital troubles of someone in his office. The items were small, and none of them completely beyond the reach of coincidence. Yet, like his impression of the minister's book, they were often so accurate and prompt that the observer wondered whether there were a psychic flow in Edgar Cayce's mind as present as background music in a restaurant. The flow seemed to be there in his dreams, as well, when he glimpsed the coming of relatives, the availability of a house to rent, a forthcoming quarrel with a friend, the commotion of moving his belongings from one city to another, and the source of new interest in his readings at a time when he needed the income.

An unusual aspect of his waking impressions was his claiming to see "little people" or "elementals" around plants. He even teased his staff for not being able to see them in a colored photograph on the shelf in his library.

How typical of the world of psychic phenomena were the hunches and impressions of Edgar Cayce?

They made a piece with claims as old as the daimon of Socrates, which had told him of danger to himself and others. They were of the order of Samuel's abilities to locate lost animals, which led Saul to him in biblical times, and not too different from Paul's precognitive dream of shipwreck. To be sure, Cayce operated without the cards, thrown sticks, horoscopes or crystal balls used to enhance impressions by diviners, in the Orient, in Rome, in Asia Minor. But his quick impressions were not substantially different from those of others in modern times, as the writer has noted in observing Eileen Garrett sensing a publisher's response to a submitted manuscript, or Arthur Ford answering in Philadelphia a long-distance call from Tucson and correctly describing while wide awake the illness of a stranger's wife. Cayce's ESP in handling a book was not unlike another clairvoyant associating to token objects, which the writer has seen scores of times in the daily life of a European psychic, and not unlike the impressions of a certain housewife who touched a book and promptly gave an accurate description of the Harvard author's Russian ancestors.

What is the scientific status of such claims of daily-life ESP?

One of the striking accounts in early research was that of the English scholar of Greek culture, Gilbert Murray, who showed that he could pick up complete book plots, or even imaginary scenes, from the thoughts of his family and friends who devised tests for him. The novelist Upton Sinclair tried similar experiments with his wife, producing results impossible to quantify but striking in their content, while the French scientist Warcollier sent impressions across the ocean to telepathic receivers waiting to draw the objects intended for them. Drawings taken from the dictionary made targets for the landmark experiment by Carington, in which he discovered that when *elephant* was the target on Tuesday night, it also turned up with disturbing frequency on Monday and Wednesday nights in the calls of his unselected subjects. He drew from this experiment the idea of "displacement" of ESP onto adjoining targets, which led him to prompt Dr. Soal to do monumental research with two subjects. Hettinger and others reported on psychometry, or the use of ESP under the stimulus of token objects, and experimenters with LSD recorded periods of ESP accuracy on a variety of targets over a period of an hour or more, occurring in subjects who had taken the drug. But of course it has been the patient work of J. B. Rhine and his many associates that has brought the order of mathematical probability into research on hunches and impressions.

Today most researchers on ESP would expect, as Schmeidler has shown, that a given subject who shows regular ESP ability will disclose a pattern of psychic perception not unlike that of his sensory perception, corresponding to the style of his personality and the character of his bonds with a sender or receiver. They would not be surprised at occasions when the subject "knows he knows," or starts strong in his calling a given set of targets and grows stronger and stronger in his accuracy and conviction, finishing flushed but exhausted. They would expect the accuracy of a subject's hunches and impressions to vary from day to day, and in response to health and general spirits of the subject; they would be surprised to have high scoring continue for more than ninety minutes at a time in a given day. They would expect an individual who scored well on one type of psychic ability to show some ability along other lines, as well, though one or two main types of ESP might be prominent and the others sporadic; a total PSI endowment rather than a narrow skill would be their expectation in a given subject. They would look for one who could do well on cards to have helpful hunches in traffic, and for one who could identify a telephone caller by holding the telephone wire to know his unseen dentist bill, as well.

But these rudimentary pictures of a total psychic process are far from constituting a theory. To be sure, theories have been attempted, such as the provocative attempt by Toksvig to account for Swedenborg's abilities, or the field theory proposed in the Ciba Foundation symposium on ESP, or the theory that Carl Jung called *synchronicity*, linking mental perception with external events by way of intermediary archetypes rather than by direct causation—in a type of theorizing also followed by the knowledgeable Australian investigator, Raynor Johnson. But a generally convincing theory of hunches and impressions has not yet been formulated.

When Edgar Cayce turned to his state of altered consciousness for a commentary on hunches and impressions, he found a great deal of material. Part of the picture from his information was an insistence that "thoughts are things," as constant investment of psychological energy in a train of thought produced fields of force that acted autonomously upon the thinker and even upon others. The Cayce source appeared to describe something similar to what a psychiatrist calls a *complex* within an individual's psyche, but to give it external reality as well. Part of psychic experience, then, was brining one's own thoughts into phase with the thought forms of others, from which events and mental states might be inferred. Though such a cosmos might be difficult to imagine, thought had force and weight beyond that which modern man usually gave it.

The Cayce source paid much attention to the work of the psyche in dreams, as a source of psychic impressions and hunches, both those that were enacted in the dream and those to which the dreamer was alerted for later by his dream. In a bold assertion, the Cayce information went so far as to insist that nothing important ever occurred to a person without being previewed in a dream; however, the body of Cayce's dream material made clear that such previewing could be of tendencies rather than of explicit objective details. While the Cayce readings interpreted much dream material along lines similar to psychiatric interpretation, stressing the efforts of the psyche to right itself, or to interpret the meaning of each day's experiences, they also went on a tack not common in psychiatric dream study, insisting that a significant proportion of the dream material of healthy people consisted of psychic material—warnings and promptings and alertings that occurred in its biological and social spheres.

The flow of hunches and impressions might be impeded, according to the Cayce readings, by fear—and this became one reason for not overloading the psyche by making it guess on problems where reason and common sense, or hard study and practice, would suffice. Further, the flow would be more flexible and accurate in mirroring external events, or the thoughts of others, where there was a wide range of experience available to the percipient. One who wanted hunches on stocks ought to study and work with stocks; one who wanted impressions for medical diagnosis should work in healing. The quick mind could be quickened to do its job even better, while the stumbling mind had difficulty in securing impressions.

As might be expected, the Cayce information insisted that the purpose of seeking hunches and impressions had a marked effect on the flow of accurate material. Cooperating created a different mind set than exploiting, which would set the seeker at odds with his own best self—the natural source of his psychic impressions and expressions. However, it was also important to actively study the various types of psychic phenomena and the laws of each. Understanding through practice and understanding through study were the watchwords. Seekers were encouraged to read such volumes as William James' *Varieties of Religious Experience*, where James first outlined his concept of the *subliminal* before Freud popularized the term *subconscious*, and Ouspensky's philosophical *Tertium Organum*, or a practical little book on the role of suggestion in focusing awareness, entitled *The Law of Psychic Phenomena*, by Hudson. Ignorance was no aid to psychic development, in the view of the Cayce source.

Because of the living example of Edgar Cayce's gifts, scores of people during his lifetime, and thousands since his death, have tried to follow his prescriptions for developing a helpful flow of hunches and impressions in waking and sleeping states. In a series of experiments called "Project X," reported in his volume *Venture Inward*, Hugh Lynn Cayce had college students try, for several weeks, a set of intensive disciplines—all drawn from suggestions in his father's readings. The students went on special diets, fasted, kept journals of dreams, used specific gems, undertook daily projects of serving the handicapped or disadvantaged, set about intensive study of their own psychological makeup, helped one another to grow, and especially undertook regular periods of prayer and meditation, some at two o'clock in the morning. The progress of these studies on ESP tests was impressive, as the writer reported at a briefing session at Duke University. Since that time in the 1950's, the methods used have been generalized to fit intensive *project* groups, not unlike *sensitivity training* groups, which have been held as part of ongoing conference programs by the Cayce-oriented Association for Research and Enlightenment.

What have these many laymen discovered about cultivating hunches and impressions? They have learned to move slowly. The cases reported in *Venture Inward* of mental breakdowns among those who sought to rush into psychic experience taught many eager seekers that opening the door to the unconscious was easier than closing it. They have learned to wait upon the flow that comes normally, in dream, in waking impression, in prayer quickening, in the heightened sense of certainty that a job is done effectively. And they have learned to analyze themselves, their motives, their states of consciousness, their drives, their energies. For they have seen that many sources in the unconscious offer imagery and imaginative material, and that some of the most compelling material is not psychic but neurotic or even psychotic. They have learned that they needed to know themselves, if they were to deal effectively with the psychic flow in everyday life.

Self-Analysis in Creativity

In its characteristic approach to religion as the cultivation of the conditions of creativity in human existence, the Cayce source took as its second theme for study and practice the task of self-analysis. The second chapter of *A Search for God* was inscribed with the words from the ancient Delphic Oracle, "Know Thyself," and the Cayce source placed the topic ahead of such topics as faith, virtue, and the cross.

No psychologist suggesting the elements in cultivation of creativity would hesitate to give priority to self-knowledge. Studies of creative individuals, both by observation and by testing for fresh approaches to problems, have consistently shown that the more creative person is typically one who has access to his inward life, to his emotions and fantasies; he is one who can produce a fairly accurate appraisal of his own abilities and weaknesses. It was self-knowledge and self-acceptance at a deep level that the sociologist David Riesman suggested might be the essential distinguishing feature of the autonomous man, able to both conform and not conform to his culture—in contrast to the overadjusted or ill-adjusted person in his culture. And of course self-knowledge has been the hallmark of psychoanalysis, whether in its forms stressing free association and dream study or its forms stressing study of daily life behavior.

It would not be difficult to picture how the cultivation of safe and reliable hunches and impressions might require self-knowledge, though popular thought might guess otherwise. The overcontrolled or repressed person, afraid of his unconscious energies and promptings that manifest sexuality or hostility or power strivings, would be likely to shut off psychic materials along with other material, in the same process that makes him forget his nightly dreams, as well as claim to be a purely rational man, master in his own psychological house. On the other hand, the person who indulges in flights of fantasy, solves problems by wishing about them or making up omens and signs, or lives reactively rather than in disciplined responses, would be likely to drown psychic promptings in the flow of other material from the darker realms just outside of consciousness.

Further research may continue to show that self-knowledge affects all creativity, and not merely psychic power; self-analysis may prove relevant to marital success, to selecting the motifs for a painting, to holding a managerial post, and to controlling the diet. But as the psychologist Erich Fromm has pointed out, most moderns know how to spot and get attention for new noises or knocks in their cars but have little skill at recognizing and attending to noises or knocks within their own psyches.

By placing cooperation at the start of religious disciplines, Cayce's source had planted itself firmly in the biblical tradition of covenanting. But in turning next to self-analysis, it picked up a strand more central to the Indo-Aryan traditions of Greece and India. Where cooperation stressed the bending of the will to serve God in the other person, self-knowledge stressed the overcoming of ignorance. Yet while the two concerns have often seemed antithetical in the history of religions, they may also be complementary. Without a spirit of covenanting, knowledge and self-knowledge may become cruel or stultifying; yet without knowledge, without truth about human life and existence, the effort to help others may become trivial sentimentalizing or vicious totalitarianism in the name of a misconceived divinity.

While the novel concept of the soul might startle the Westerner approaching Cayce's materials on self-knowledge, the actual emphasis in these materials was upon the biblical "heart" of man—his intentions, desires, purposes. Evil, in the view of the Cayce source, was that which put a man out of relation with his brother, with his God; evil was that which made man separate—sin was selfishness. By contrast, man in his proper stature was seen in this view as having what Paul called "fruits of the Spirit:" patience, long–suffering, kindness. To undertake self-knowledge, then, was to learn to distinguish among the impulses in the heart of man.

In the Cayce readings there was no dualism of impulses. The evil in man was essentially misplaced good, to be treated as such and raised to higher levels of effectiveness. Man's animal passions were not in themselves evil, for animal creation was good; they were only dangerous to man if he limited himself to this kind of expression forsaking his larger inheritance of becoming, for then his very soul would rise up against him. Two inner processes, instead, in the Cayce readings, first contributed to putting man out of relation with his God, and did so today: fear and doubt. Human wickedness was real, as seen in cravings for lust, power, position, and possessions: but such drives could be harnessed for effective expression, if man would turn to the Source too often obscured by fear.

Why man's fear? In the Cayce perspective, fear could be either destructive or helpful. As "the fear of God," it could be "the beginning of wisdom," a limiting, focusing element, the instrument of education of the soul, the bearer of what Eastern thought calls *karma*. What a man did to himself or others that was wrong, selfish, or contrary to the loving force in his own soul became his problem, his panic, his puzzle. He was held to his wrong activity by his very fear and defensiveness about it—whether his problem be with knowledge, power, love, or things—until he finally learned to work properly with it. He might overcome such karmic fear by a slow path of suffering or by a swifter path of grace—involving insight, forgiveness, and giving to others at the very point of that fear. Learning about oneself, then, meant learning about one's evil and its cure, and discriminating among one's fears.

Yet the emphasis of the Cayce materials was typically on what was right with humankind, on those resources for good that could be studied under three ancient headings: body, mind, spirit.

Because for forty years the Cayce source was chiefly occupied with giving medical aid, it produced an immense amount of material about the human body, its systems and organs, its diseases and their cures. But on the subject of self–analysis, this source turned to the question of how the body could respond to the promptings of the soul and of

Christ. It urged a distinction between the "flesh body" of cells and molecules and the "real physical body" that existed as a field in and around the physiological body and that mediated impulses from the mind and from the soul. Because of the delicate interactions possible in the real physical body, one might see as a literal truth the claim that "the body is the temple of the Living God"—and it was a truth often repeated, together with the assertion that "there He has promised to meet thee." Man need not, and should not, try to leave his body aside nor rise above it, but rather should seek to quicken and use it for others, until it could respond to unseen impulses as though it were a finely tuned electronic instrument. By seeking "the mind of Christ," man could find "the Christ consciousness" present "in, with and under" his flesh—the last phrase being one that the Cayce source borrowed from Lutheran teachings of the presence of Christ in bread and wine, to suggest that holiness was possible in human bodies, not reserved for other planes.

As self-study meant investigating the body, it also meant investigating the mind. In the 1920's, when psychoanalysis was limited to sophisticated intellectual circles in the U.S., Cayce was insisting in his readings that exploring the mind through dreams, as they led one into awareness of the spirit, would be a central avenue for modern man's growth in spirituality. In dreams would be found the drives and impulses that made up desire in man. For the Cayce source, the mental realm in man was a bridge between his body and the soul, but not as a simple conveyor belt. The mind had formative power greater than most men realized, although that power was sometimes apparent in hypnosis (as in Cayce's own instance) or in crisis, or in the puzzling endowments of a genius. What man had first to discover about his mind was its dynamism, its tendency to construct whatever the person set before himself. What one thought about and sought, he became. Indeed, the heaven and the hell of the afterlife literally existed in one's own subconscious, no more, but no less. The key to the life of the mind, then, was the choice of one's ideal. Whether an ideal were animal cunning or selfless spirituality, the mind would try to build what was constantly set before it, though the building would be harder when the ideal was out of phase with the soul. In the view of the Cayce source, the living mind had two spheres always before it: the complex signals of the physical body and its interlocking cells mediating the outside world, and the rich signals of the ancient and godlike soul, infused with the particular qualities gained on the long journey of reincarnation. Each night, the mind of a man would struggle in dreams to reconcile and interpret the current events of his outward life with the deeper ideals and directions of his soul.

Yet the mind was not purely private. Because of its ability to be tuned like an instrument, it could be put in rapport with other minds and events, yielding an endless supply of helpful psychic experiences, where the mind was in harmony with the individual's own developed talents and soul. Because of its psychic powers, the mind was an active system, affecting the universe with its every reflection; over and over the Cayce source insisted, "Thoughts are deeds, and may become miracles or crimes," depending on how mental energies were used. To find religious parallels with the emphasis of the Cayce source on constructive powers of the mind, one would have to turn to Jesus' morality of intention, where thinking adultery was ultimately the same as doing it. Or one would have to turn to the "right mindfulness" of the Buddha—if the mind were set aright and properly fed, it would lead man out of his suffering.

Finally, according to the Cayce readings on self-discovery, there was need for study of the soul—a structure that had little stature in modern religious reflection in the West. The approach to the soul should not be made, in the view of this source, from what man might produce in one lifetime that could endure. The Cayce picture, which seekers were invited to verify through dream and vision and quickenings in daily life, was of a soul that dated with other souls from the beginnings of creation. Every man on the street was millions of years old, in his essential being, however far from the surface that essential self might have been driven by his actions. Every man on the street was inwardly a veritable universe, staggering if one could visualize it.

According to the Cayce source, when God made the human creature, He gave to each as a soul treasure every pattern of creativity found as yet in creation; the Cayce term for them was *Creative Forces* or *Universal Forces,* and the readings used these terms as synonymous with *God Himself.* God was not just another *Person doing things;* He was in some sense *Doing Itself,* the unspeakable creativity working itself out in all things and planes and realms, whose extravagance and brilliance were graciously shielded from individuals except in visions such as the one that overpowered Job. But God was no blind principle of evolution, either, as people had found in the swift intelligence and loving, personal responses of the Christ, or of their own souls. Each individual could make what she or he willed of the body, through lifetime after lifetime, for its destiny was given unto the self. And each might turn the mind in directions beyond counting, for it was a great storehouse of abilities, and could bring what the heart was set upon, if not at the expense of another or personal integrity. But the destiny of the soul, said the Cayce readings, was with God. The proper end of the soul was not past finding out, but only God could establish whether an individual soul were reaching its opportunity or betraying it.

Where would an individual turn to learn about the soul? Would he or she seek some special tradition, books, teachers? The Cayce source did not belittle these resources, but it placed an astonishingly heavy emphasis on what could be known in self–study, when conducted in prayer and disciplined meditation: "All that ye may know of God is within thyself." Very often, too, the Cayce source quoted from the last speech of Moses to his people, in Deuteronomy, where Moses told his hearers not to send over the sea or into the heavens for the word of truth, since the Law could be found within, "in thy mouth, in thy heart." Openings, disclosures of God, were every individual's right, not limited to prophets, priests, founders or reformers. If one sought to find her or his own soul, sooner or later it would be found, and its Author, as well. For both were of the realm that Cayce called *force*, using the term synonymously with *spirit*. So conceived, force was not a higher realm detached and floating above matter and mind, but the infusing, activating, directing and striv– ing quality found everywhere in matter and mind. To be spiritual was not to discard matter and mind; this was impossible, though one might indeed discard a body by dying. To be spiritual meant to become more perfectly aligned with the essential quality of this force, with the One Force, which poured forth from itself all Creative Forces. This formative word or pattern–giving element in the Godhead was to be given flesh in each person's real daily life, not alone by moral propriety within cer– tain established limits but by being alive, productive, a full child of the Creator, a light within the Light.

Tracing out the body, the mind, the soul were the essential tasks, then, of self-knowing. The method was to be not merely introspection but experiment. An individual was best known, in the view of the Cayce source, not by what he or she had, but by what he or she could give. No course of study alone could reveal this potential; a person had to act, to serve, to love, to dare, if the self was to be known. While in action, as this source so often urged, one could "step aside and watch self go by." One could examine his effect on others, to see whether in truth they were "glad to see thee come and sorry to see thee go"—a devastatingly simple criterion of spirituality. The evil that one saw and bemoaned in others could also become a useful tool for self-understanding, insisted the Cayce readings, since such annoying traits were irritating because they were in the beholder—precisely the psychoanalytic concept of projection of rejected unconscious material. One's mistakes, errors, and failures could be food for study, as well, because they could disclose laws at work and show the mercy of God in his tempering of the soul: "Whom the Lord loveth he chasteneth." Yet the ultimate resource for self-understanding was not an achievement but a gift—the quiet prompting of the soul. As one slept or awoke, worked or paused, the soul could be trusted to bear its witness with the "still small voice that convicts, convinces," and to bring its everlasting promise of goodness, in oneself as in another.

Could self-analysis actually affect the flow of psychic hunches and impressions in daily life?

A young English teacher, much taken with Cayce's readings on psychic ability, set out to awaken his own abilities. He concentrated his thoughts, tried special methods of breathing, fasted, studied his dreams for evidence of psychic awareness, meditated, prayed, used candles, took ESP tests, read books about psychic phenomena, joined groups interested in the psychic realm, and went among psychics. Still, his impressions were sporadic, his hunches hardly reliable. He worked harder at his teaching, spent much time with his students, tried to improve his school and his church and community. His psychic awareness improved a little. But he knew that if there were anything to the Cayce picture, he was far short of his potential for reliable promptings.

He attended séances, he tried automatic writing, he sought to bring out the psychic abilities of others, and he talked with researchers such as the present writer. But his experiences were still few. Finally, his family problems drove him to psychoanalysis, a step that humiliated his pride. With his analyst he began to face crippling patterns within himself that he had only dimly glimpsed before. He worked on hundreds of dreams, and he kept his religious sensitivities alive through his religious painting, an avenue that always awakened deep and good currents within him. He became so absorbed in his growth toward balance and wholeness through analysis that he forgot about psychic abilities.

But then the hunches and impressions began to come in dreams, in visions of the dead, in nudges about the affairs of daily life, in seeing auras, in experiences of healing within his Episcopal church life. Without any dramatic turning point, he reached the time when he could sit down and take inventory, discovering that not a day passed without helpful psychic impressions to meet his increasingly effective work as a teacher, and his efforts as a husband and father.

What had changed? Like Peter of old, had he been required to study himself until he could distinguish within himself Satan and rock, the voice from "flesh and blood" and the voice from the Father?

~ FIVE ~
Auras

Thirty people were crowded onto couches and folding chairs in the library adjoining Edgar Cayce's home, part of the frame building housing his offices and files. Although some had come to Virginia Beach from as far as California, nearly half were from points in Virginia. All were in a mood of expectancy, and in good spirits, though most were also self-conscious. It was a Saturday morning in early June, part of the long weekend called the annual Congress of the Association that sponsored Edgar Cayce's work. Cayce was going to read their auras as he did each year at this time.

Most of those in the room had received trance readings from Cayce. Some had even received scores of readings, on medical problems, vocational problems, spiritual ideals, business problems, and influences from past lives. Some had shared in the readings for a study group. But even those most familiar with Cayce's work felt a touch of apprehension. What would Cayce see, wide awake and looking at them? It was one thing for them to come under the inspection of his altered consciousness while he was in trance and speaking impersonally. But it was something else to have him inspect them, wide awake, and describe the fields of force that he, like so many psychics before him, reported he saw in patterns of shapes and thrusts and colors. From these auras, as he had shown in Congresses for some years, as well as from informal moments with those close to him, he seemed to discern the quality of a person's life at

various levels. Would he warn of illness? Would he hint at marital infi-
delity, which a couple had so far concealed from others and almost from
themselves? Would he find an outer shell of spiritual talk covering self-
righteousness? Or would he mention a hidden talent, so far overlooked?
Or growth of soul that was permanent gain? Everyone knew that Cayce
did not expose people in front of others in these sessions. But they also
trusted him to indicate something of the truth he saw as prominent for
each. So they spoke nervously with one another, chatting of little things
and then lapsing into introspective pauses. Had Cayce asked around
the room, just then, he might have received fair readings from each one
about himself, as the responses to his comments would shortly show,
when individuals spoke here and there with evident depth of feeling.

Cayce explained briefly that he could see only what he could see and
report it. Like so many other aspects of his abilities, there was much
about his seeing auras that he did not understand. But he knew that
others had found this experience helpful, so he would try it for them.
He kept the mood gentle, often playful as he went around the room for
nearly forty-five minutes, making certain that laughter protected people
from feeling too exposed.

To a woman who had been in and out of hospitals for several years,
he described colors and shafts he saw in the region of her lower body
and assured her that the surgery recently undergone had done its work,
with no relapses coming (and the months that followed proved him correct). For a doctor he described the colors and patterns that conveyed to
Cayce a sense of intense energy; then he added with a laugh, "But you
should never run for political office, for you will surely lose." (Though the
doctor came from a family of social philosophers, he had no intention
at that point of giving up his practice for politics; yet within a few years
he ran for a state office—and lost.) On around the room Cayce went. He
saw a field of golden yellow around one person whom he described
as outgoing, helpful to others. He saw an intense blue over the head
of another and reported that she always meant what she said, that she
was a person without guile. To another he mentioned the little crown
of white, almost like the headpiece of a bride, which to him meant that
her prayers and meditations were reaching "unto the throne" and beginning to change her whole life and feeling about herself. To a young

housewife he reported a divided field, almost like an egg with two yolks, which suggested to him that she had not yet resolved the tug between home and career but that she was making it. For a young student there were flecks of grey for disappointment and some patches of angry red for frustration that needed to be worked out. For a middle-aged man there was a swirl that warned of a potential ulcer if he did not revise his attitudes and diet. For a gray-haired woman there was an indication in green that she would find peace and self-expression in gardening. On he went, speaking of health, travel, friendships, money, faith. As he spoke, people responded with comments indicating that in most cases they had some idea of what he was describing—at times a very clear idea—or facts to report that delighted the room and wreathed Cayce's face in smiles. Some shook their heads in bewilderment but promised to think about what he had said. Those whom the writer interviewed later produced considerable corroborative detail. It seemed that in at least some instances Cayce's psychic abilities awake had been as accurate and helpful as when he was in trance.

How like the experience of others were Edgar Cayce's glimpses of auras? They appear to have been of the same order as those that prompted medieval artists to paint halos around saints, or led observers of Loyola in prayer to insist that there was a light around his head. Whether a similar phenomenon may have occurred to the disciples of Jesus on the Mount of Transfiguration is problematic, as is the question of the energy field around the quaking shepherds, which made them see light on the night of Jesus' birth. But there are abundant anecdotal reports in contemporary Western biographies of psychics to suggest that some phenomenon actually occurs under the name of *auras*.

Although the subject was studied in the early days of psychic research by a German investigator and by an Englishman named Kilner who worked on a filter to enable ordinary percipients to see the aura, the phenomenon has been less studied than most other forms of psychic experience. This is unfortunate, for it may hold the clue to a number of processes to which it has not yet been connected by experiment. Were the strokings or "passes" of Mesmer in early days of hypnotism a process of affecting the aura of the subject, as Hugh Lynn Cayce suggested from his research on hypnosis? Is the meeting of aura fields an important part of healing by laying on of hands? Are there fields of force similar to auras, which inhere in objects and account for object reading or psychometry and perhaps even for some forms of hauntings, as well as for part of the healing effects of shrines and holy places? The area of auras should not be too difficult to investigate, for it is one of the most familiar experiences of gifted subjects, as the writer observed in studying a number of noted psychics from the U.S. and Europe, as well as a number of gifted but unknown subjects.

An excellent beginning on such research has been reported by Shafica Karagulla, a physician with credentials in neuropsychiatry. With the aid of a foundation grant, she spent several years seeking out individuals on both sides of the Atlantic who could see auras, and then developed a clinical procedure with several gifted subjects. Her reports in *Breakthrough to Creativity* make an intelligent whole that appears to confirm and extend what the writer and others have observed in individuals such as Cayce. Her best subjects saw the shapes and colors of several different interpenetrating fields around the individuals on whom they concentrated; from these fields they were able to make remarkably accurate medical diagnoses of individuals with glandular ailments, as well as of other illnesses. Particularly interesting, in the light of Cayce's claims about the real physical body, were the reports of her subjects that they saw distinct vortices in the auric fields of subjects, located in areas roughly corresponding to what Cayce called "centers." Dr. Karagulla's reports of how individuals could be seen to draw energy from other fields or to give energy or to change the quality of others' energy corroborate the tentative reports of those who have worked with the Cayce ideas on auras, as have her studies of force fields associated with certain gems.

The Cayce source produced considerable material on auras and related fields of force, over the years. Individuals were sometimes encouraged to look for auras or were told that they had always seen them without recognizing what the colors and patterns meant. The workings of auras were closely linked to the operation of the kundalini centers in seven areas of the body, and some were advised to wear specific gems in the area of one of these centers to heighten and focus psychic ability—provided that their bodies and lives were in good balance, and their purposes for psychic experience creative rather than exploitative. An instrument using crystals to enhance the seeing of auras was described for manufacture. The impression left by this material was that all such procedures could heighten abilities developed in past lives more readily than initiate new psychic ability in one who had previously tried to use it.

Along with psychic perception in dreams, those who have worked in small groups with the Cayce materials since the early 1930's have placed the seeing of auras and their interpretation as one of the most helpful and safe forms of psychic perception for most people to try. Starting with impressions about the aptness of an individual's clothing and colors, one might seek in a relaxed yet attentive way to imagine and respond to various fields of color about another, especially while the other was concentrating and trying to express himself. For many people, areas and hues of color would eventually begin to appear in the mind—and very often be similar for several independent observers of a speaker or per-forming musician or one conducting healing services. Over the years few have shown the ability to see fields at will as did Edgar Cayce, although some who have grown up accepting auras as natural seem to be able to do so. So far, none has been reported who saw auras as Cayce appeared to do in trance state, when he described level on level of color from an individual, together with associated symbolism that constituted an "aura chart," and which have in a number of cases been painted according to the instructions of the readings, for study and for use as an aid to attune-ment and the strengthening of ideals by those who secured the special readings. These charts might carry such symbols as the all-seeing eye, the sunrise, the cross, the lotus, which might also appear in the individual's life-seal as described in Cayce's life-readings—incorporating themes from the best choices and experiences of an individual's past lives. But the aura charts were less representational, more purely esthetic in their dependence on tongues of color shading into one another.

Is it possible for ordinary people to learn to see auras? Could such impressions guide a mother on the degree of illness of her child, or a foreman on the disturbed state of an accident-prone employee, or a physician on the location of an infection (as the talented healer Ambrose Worrall reported to the writer and recounted in his biography, *A Gift of Healing*)? Are processes involving the aura incorporated in such sacra-ments as baptism, confirmation, ordination, and extreme unction – not to mention the force fields in the communion elements? Has the ancient practice of crossing oneself, or the threefold gesture of Moslem piety, some basis in affecting the outreach of one's aura to another, as in all gestures of prayerful blessing? Fortunately, the literature of LSD research affords cases of apparent inspection of such fields for brief periods, mixed in with accounts of imagery that seem more like sensory overloads; new approaches to the study of auras may soon be found, including correlating the color material in dreams with other impressions of color about individuals dreamed.

Out of the reports of many persons in prayer groups, AA groups, therapy groups, sensitivity-training groups, it has begun to appear that at least one factor in seeing auras is important: the percipient must look to see what is really there in the person being observed. To do this, one must look with an open mind and receptive attitude, relatively free of the constricting force of his or her own conscience, standards, ambitions, and evaluations, except insofar as these may sensitize him or her to matching concerns in the other person. One needs to have a conscience structure, a value system, which enlivens personal perception but does not cramp or dictate it. What would such a conscience be like?

Conscience in Creativity

The third area of religious concern that the Edgar Cayce source identified as essential to consider in creativity was the general area of conscience. The Cayce source headed the third lesson in *A Search for God* with a question, "What Is My Ideal?"

To link the psychic perception of auras, or any other targets, with conscience structures would seem arbitrary only to someone not familiar with the abundant literature linking sensory perception to the selective attention and image-making processes of the unconscious. The famed Rorschach tests with inkblots or the less well-publicized but equally dramatic projective cards and drawings show how individuals perceive ambiguous situations according to patterns below the surface of consciousness, though often within reach of consciousness and fed by it. Repressed people may see others as controlled or uninhibited. Perfectionists may see others as ambitious, driven, or despairing. Self-indulgent people may see others as selfish, lazy or missing life's fun. What we perceive in others is located somewhere on an axis of our own concerns, interests, defenses, fears, wishes, conscience. A large part of psychotherapy is the reevaluation of these conscience controls systems, bringing them into line with realistic goals and limits in a given culture. Whether approached in terms of Freudian superego concepts, or the "parents" within so neatly described by Eric Berne in *Games People Play*, or in terms of compensatory strivings and "guiding fictions" postulated by Adler, or in terms of dominant archetypes in Jungian language, or in terms of masculine and feminine values described by Erich Fromm as fatherly and motherly conscience, the drama of conscience development and operation within the person holds a critical place in theories of therapy and education alike.

The problem of all creativity is to stimulate and tolerate the flow of relevant material from the unconscious, delaying selection until likely options are identified, and then following through with the creation of necessary products or events to embody the desired values. For this process a certain playfulness and tentativeness is needed, with an ability to endure the strain of no solution, crowned with drive to finish up and follow through. There are a number of reasons to suspect that psychic ability may operate in this way, involving the creation of special states of altered consciousness and the matching of inner material with outer events, rather than operating on an inspectional basis as do the usual senses. For this reason, parapsychologists have long wondered whether the term *ESP* may have misled researchers by suggesting too strong an analogy with sensory operation, rather than an analogy with problem solving.

In taking up the question of ideals as a spiritual contribution to creativity, the Cayce source addressed the thorny problem of bringing together God's controls and man's. It was a question as old as religious commandments in any culture, as pressing as burning at the stake, as modern as stands against war or contraception, as personal as love and child rearing. It was a question addressed by Jesus as well as his Jewish ancestors and contemporaries, some of whom took positions like his on both moral and ritual law—and all religious laws tend to be both. It was a problem that has split Buddhism into two great camps or "rafts," over the adequacy of a religious ideal of personal fulfillment and perfection versus an ideal of serving others and even the very blades of grass.

As the Cayce information approached the question of ideals, it was insisted that *idea* be contrasted with *ideal*. An idea was the product of purely mental activity, whether stimulated by the needs and activity of the body or by the soul; an idea was a creation of the imagination and the heart of man, which might or might not be in line with his ideal. It was just a unit of mental activity. On the other hand, the ideal was a pattern–giving structure of great importance, the character of the soul's energies available to the person. The ideal was not the same as a goal, which a person might invent and set for himself, but was in the last analysis a gift from the soul, which a person might welcome and use well or answer indifferently or perversely. In the language of Hebraic thought, an ideal had to be thought of in terms of being called and answering. Yet an individual might take a call from her or his own soul, in it godliness, to be just, and turn this very justness into condemnation of others—eventually of self, as well. Or one might take an ideal of beauty and answer it with manipulative entertainment. Or one might take an ideal of wisdom welling up within self and answer it with craftiness in crime. The value and the energy and the interest were given in the mystery of becoming, which followed laws not always clear to human sight. But each person had the free will to recognize or ignore the beckoning of each ideal within or to perfect or distort its promise. Each person's soul had its own crest, its coat of arms, made of the ideals he or she had truly chosen to answer when the soul spoke to self, though some crests were smirched by misuse.

Approaching the high value given to conscience in Catholic tradition, the Cayce source insisted that each individual was judged by God only in terms of personal ideals—not in terms of the ideals of someone else or the norms of a church or culture, however valuable these might be for orienting the growth of a person or for sensitizing that individual to what was unfolding within. But the ideals or standards that each chose, deep within her or his own being, when in some lifetime was sought one or another human quality, talent, virtue, were ever after used upon her or him; they were the soul's private bar of justice, though in a given lifetime it might be ignored or repressed. To be sure, these ideals were not simple verbal labels but dynamic wholes containing within them the seeds of opposites and of ever richer ideals. One who chose justice as an ideal inevitably chose its twin, mercy, as well, though it might take long to discover this and respond to it.

Someone who at some point in the soul's journey set an ideal and then later ignored or defiled it might find self destroyed or crippled in body or mind by the negative action of a force so great that it overrode personal thoughts and psychosomatic controls. For these ideals were described as dynamic structures, unleashing the creative energies of the universe itself through the soul, and as capable of producing insanity as sanity, sickness as health, if not properly handled. This was the working of karma: sooner or later each individual had to face what was chosen, what was held up for self, as well as for others. Over and over the Cayce readings insisted, "Be not deceived, God is not mocked. Whatsoever a man soweth, that shall he also reap." Far from being mere trappings of the mind, then, ideals were dangerous and important business, central business for every life. In the view of the Cayce source, each soul came into each lifetime with one overarching ideal or cluster of ideals before it, always both personal and social. "For no soul enters by chance," it was insisted, but always on trajectory of encounter and discovery to enlarge its treasurehouse of becoming, on the long journey to conscious co-creatorhood with God.

Ought one then to leave ideals alone, just living life from day to day and speaking only when spoken to? One might take this path, to some degree, for God is merciful, and in words from the New Testament repeated often by this source, "God hath not willed that any soul should perish, but hath with every temptation provided a means of escape." It was an affirmation, which came as fresh air to many an anxious person who sought aid from Cayce—this categorical affirmation that God was no impatient perfectionist, no tester of the human creature. Yet the warning was there, too, that every soul would sooner or later find its temptation, its choices to make, its moments of truth, when it would either answer or betray its chosen ideals or those aborning in its deeps. For creation itself, the Creative Forces, the One Force, was pouring itself through human soul, bent on making companions for Itself; and though the process might take uncounted eons, it never ceased. Each individual would face self, sooner or later.

When such choices came, one had two options. She or he could "come under the law," which meant relentlessly being drawn into exactly the situations she or he forced upon others, in secret or avowed ideals, until it was finally known with acute participation just what true and merciful justice meant, for instance, as distinguished from condemnation of self or others. But there was an alternative. One could choose the "way of Grace," could enter into the full mystery of a chosen ideal by sharing it with others. Even when one betrayed an ideal, he or she could be freed of its destructive consequences, though not of all its consequences, if he or she turned again and sought to give of that very ideal to others in a spirit of humility and generosity. A man who set for himself an ideal of loyalty, and then broke it by taking another's wife, might go two routes. He could become so transfixed by his own ideal, within, that he would become defensive about his own wife and eventually alienate and lose her, learning about loss the hard way—in one life or another. Or he might recover his true ideal and begin to help others live out the severe task of loyalty, not narrow bondage but convenanted loyalty to the best in each before God—whether he did this in aiding others with marriages or in political bonds or in theological loyalties.

Yet in the view of the Cayce source, no one was expected to wrestle alone with personal ideals, nor with the consequences of ignoring or violating them. There were social structures and traditions, such as the church and the principled idealisms of national heritages, to help reorient. But the greatest aid was always the Christ, who had gone before as the "Ensample," the "Elder Brother," and who represented a kind of ever-present Field below or beside one's own that might tug one's own being into shape, if self would allow it. So the Cayce readings repeatedly urged people to "know in Whom you have believed, and that He is able to keep unto the last day that which ye have committed to Him." Of self, an individual could not really choose the best ideals, nor live up to them. But in the most literal sense each had help, if it was chosen. Every ideal needed to be thought out to its ultimate grounding in God; every ideal needed to be given living footing in one's best understanding of the Christ way, the Christ life. Every ideal should be set "in Him."

Far from producing a religious legalism, or perfectionism, then, the Cayce approach to conscience was meant to set before each individual the hope of controls as flexible as the next moment, as living as the Man. It was an approach similar to that of Augustine in his famous dictum, "Love God, and do as you like." The Cayce way of putting it was to say the Christ so fulfilled the Law that he became the Law—so that even the elements of storms and sickness obeyed Him. Not that He achieved some totalitarian authority over natural and moral law, but that He was able to so live that all things worked together with Him. This goal, the Cayce readings firmly asserted, was the destiny of every soul—not alone to obey the Law and laws as a child obeys a parent, but to choose becoming, and to understand by doing and creating until one became the Law.

Working with ideals was made complicated, in this view, by the fabulous creative powers of the mind, which would tend to build for a person whatever that individual set personal desire upon. If one chose to become a crook, the creative unconscious, "ever the Builder in man," would take her or him a long ways in that direction, until the individual was finally faced in some way with a question—such as integrity in workmanship even for a criminal—which might force the person to face self and grow a new ideal. For the soul never quit trying. If, however, the same individual finally answered the call to strategy within self by becoming, for example, a legal strategist, the person might go through experiences in one or many lives that would enable that individual to draft the very constitution of a people and to frame the temper of their laws so as to minimize crime. Constructive ideals would be found to come more quickly to realization than destructive ones—though the universe was big enough to hold plenty of the latter and made room for someone to hobble self with a personal lasso. The Cayce source insisted that no ideal was beyond the reach of a soul, in the fullness of time: "As ye abide in me, ye shall ask what ye will, and it shall be done upon you" was a typical Cayce variant on a saying of Jesus. Power, love, possessions, wisdom, patience—the possibilities were endless, if one began by being true to the ideals he already had and used their energies and resultant imagery and interests in service to others. However, one need not expect to do all of this in one lifetime; the Cayce source was no exponent of riches by positive thinking (though ready to explain in terms of reincarnation and past ideals why some had so little difficulty in achieving riches in a given lifetime).

Where ought someone begin, who sought to grow with respect to those treasures of the soul, self's true ideals? The rule of thumb in the Cayce materials was always "Be true to the best you know, and the next will be given to you." Being true to what rang clear in one's own depths was critically important and must be followed, even at the price of social rejection; it was the point at which the person would be judged, or judge self from the standpoint of the soul. Yet one had to sort decisions with care, for there was often a way that seemed good and compelling to someone whose end was destruction. The Cayce information was as clear as psychoanalysis that the human unconscious is a wily thing, a natural force not wholly subdued to the soul in any but Christ, and in those who achieved at times perfect attunement with Him. One must judge one's own promptings, even the strong ones, by the legacy of one's own people—as the Cayce materials so fully used the Bible—and ever keep in mind the commandment to serve the other, to be the keeper of one's brother or sister. But against this background, the seeming imperative had further to be checked by attunement, by waiting upon the still, small voice, by prayer and reflection and the weighing of dreams and impressions. When an individual sought such counsel as to whether one was hearing from self's own depths an idea or an ideal, that individual could—if one's purposes were sincere—unfailingly count on guidance, for "God hath not left himself without a witness." The guidance might take time and be crowded out by other impulses at first, but it would be there, and each individual could count on it—even as Edgar Cayce could count on aid to give his readings, so long as he gave them to be helpful rather than to advance himself alone.

The Cayce source was ready with practical steps in working with conscience and its ideals. One should take a piece of paper and draw upon it two lines, making three columns, to be marked "spiritual, mental, physical." In each of these columns one should set down as honestly as possible real ideals, from keeping the body at a fitting weight to loving one's enemies—the whole gamut of what made sense for sure, right then, to the person. Then the entries in these columns should be worked with, checked against the life, made clearer. "Often you will find yourself rubbing out," the Cayce source warned, for some ideals would drop away or be incorporated in better ones. In time, each column would begin to show the real uniqueness of that soul, on its special pilgrimage, with its strengths and weaknesses appearing side by side in specific ideals. At the same time, each column would be cast more and more in ways that to the person meant the mind of Christ: the ideals would be "grounded in Him" —not by imitation but by intent, quality, direction. In time one would come to see, said the Cayce readings, that there was no way forward except the Way that Christ showed and was a living way, not a book of rules or behaviors or taboos or formulas. It was so not by special decree, or any excellence of Christians who often missed the point by identifying with Christ as a hero rather than as a personal challenge, but it was so because of the way the universe was built—a way of wise love and radical creativity that Christ walked and opened out for others. Setting the ideals in Christ was not a merely rational matter, in this view. As one chose to organize and think ideals in this way, she or he automatically set the unconscious building in His direction and called into being native psychic ability to seek and find that reality in the present universe, not merely in history, which was the Christ Spirit. The soul would seek its own, by the most valuable kind of psychic capacity, and find it.

To be sure, some souls might require much time to build their ESP awareness of the living Christ, so that they could daily orient themselves by this lodestar. In the meantime, there was a practical method by which they could check their actual, functioning ideals. They could look to see to what they responded in others. Each would find that what self weighed and measured in others, or was drawn by, was the standard actually at work in her or his own soul. If one saw beauty, then beauty called him or her; if purity, if play, if patience—each was nudging the self for decision or action within. If one saw mostly evil, or selfishness, or betrayal, then the individual should know that his or her own soul was holding self tightly to the same ideal, pressing one to it until one's ways were changed or until the mind was broadened. If, in time, something new was found—a new thing, a new hunger, a new longing arising from the soul—it could be made one's own, not alone by praying for it nor by studying about it nor by associating with the like-minded—although all of these things profited the birth of ideals. But above all, the new treasure could be given life by giving it away. Money might not be buried but must be invested in life, said the old parable; it was so with ideals. Said the Cayce readings many times, "If ye would have love, give love; if ye would have friends, be friendly; if ye would have mercy, be merciful; if ye would have beauty, make your world beautiful for others." For this was a law, not just a good thing, but a law.

It was important, too, to think of ideals in positive terms, rather than negative: Better to seek to love than to omit hating. Even in matters of physical health, just avoiding illness was not enough. Not a few times the Cayce source put a direct question to a sick person, "What would ye do if ye were well?" It was made clear that the very body would not respond sufficiently to the life–giving patterns destined for it, unless the life were under the guidance of a fitting ideal, one that belonged to that special soul. Someone who had no notion of what to do with health might not receive it until she or he did. For those responsive to the Christian ideal (and the Cayce source said that by the 1940's there were no souls anywhere in the earth who had not been faced with the Christ way in some lifetime; the rest had been separated out for other paths), one might find the way to think personal ideals by asking in a given situation a simple, blunt question, "What would the Master do?" No pat answer should be expected, but the question, truly put, would start the seeker in the right direction.

Auras and Conscience

Are there cases that seem to link the seeing of auras with maturity of conscience development?

A busy young congregational minister set about building the membership of his Southwestern church. He drove himself to make calls on homes; he raised money for a new organ; he attended community functions; he worked on his sermons. The membership increased a bit and then leveled off. He pushed himself harder. There were denominational conferences to attend, inspirational books to read, causes to espouse, including the reality of psychic experience. He became known as a promising young minister, and denominational executives looked on him with favor, assigning him to city and state committees.

But his wife was lonely, his children difficult. His prayers of thanksgiving sounded forced, even to him. Then he went to a pastor's conference at his seminary where an older pastor preached and simply talked with the young ministers. The older pastor reached him, not by claims about his ministry—though his church was immense, with a full staff of ministers—but by using the language of psychotherapy. He spoke of self-acceptance, of insight, of the treasures hidden in the sick complexes of a man. And he put the ministers at the conference into small groups, where many dared to speak freely with one another. At the same time, he spoke of prayer and showed in his own unforced praying an emblem of one man's relationship with God. The young preacher went home and took stock of himself. He did not like what he saw—a driving perfectionism that was killing whatever he sought to create. He began to read, to confront his own conscience with the materials from psychiatry. Cautiously, he introduced a few small study groups in his church and began with his wife to set a pattern of speaking honestly in them.

The first development was that his parishioners seemed to go to pieces. Or at least more went through breakdowns and near breakdowns than he would ever have expected. It was as though they had been waiting, holding on by force of will, until someone was ready to hear and to help. With each new set of problems, he thought he saw more of his own weaknesses, new symptoms of his own failings. He was near distraction, many times, and even contemplated suicide. But he stayed close to his people and listened to them and prayed in his own way. Some of his sermons were poor, and he missed enough meetings to make a few church stalwarts angry with him. But a new spirit began to show in worship. People sang from their hearts, every now and then. An alcoholic family changed, and the husband became an active building force in the community and the church. People came from nearby housing developments to see what made members talk about the life of the church, and often found the answer in the small groups.

The young minister forgot psychic abilities for weeks at a time. But then he noticed that faces were looking softer to him, people were looking to him like individual adventures, like paintings of themselves. And one day he was noting colors about them, rather absent-mindedly. He joked about the colors with a few of his laymen and was surprised to find they were seeing the same things—especially two who had worked for years in Alcoholics Anonymous, and one young bookkeeper. They

compared notes and found themselves seeing similar colors and intensi-
ties, over and over again, with similar meanings. As time went on, seeing
auras became as natural for the minister and for other leaders of the
church as making phone calls to see how friends were doing. They made
no special claims about it, yet enjoyed it among themselves, as was clear
when the writer came to attend a conference in the same city and became
acquainted with the minister and leaders of the church.

What had been involved in one man's coming to see auras? He had
come to see faces. Out of his own searching, his own sorting out of himself, he had begun to look at others, to care about them rather than to
process them for church functions. And their faces and forms had lit up
for him. He had meant more than auras when he spoke in a small group
one day of "the true Light that lighteth every man in the world" as the
inner radiance men had to seek in one another, rather than constrictive
consciences. But he suspected that the true Light showed itself in colors,
as well—helpful colors, physically perceived.

~ SIX ~
Automatisms and Quickenings

"Holy Father," Edgar Cayce began to pray, using the phrase with which he often started his prayers. "We ask Thy presence here with us today, now." His voice was low, contained; his hands were folded on the library table before him, beside the large Bible from which he had read aloud.

"We have no secrets from Thee, for Thou knowest us altogether. Thou knowest how each of us has sinned and fallen short, even as thy servant David, of whom we have read." The words were earnest, steady. It grew very still in the room, for the mention of sin struck home to those gathered with him at the regular two o'clock prayer period of his family and office staff. There was silence around the library table, and heads were bowed.

Only a few days before, Cayce had recovered his voice after a month's illness and had taken a reading on his own health. He had been rebuked for not keeping better balance in diet, for not keeping more quiet times, for not preparing himself for each trance session—even for not showering and changing clothes before entering the reading room. Then his voice, still hoarse, had suddenly changed to ringing tones of unbelievable loudness, and the source of the information had come right to the point. It was not Cayce alone who had broken the law, lost touch with his spiritual center, and contracted illness under the strain of giving so many extra readings each day. The weight of the trouble fell upon the entire staff, who were—with Cayce—called "ungracious, unrepentant" people who made a "garbage pit" of their negative emotions. With a severity the writer—who was present for the reading and included in the rebuke—cannot exaggerate, the stentorian voice had said, "Walk in the way of the Lord, or else there will come that sudden reckoning, as ye have seen. But don't be pigs!"

Nobody in the room doubted what was meant. Under pressure to handle the stream of mail, phone calls, and visitors, Cayce had hired extra typists and pressed volunteers into service until the small office quarters were jammed with people at makeshift tables and desks. People got in one another's way, bypassed one another's authority, strove to feel important. Tempers rose, bodies were weary from long hours of work, quiet times were lost. Bickering and jostling for position became so common that it was unpleasant to come to work. Edgar Cayce became entangled in the turmoil, growing morose in those few times when he stopped for a cigarette. Then he had become ill, and there had been no readings at all for a month, followed by the searing reading heard that day.

Now, a few days later, things were more controlled, and Cayce was praying aloud.

Then something strange occurred. Usually his prayers aloud were simple, biblical, and somewhat halting; he once told the writer that "the man who prayed without stumbling very possibly doesn't mean it." But at this point Cayce's speech became steady, sure; each phrase was a finished thought, each word fitted securely into place, each image seized and focused the attention. Without raising his voice, Cayce was listing the sins of those in the room, including himself. He named no names; he made no charges. He simply spoke the truth about one person after another, and all in the room knew it. There had indeed been pettiness, boastfulness, backbiting, impatience, unforgiveness, indulgence—and more. Yet there was no condemnation in his voice, no reveling in trouble. For his prayer continued, "Thou hast made it known to us that the effort to serve one's brother covereth a multitude of sins." He gave thanks that each in the room could aid in relieving pain, could light a path for the troubled, would "make the heart of many a man to sing." And in the same quiet, sure voice, he closed, asking "that we might be given the grace to follow Him, the Master whose Name we have named in our hearts, and for Whose sake we pray."

Something better than a lecture had taken place. Talking and thinking about David, who as the Lord's anointed had still so often sinned, and had repented, the staff had gathered into a common mind. The tight controls of the past few days since the painful reading had eased, and bodies leaned back a bit. Then had come this cleansing prayer, catching up each person in the room, enacting a shared confession with the assurance of an absolution as real as the wrongdoing. Later that afternoon people were humming and whistling, as they had not done for weeks. And in the days that followed, something like teamwork began to emerge from a crew whose understanding of Cayce's work varied from almost nothing to years of experience, whose education varied from grammar school to graduate school, and whose devotional life varied from fishing to choir singing.

Had Cayce been taken over by another entity for this prayer? His vocabulary had not changed, although his sentence structure had tightened. He had said little that he could not have compiled in a conscious checklist of problems around the room, and yet he had said it with striking speed and fitness. His voice had not changed, except to reach the timber and depth that those who loved him associated with his best self. No revelation had been given, and yet his speech had revealed each one in the room.

Was this automatic speech? Was it of the same order as the biblical speaking in tongues? Was it like the automatic writing, so commonly reported in psychic circles, where the words streamed forth from a pencil moving without the subject's intent, yet using his hand?

Those in the room would rather have described Cayce's incisive prayer and catalog of penance as a *quickening*, a meeting of Cayce's psyche with a field or force or spirit wiser and richer than his own. He had, they would say, been "lifted up," in accordance with the promise so often quoted in the readings, "My Spirit beareth witness with thy spirit, as to whether ye be the sons of God."

It would be no surprise to those familiar with Edgar Cayce's work for his consciousness to change, allowing some new center of his being or some other center of being to guide his thoughts and speech. This was the substance of what he did twice a day when hypnotized and speaking in trance.

Moreover, he came from a family where he had seen his grandfather, in his childhood, make a broom move around the kitchen, and where his father had proven his ability to dowse for water with a forked stick. Those who had worked with Cayce in trance claimed that once he had even levitated, risen up from the couch in response to an urgent instruction meant to lift the level of his voice: "Up, up!" Not having seen this, Cayce did not have to believe it. But he had seen the little planchette fly, the night he and his wife had tried a Ouija board.

Cayce's experience of being fully conscious and yet having his vocal cords seem to leap to form phrases in prayer placed him in the midst of a wide variety of psychic practices that had for centuries employed spontaneous muscular action. He was experiencing a variant of what the writer and many others have seen and studied in table tipping, the divinatory use of swinging pendulums, ecstatic speech of glossolalia, address in unknown foreign tongues, speech in what was claimed to be the language of angels, opening of the Bible to let the eye fall on guiding passages, staring at imagery in crystal balls, arranging Chinese sticks in symbolic patterns, turning up cards in fortune telling—and still other practices of individuals seeking to let unguided activity mediate the messages of the gods or fate or spirits.

The literature of parapsychology includes many investigations of automatisms and quickenings, where the response of muscles appears to precede or accompany conscious thought, rather than to follow it as is usual. Researchers on both sides of the Atlantic have spent hundreds of hours observing and interpreting automatic writing, reporting it to be often trivial, sometimes sensible, and occasionally erudite (as in the famous cross-correspondences) or artistic (as in the poetry and prose of Patience Worth) or inspirational (as in the Betty books of Stewart Edward White). They have also shown that more material proceeds from unconscious complexes of the writing subjects than most lay individuals would believe, to the degree that some psychiatrists today employ automatic writing to disclose a patient's real responses to touchy material that the conscious mind denies.

The novelist Kenneth Roberts has reported on the water dowsing of Henry Gross, and investigators such as the present writer have watched psychics accurately locate underground water and minerals by touching a map or drawing on it. A considerable literature and interest in automatic speaking in tongues, long practiced in Holiness churches, has emerged in such staid church circles as Episcopalian and Lutheran.

If there is any agreement at all among seasoned investigators, it might lie in warning against wholesale abdication of consciousness for automatisms, because of risks as dangerous as playing with hypnosis. Many have personally observed cases of mental illness, such as those described by Hugh Lynn Cayce in *Venture Inward*, which began as harmless dissociation with a Ouija board and turned to engrossing automatic writing, then finally to uncontrollable hearing of voices or experiencing sexual sensations. Few investigators would suggest that the dissociation or automatisms caused the illness, for underlying neuroses seem always present in such cases. But the method appears to be a problematic approach to dealing with unconscious contents.

Yet other investigators, including such psychics as Arthur Ford, who have reported on their own experiences, have argued that automatism can be safely attempted by anyone who first does a responsible inventory of his own problems and attitudes.

Over the years of Cayce's trance activity, many sought from his information some guidance on automatic writing or other automatisms and quickenings. The answer often given was that anybody could develop such abilities, if he set about practicing properly. But with the answer always went a question: Why? In part this was a question of motive, for impulses to self-glory or power over others were potentially dangerous impulses, according to this source; such attitudes might release unwelcome contents of the unconscious that would be difficult to control and might draw to the person disturbing forces in the form of discarnate entities enjoying full or partial takeover of willing subjects. But the question of why was also the posing of a choice. For the Cayce source insisted that the same energy used to achieve automatic writing, for example, could achieve inspirational writing. The former would be limited to discarnate entities, at best, while the latter might give the individual access to the best of her or his own soul, and whatever additional resource might be needed from the treasure house of the Universal Forces. Not Uncle John but the Christ was the better focus in this view—and not abdication of consciousness but alignment, attunement, elevation of consciousness until it was infused from beyond itself, rather than displaced or destroyed. Yet various twilight stages of consciousness had their usefulness, as the trances of Edgar Cayce showed. One woman was urged to cultivate along with her prayer life the ability to talk in her sleep, for some of the counsel she would give would be found similar to Cayce's readings. In the view of the Cayce source, many variables had their effect on what came through a person who sought to open himself or herself to other energies and insights than those afforded by normal consciousness. Any injury or illness affecting the endocrine gland operation (and associated centers in the real physical body) might turn quiet times into nightmares of unwanted promptings. So might habitual dwelling on sexual or hostile material, creating thought forms that would trouble the percipient as though they were separate beings. So might participation in a group whose intentions were thrills or distractions, bringing forth responses in the dissociated person, which were not his own intention.

But one whose physical and mental life were in some balance and whose intention was to secure aid to increase rather than supplant waking gifts might find that through quiet times, prayer, Bible study, and the cleansing–arousing flow of meditation, she or he could be lifted beyond usual conscious abilities. According to their gifts, some might recall scenes of past lives and be able to write them as stories; others might hear music as though from the spheres, to incorporate in their music-making or poetry; others might have flashes of light, where the face and form of a loved one, acutely real, came momentarily before their minds, together with a helpful impression or prompting for daily life.

Over the years since Cayce's death, individuals interested in his approaches have tried various forms of dissociation and focusing, attempting to stretch their consciousness to levels beyond its usual function. A few have interpreted dreams and performed well on psychic tasks under hypnosis, though most who have tried it have not. Some who have tried automatic writing have found bits of helpful or evidential material, though most have not, and a few have found to their horror that they entered unconscious depths that they could not control. Others have tried writing out Bible passages in their own words by inspiration and have achieved results varying from good poetry to gobbledegook. Still others have tried to let messages come from them while laying on hands in healing, and a few have experienced apt leading, while others have produced wordy generalities. In all of this experimenting, there has been highlighted the problem of initiative: What are individuals supposed to do, and what are individuals supposed to let God do?

Initiative in Creativity

The Cayce source took up the difficult problem of initiative in its fourth lesson for trainees seeking psychic and other creativity. It titled the chapter "Faith" in *A Search for God.*

Emphasizing initiative would seem appropriate to a careful observer of the phenomena of automatisms. In any major city, and certainly at a Spiritualist summer camp, one can find individuals practicing automatic writing to secure messages from discarnates and sometimes to see counsel for problems of daily life. Some of these practitioners report themselves authorized by heavenly beings and present their materials with boldness and fervor. Some present their materials with a touch of whimsy, as surprised as any at what seems to "come through them." Others wait until "caught up in the Spirit" to do their work, in accustomed piety. What seems to be evidential material at times results through any of these methods. But in all of them the psyche appears to take its stand on some flow, whether personal or transpersonal, which the individual has learned to trust. What is such trust, such faith, and how does it act to free the psyche for useful parapsychological material or to flood it with irrelevances?

Erich Fromm has argued that faith in the orderliness and helpfulness of the universe and other people must under any creative loving and working; he has distinguished what he calls *rational faith* from *blind faith.* Gerald Heard, writing of the Buddhist call to right belief, has insisted that an individual's "deep mind" must be convinced of what he or she sets out to do, or it will not build in the direction he or she seeks growth. Both have touched on the relation between understanding and trust in probing the issue of faith. It is an issue as old as religion. In Christianity, the issue has been approached by those who, like Tertullian, rejoiced in believing the absurd, and those of scientific temper who reserved belief and trust for things demonstrable through the senses. While these viewpoints may seem at times merely theological, it is clear that important issues in any kind of creativity—whether psychic or political or laboratory or philosophical—can be involved in the controversy. To be creative often involves some suspension of judgment, in the trust that a solution will present itself—but from where? It involves also the commitment to take action on a solution, rather than daydream more and more solutions, in the trust that such action will be worthwhile—for whom? It involves the ability to overhaul one's functioning after repeated failures, in the trust that one can arrive at better patterns of problem solving—from where? Repeatedly the issue emerges of what an individual can trust when habit and experience, counsel and expedience fail, whether in child rearing or moneymaking or facing death—where no one has conscious experience.

The approach of the Cayce source on the initiatives in faith was remarkably literal. Faith was described as a flow of promptings with definite content, coming into consciousness from beyond itself, ultimately from the soul as it answered the force of the life. One might learn to recognize the flow, to respond to it with assent, to improve it with a godly life of service. But the flow of faith might neither be taught nor learned, could not be forced, and could not be destroyed – though it might be ignored. For it was a gift, a fundamental attribute of the soul welling up from the soul's intimate knowledge of the Creative Forces. In every realm of an individual's life, from the most practical problem of starting a stalled car to the blinding problem of handling the sudden death of a loved one, each person could count upon a quiet flow from within, trying to show patterns, meanings, connections, directions, until that individual could say in a click of recognition, "So that's how it is!" Faith in this view was not a specifically religious or churchly phenomenon but the evidence of many things unseen, as wide in range as God's love for humankind or a parent's love for a child. It was the everlasting prompting of the next step, the next insight, the next commitment—not a series of tests nor a series of propositions. It was a steady flow of inward knowing, a living business, to be tried out daily. When Jesus described Peter's insight about His Messiahship by saying, "Flesh and blood hath not revealed this to thee, but the Father," he meant, in the view of this source, the kind of helpful certitude that did not overwhelm the person nor displace him but quietly fed and strengthened his understanding, in little moments or in crisis of judgment. Such moments as Peter's declaration might be elevated when the human spirit was fused with a Spirit from on high, but there would be other moments of prompting, equally the flow of faith, when the certitude would seem more ordinary—as when a mother or father was prompted to trust that a child told the truth. Whenever something within seemed to say, "Yes, you can trust that," an individual might be brushing against the gift of faith.

Yet in the view of the Cayce source, faith was not an all-or-none business. An individual's proper prayer was "I believe; help thou mine unbelief," for one had to grow in faith. One had to learn to empty the heart of selfishness, which could block the flow; one had to learn through meditation and often-repeated prayer to become a channel—and then act as one prayed. One had to learn to distinguish faith from unconscious compulsions, for faith would not come as a noisy absolute, taking over, but as a steady beat, an assurance, an awakening, a shadow cast by real events over the mind of the seeker. One had to learn to use constructively the quiet, steady assurance of faith—and even to be willing to make mistakes; it was "better to do wrong with good intent than to do nothing at all."

Over and over the Cayce source insisted that individuals could count on the divine initiative within to stir, to guide, to strengthen. Faith was a "gift from the Throne, implanted in the soul." Yet no more could rightly be sought than the next step and the next—although sometimes far vistas might briefly show, in dream or vision or reasoned understanding. For the gifts of faith were always contingent upon using what one has now: "Use what you have in hand, and the next will be given to you." This contingency was not a matter of God's being despotic or arbitrary in his self-giving through the soul, but of lawful processes that kept the person from destroying self with the knowledge and power that could be attained through faith. In general, a person would recognize only those opportunities she or he could use, if self was not deluded by one's imagination, while others would also be prompted by their faith to recognize and honor opportunities—though not always, if they ignored their inner promptings. Likewise, one would not be led by faith into more than could be handled, for "God hath not willed that any soul should perish"—though a person could trap one's self by the will and the imagination.

How might one distinguish between faith and imagination? The rational mind could help by providing clues to a Christlike life and by orienting one's native psychic ability towards attunement with the Spirit of Christ. The Cayce source offered no encouragement to discard thinking, but urged people to "get understanding," both by study in all its forms and by experiment or application in real-life situations. Faith was not a flow to be damped or disturbed by responsible reasoning; it would give life to reason by supplying connections, inferences, even factual data in psychic perceptions. But the ultimate task of responding to faith was not formulating facts or dogmas; it was seeking and hearing the Father, not announcing that God was a fact.

How might one help the flow of faith in others? First of all, by trusting that God was working to fulfill His purposes "in the other fellow." Second, by fulfilling the duty of having faith in oneself, in the action of God in one's own life—for one who doubted self soon doubted others. The life lived in this vein would soon begin to shine with good energies—as in the aura—and with effective deeds or good works, and such a light should be trusted "to so shine before men that they may glorify your Father in heaven." There was no need to set out to work miracles, though remarkable things could come about under the quiet stimulus of promptings called faith. For the Cayce source insisted that no material emergency was beyond solution by spiritual inspiration; God would be found fantastically creative, if each individual would learn to listen to Him. For example, the Cayce information insisted that there was no disease that did not have its cure available somewhere on earth, a cure that could be found and used through the psychic capacities that were an integral part of faith. There were no incurable diseases, although there were specific cases of deterioration that had progressed too far to be reserved, when the soul would soon leave the body.

How might one cultivate the lively flow of faith—of practical, helpful promptings as well as ultimate assurances about the meaning and place of suffering and freedom? "Let us humble ourselves," began one reading. Individuals must use their initiative, their will, their consciousness, to set themselves before God and to bow their will to the One. "Let us open our hearts in meditation," the reading continued, stressing that extraordinary state of altered consciousness that could come from daily quiet focus on a biblical prayer or affirmation. Further, one could set the mind to remember, in times of stress, the faith of others in distress, their trust and steadfastness; for this purpose the study of the Bible was one's best resource, though every great life or biography might carry assurances—as the Cayce readings often referred to Woodrow Wilson and at other times to such figures as the Buddha, Lao Tse, Swedenborg, or the founder of Zoroastrianism. As part of cultivating the flow of faith, one would have to analyze self, not forgetting the loving help of others, and seeking to find the typical weaknesses. One would need to determine where he or she actually put trust, lest one proclaim faith in God, but enact faith in power, or wealth, or charm, or some other ultimate. And in moments that seemed to contain assurance, one could learn to distinguish, said the Cayce source, between confidence, which might be based on sensory data or emotional vigor alone, and faith, which came in quieter, deeper tones but allowed acting in no fear at all. For as an individual grew in awareness and response to this flow, that person could become as a rock, and upon such a rocklike trust Christ Himself could build a Kingdom.

Automatisms or Quickening and Initiative

Can building a living awareness of the gift of faith affect psychic performance with the muscles and nerves, in automatisms and quickenings?

A young choral conductor, trained in Navy musical groups after his college experience in singing and conducting, tried repeatedly to find the way to a larger guidance than his own in his work. He tried closing his eyes and losing himself at important passages; he tried concentrating intensely on the score, on the singers, on his conducting technique. He tried sitting in silence before performances, and tried fasting and special breathing techniques on days of concerts. Learning of Cayce and other psychics, he sought and achieved the ability of automatic writing, securing a variety of messages that purported to come from entities wiser than himself. Still, his conducting was erratic; trying to lose himself, he sometimes lost the choir.

He joined a weekly study group, some of whose members were church people and some not, but all of whom were serious. He tried meditation and at first made of it another attempt to abandon himself to the unconscious. But he worked hard in the Bible study of the group and in the shared discussions during the next four years. Slowly it began to come clear to him that creativity was not leaving himself out of favor of something better but using his every skill and understanding to answer the quickenings to beauty that might come within him. He worked harder at his music and began to listen ever more carefully to chords and balances, to the contributions of each section of his choir. One day he caught himself knowing, really knowing, exactly how the sopranos would sing the next phrase, though they had never sung it before in such marked accents. Spontaneously, his arms joined his consciousness in conducting the sopranos through the phrase, adding his force to theirs, and then carrying the force onward with the tenors. The effect was electric. It had come after long practicing, but it was new. Neither conductor nor singers had created the result alone; it had flashed to life in all of them together, using all their training and skill.

For a while the conductor could not find the way to the same state. But in time he did, learning that he could sense not only the strengths of his singers but their weaknesses, and respond accordingly. He thought at times he was using his rational inference alone. But how would that account for his knowing when a given singer would be absent or when a choir bus would miss its route and be late or when a recording date would be called off? These items came into his consciousness in the same stream as the signals to create beauty. And how was he to account for something the choir itself noticed and commented upon, that at times—and he knew the times—he could add a vital force to the singers, feeling a flow go forth from him that helped the basses reach notes usually out of range or prompted deftness beyond the usual reach of the second sopranos? It was not that he did something to the singers, but that something good in him seemed released to trigger something good in them and to guide and shape it with them. An important part of the process was listening to the singers, training them to sing, to be artists, to answer the call of each performance from their own creativity. "We hear each other all the way down; we really do," he once told the writer.

"If men could act out with one another the way God hears and responds to us, this would have to be something like it."

Had he found his way to a process to which Jesus pointed when His touch brought movement of a withered limb or sight to a sightless eye? Jesus' typical response had been not to take credit nor reject it but only to strengthen the flow in the person before Him: "Your faith has made you whole." Perhaps this was the psychic quickening, the ecstatic speech, the spontaneous movement that could be trusted.

~ SEVEN ~
Action on People and Things

The idea seemed ridiculous, but Edgar Cayce was confident. "I'll waken you," he said. He was offering to waken the writer and a few others at the same time every night by thinking about them. "It will work," he added; "I've done it before."

The group was studying *A Search for God*, attempting to keep daily meditation times with the specific procedures outlined in the Cayce readings for stilling the mind and body. But the distractions of daily life in wartime seemed too much. Nobody in the group was meditating every day, and few were doing it at the agreed-upon times when all would be invisibly together. As a consequence, nobody's meditation was going through the complete arc or cycle, but instead each person was being sidetracked into introspection or unconscious imagery or psychic promptings. At last the group had decided to follow a method suggested in many a Cayce reading. That method was to arise at two a.m. for thirty days and keep first a half hour of prayer—drawing close to God in adoration, petition, dedication—followed by a half hour of nonreflective meditation, in which the effort would be made to empty oneself of whatever hindered the divine force from rising within the individual. Several, however, confessed that they could not awaken from a sound asleep, even with an alarm clock, lest they disturb a spouse not so interested in the devotional life. They were discussing the problem as they stood in Cayce's hallway after a Bible class. It was then that he offered to waken them for a time, until they became used to the nightly hour.

But the idea was certainly strange. The sleepers would be scattered over a twenty-five mile radius, in Virginia Beach and Norfolk and Oceana. The thought that Edgar Cayce or anyone else could exert a force to awaken all these people at the same time was farfetched, even to those who had become accustomed to fetching far with Edgar Cayce.

The experiment was begun the next night. As did the others, according to the shared reports at the next meeting, the writer found himself wide awake at two a.m., roused from a sound sleep, and feeling no inclination to return to sleep. Was it the power of suggestion? Experimenters with hypnosis have shown that every adult has a sense of the hour of the day, accurate within a few minutes, and the posthypnotic suggestion can awaken a person at a desired time—or put someone to sleep in the same way. But posthypnotic suggestion usually does not work night after night without reinforcement and frequently disturbs the depth of sleep. Yet here were the group members popping awake night after night to keep their appointed devotional hour, free from telephone calls or children or business demands. And nobody was hypnotizing them, although everyone was voicing their desire to cooperate. During the experimental period when Cayce added his aid, two reported thinking that on given nights they would skip the time, because of illness, yet were unable to keep from waking up. Later, when Cayce discontinued his efforts, some members of the group found they had to try harder to wake up or could sleep through the time if they chose.

Nothing was clearly proven by this little experiment. But those who took part had an eerie sense that the mind might have more powers of outreach, of action on people and things, than was usually assumed in daily life.

For Cayce the experience was less strange. Years ago in his photographic studio in Kentucky he had taken a dare to summon a man to his studio by concentrating on him, and had seen the bewildered man enter, within a relatively few minutes, apologizing for coming up without a definite reason, yet feeling that Cayce wanted him. It was one of a number of experiences that had taught Cayce the power of thought to affect events—as had the events that he relayed to the writer, involving two men at Virginia Beach. They had wanted $1500 for a business deal by a certain date and had begun concentrating on bringing the money forth, "manifesting it." Not praying, they were simply willing the money to appear. Day and night they "held the thought." The appointed day came and there was no sign of the money—but that day a severe automobile wreck hospitalized them both. An insurance agent came to the hospital to offer them a settlement at once, protecting his client who was also in the accident. The amount? $1500.

Cayce trusted the flow of energy going out from his being, so long as he kept his attunement in prayer and his purposes those of service. He was immensely successful in vegetable gardening, as his friends were reminded by an abundant crop of asparagus that spread over an adjoining lot after Cayce's death. It was not strange to him that plants should respond to loving care. Nor did he consider that healing by touch was impossible, although he felt it was not his gift for this lifetime. The only form of direct action on the body that the writer saw him attempt was a bit of folklore practice: stroking someone's warts to make them go away—which they did (as research has shown they will also do under suggestion). But the outreach of psychic ability was as real to Cayce as the inreach. There had been those times in his life when it seemed that people were acted on in ways that completely passed understanding. For example, there had been the time—one of many—when he had been anxious for money to meet household needs and had prayed earnestly for aid. Taking a reading on the subject, he was told the he should have no fear as long as he kept close to God; it was the same counsel he was always given by the Information, except with a slight addition this time. He should watch what happened now for thirty days, to learn the truth in the biblical phrase often repeated by his trance source: "The silver and the gold are mine, saith the Lord: the cattle on a thousand hills." He watched, and his whole household watched with him, as something developed that none of them has yet explained. For exactly thirty days there was some form of money in every letter he received. People long forgotten remembered to pay for their readings (about twenty-five percent, in the author's experience, never paid, and Cayce never dunned them). Friends sent a dollar bill, or a five-dollar bill "just to help out." Creditors sent adjustments on accounts. One way or another, everyone who wrote, from points all over the country, tucked in some money—

even coins for return postage. Then at the end of thirty days the phenomenon stopped, and money came irregularly as always—somehow
enough, never too much. Had a signal gone forth from Cayce by some
form of psychic ability? Or had he reached unto "the Throne" that his
readings described as in touch with every individual, according to that
person's desire and intent?

Cayce's seeming ability to affect people and things at a distance from
him was a reminder of claims as old as antiquity: of Joshua making an
ax to float, of Jesus stilling the waves, of Peter triggering the death of An-
nanias when the latter held back money he had agreed to share. It had in
it elements of the claims in firewalking, of mediums claiming to produce
fresh roses from out of the air in séance rooms, of Haitian needles stuck
in Voodoo dolls. It raised questions long raised in the human family
about the powers of mind over matter.

Parapsychologists have tackled these questions in different ways. Dr.
Karagulla set her psychics to observing auric fields of force sweeping out
from a compelling speaker to embrace a room of people and pull their
fields into a shared unity. The present writer studied a European psychic
as he held his hand near sections of the backs of volunteer subjects,
making the subjects' flesh jump and muscles activate at his will—but
only by dint of exhausting concentration on his part. He said it was the
same ability that he also used to produce images on unexposed film
held in his hand or—when he failed—to produce peculiar flecks of light
that ruined packs of film. J. G. Pratt and others investigated the action
of so-called poltergeists, seemingly disembodied centers of activity that
threw furniture and objects around a home by undetermined force.
Gerald Heard analyzed in his technical studies of prayer how asceticism
may have produced in certain subjects, such as the Cure d'Ars, a piled-up
charge of psychic energy that spilled over in the movement of objects
around them.

But by far the most careful and valuable work on psychokinesis—PK—
has been that done by J. B. Rhine and associates at Duke and elsewhere
in the U.S. and Europe, exploring the effects of concentration on the
fall of dice down chutes onto marked tables. Thousands of runs have
been conducted by a score of investigators, including engineers and
professors of biology and physics. In general, their findings have been

less spectacular than those on telepathy or clairvoyance, yet still statistically notable and showing lawful patterns that have convinced at least the dedicated workers that they are dealing with a measurable force. Yet the difficulty of conceiving of such a force along lines of presently know forces has challenged philosophers such as Professor Margenau of Yale and physicists such as Professor McConnell of Pittsburgh, as well as engaged that wide-ranging intellect, C. G. Jung, who undertook his doctoral dissertation on the seeming direct action of the mind upon a table, a knife, and a bookcase.

From time to time the question of the direct impact of the mind upon external events, objects, and persons came up in the Cayce readings. Here such phenomena were treated as further exemplification of the claim that "thoughts are things," and at least one researcher was encouraged to believe that he could train himself to move such objects as a spoon (he was told to start with objects made of silver), which he saw himself affecting in a dream. However, he was warned that such activity was much more taxing for the body than ESP, and that he would have to cleanse his body and emotions alike to accomplish it—as well as to hold to a purpose that did not include impressing other people, whether for the sake of his own ego or to advance a supposed religious cause. In the Cayce view, the actual energy involved in psychokinesis came from the action of the delicate centers of the body, the same ones involved in psychic perceptions; the training of these centers was a matter of training the whole person, not simply a training of psychic musculature. Once the way had been found and the gift used in service, probably over many lifetimes, it would be reliable and could even be used spontaneously as Jesus had used it to change water into wine (in a process, the Cayce source noted, during which the actual change had not taken place until the water was poured).

During Cayce's lifetime and since, his associates and those who have together worked with his materials have concentrated chiefly on absent healing through prayer as their means of using psychokinetic force. In developing this ability, as in developing other forms of psychic phenomena, they have been mindful of the Cayce source's injunction to seek "the mind of Christ." Repeatedly it has become clear that no form of ritual, no method of concentration or breathing, no circle in the dark or in daylight, no chant or incantation, would bring about an apparent operation of energy flowing out to people and things, except as the individuals brought their whole lives into harmony with the spirit of their prayer. It did no good to ask for God's help unless one were willing to offer one's own—through a telephone call, a visit, the securing of a good doctor, the giving of a massage. Those who sought the capacity for sharing with others an energy broader than the body and consciousness had to "live as they pray," as the Cayce source so often put it. Integrity was crucial.

Integrity and Creativity

The Cayce source took the issue of integrity as the fifth area of religious concerns in training for creativity. The chapter of *A Search for God* on integrity was named after two components of integrity, "Virtue and Understanding." In this view *virtue* was consistent behavior from pure motives, which freed the flow of insights that made *understanding*, leading in turn to more effective behavior.

That personal integrity affects the flow of psychokinesis in everyday life would seem reasonable if in fact psychic activity is a total creative act of a person, rather than a trick of an obscure nerve or gland. One living without integrity by a double standard might be subject to the same censorship that disguises the contents of dreams; psychic energy used to justify oneself with others could hardly be expected to work effectively. A man with hidden and unresolved anger or sexuality could hesitate to broadcast his force by PK, just as he might be guarded in other areas of life. And an individual whose behavior led him or her to fear punishment would be as likely to have the "will to fail" in psychic matters as any other. At the same time, a self-righteously virtuous person, whose proper behavior lacked human understanding, could not expect to mobilize PK for others more readily than she would her handshake or her money.

A number of individuals with what appear to be healing gifts—for example, Ambrose Worrall—have told the writer that the use of such energies for show or personal advantage tends to limit their availability the next time they are needed. For Worrall, this has meant making his living as an executive for the Martin Aircraft Company and accepting no fees for his healing work. For a psychic from China whose psychokinetic abilities with coins, dice, living tissue, and chemical solutions have seemed to the writer to be extraordinary, the question of stability of his talent appears directly linked to his motives. What he does for research or as a contribution to healing seems to leave him peaceful and ready for the next assignment; what he does for entertainment, or for publicity, seems to render his next efforts less reliable.

Insofar as many psychics can describe the difference between natural everyday psychic experience and elevated psychic experience, where the sense of a cooperating divine reality is unshakeable, the role of integrity seems to them prominent in making the difference. Edgar Cayce once lost his ability for a year, after it was used to predict the results of horse races. At another period when it was used for mixed motives in locating oil wells, it seemed to describe oil accurately as it had been present thousands of years ago. Something beyond Cayce's consciously feeling worthy or unworthy may have been at work in such experiences, for those who have elevated psychic experiences do not typically claim to be worthy of these at all. Instead, unconscious processes may be chiefly involved, where the entire psyche takes account of its controls, ideals, and defenses—its integrity.

Investigation of creativity in problem-solving and the arts has not always shown a high correlation between public norms of virtue and the productivity of the creative individual. However, when one's productivity is measured against her or his own consistency with inner stances disclosed in dreams and introspection, another picture emerges. Individuals who prostitute their art or solve strategy problems for industrial spies may produce results, but there are often suggestions that they operate below their best capacities. An experience such as Samson's, where an individual recovers his full potential in a burst, after breaking vows he has made, also raises the question of integrity in the generation of creative energy. On the other hand, those who practice proper but stale virtue, as the story of Job may suggest, may find that only crisis and accompanying vision may free their best energies. Understanding, or wisdom, may indeed be the twin of upright behavior in all creativity. Carl Jung and his associates have traced the spontaneous emergence of archetypes from the deep unconscious as occurring in an orderly sequence of "understanding," which is the accompaniment of productive essay. Jung has suggested that Paul's phrase might read, "For now abideth faith, hope, love—and insight." Virtue seems to require understanding.

In taking up the question of integrity, Edgar Cayce turned to the ancient religious question of how one may do that which one knows to do. In the Cayce view, no individual alone had sufficient resources to keep true to present ideals and open to new ones at the same time; one must have the continuous aid of one's own transcendent soul and seek the help of the ever-aiding Christ Spirit. "None can choose aright without the Holy Spirit" was one statement on the problem. Yet those who patiently hoped and tried to do the best they knew would find help, until one day it might be said of them as the Cayce information occasionally observed of an individual who asked guidance: "Who can tell a rose to be beautiful? Who can tell the wind to blow? Who can tell a baby how to smile?" Purity of heart was not beyond reach, with God's help.

Part of God's help would be understanding—not necessarily learning, or knowledge of facts, but the sense of meaning, of design, of the connection in behavior. An individual who tried to control anger might learn how the energies of anger can work effectively, so that one can "be angry but sin not," and in the process learn how to convert hostility to courage, violence to vigor, aggression to boldness, explosive episodes to steady fierceness over poverty and bigotry and epidemics. For there were laws for the operation of the adrenalin glands, just as there were laws for everything else in the universe. Man could learn how he uses anger for cheap catharsis, or to cover up threatening sexuality, or to impute his own guilts to others, for these things were not past understanding—just as he could learn that "a person without a temper isn't worth much." Virtue could be grounded in intelligent understanding. By self-study, even by the study of the glandular function, as well as by the study of literature and the Bible, one might grasp little by little the essential truths of any area of his behavior. But introspection alone would not take an individual far, and knowledge not tested could be a pit, a snare. For the primary activity of human consciousness was comparison, correlation—and these processes could only be brought fully into play in activity, in experiment, in trying out the laws of being. No virtue worth having would be mere artificial control. As already noted, the Cayce materials insisted, "Don't be just goody-goody, be good for something"—for in productive creativity, in shared making and loving and giving, one could find the precious wisdom needed to conquer self.

Part of every person's task of integrity would be making sure that one's personality was in alignment with, and grounded upon, one's individuality. By *personality*, Cayce's source meant the public self—the offices, roles, trappings, standards, station, titles, vestments, and the rest of the image that one asked the world to accept. By *individuality*, Cayce's source meant something not so easy to inspect but evidently the unique thrust of a soul in a given lifetime—with certain ideals to the fore, certain vows to be kept, certain talents to be used, certain life-riddles to be solved. Individuality was what the Cayce information probed in life readings, as well as in mental and spiritual readings. Dreams, prayer, meditation, the tiny daily promptings of the stream of faith—all might bring to consciousness the true individuality upon which the personality might be properly grounded in virtue. Other aids to discovering individuality could also be found in the loving responses of group members, in the ring of biographies within the self, in the construction of "life seals" based upon the best elements in past lives, and even in travel to sites where one had grown most beautifully in former existences, or in cleaving to associates who seemed to elicit one's best self. For the individuality upon which virtue must be grounded was not hopelessly hidden; what covered it over would be so acting toward one's brother as to blind oneself from the light of one's own soul, in the very act of blinding one's brother. To grapple with virtue and understanding, then, one had to work to see behind the vice of others, had constantly to discover what good thing sought to work itself out in another, however clumsily. Always, one had to go beyond vengeance to compassion for the offender, for it was a law that the psyche would exact upon itself the same standards used upon others. "Judge not, that ye be not judged" was more than good advice; it was reality as sure as gravity.

Yet not every trial that came upon a person meant that the individual was being judged, that one's virtue and understanding had failed. There were, in the view of the Cayce source, those times when—as Job discovered—tribulations were the mercy of God. Weakness might yield to strength, timidity to certitude, hope to performance, under a duress that had its origin in what was to come as much as in what had been. "Whom the Lord loveth He chasteneth" was used by this source to forestall the endless computing of karma by those who sought, like the friends of Job, to rationalize all stations and developments in life. A soul's journey was ultimately known only to God, and to be measured only by God and the individual's own soul, born of the same Godhead; it was possible (as Jesus said, according to the Cayce readings) for one to be born blind "that God may be glorified" by the choice of that soul. Hardship was not always the sharp justice of karma for deserting virtue and understanding (which was in the minds of those questioners who asked whether it could be the soul's fault that one had been born blind).

How might one begin to cultivate integrity? There was that remarkable creative power of the subconscious, which would build whatever it was consistently offered. Therefore, "whatsoever things are true, beautiful, just, of good report, think of these things." And one could make choices of thoughts, beginning again and again. The power to choose, to throw the switch of meaning, to pick, to determine, to take a stand, was in the view of the Cayce source a final attribute of the soul, never fully lost. This did not mean one could invent or imagine life to be what was pleased; the universe was not that chaotic. But in the real choices that faced individuals, not hypothetical ones, they would find they had the power of choice and a tiny bit more each time they used it constructively, in the way or mind of Christ. Such power of choice, to recognize and answer calls from the soul and one's brothers or sisters, was of more value than attainment of skill or position that men prize. On that account, each would find that what God asked in any lifetime was not that one succeed in some notable way, or that virtue and understanding bring public results; God's ultimate question was only whether that individual had tried. "Try, try again," the Cayce readings urged upon alcoholics, quarreling lovers, struggling scientists, repentant parents, regretful politicians, fumbling artists. This was the commandment: not to succeed, not to be perfect, but to try—with all the heart, mind, soul, strength—until the whole being burned with single light in the effort to glorify God. That alone would be gain, eternal gain, if the effort were made in order to be a channel of blessings—that blessed channel—to others. For one would not get "into heaven," into new and free consciousness of creating daily with God, except "leaning on the arm of someone ye have helped." This was the refrain of hundreds of the Cayce readings.

Integrity and Action on People and Things

Can growth of integrity actually be accompanied by growth in psychokinesis, in capacity to direct an unseen flow of energy towards people and things? Do virtue and understanding play so large a part in the development of psychic gifts?

The writer interviewed a psychiatrist who has practiced in New England for years, working long hours with troubled people. A student of parapsychological research and of dream research, he described a process that he had found emerging in recent years of his practice.

Early in his practice he had conceived his role as explaining people's problems to them, helping them name the goblins of the mind, equipping them with the courage born of knowing that others had faced and met such problems, and sharing his professional treasure of procedures that they could use to meet and tame their demons. In this process, he often found himself touched to the quick by the situation laid bare in a life before him, which so closely paralleled his own weaknesses that had led to divorce in early marriage. As many another therapist has done, he found himself as much healed as his patients, through what he came to face and to understand, as well as in the impact of those telling moments when his patients chose fidelity or trust or risk, and showed the human spirit shining, even out of sickness.

His perception of unconscious contents in his patients grew keener, his empathy warmer, as he brought his own life under the same standards, the same disciplines, the same covenants he fostered in his patients. But more, he had found recently in his practice that something beneath the level of words was occurring at critical moments in therapy. He was slipping into a total stance of prayer, like his own best private devotional life, while before him a father chose whether to forgive a son, or a painter whether to live in reality, or a child-molester whether to face his own childish aggression. And in those moments he could feel a flow of energy go out from him that seemed to have an almost physical impact on the patients. Tears came more freely when they were needed by a patient, a patient's anger reached catharsis rather than staying sullen poison, fear sharpened a patient's desire to dig out his deceptions, truth recognized by a patient could resonate into a huge laugh. Patients repeatedly com-

mented on the vital boost of help they felt at turning points, and relatives even mentioned hearing of the incidents. Not every sick person
recovered. Not everyone was significantly helped. Yet there had appeared
what seemed to be a force that could be relied upon in the consulting
room (though not for too many hours in a given day), a force that at
least triggered or restricted responses in others, if it did not act directly
upon their minds and bodies.

The psychiatrist did not abandon his psychiatry. Instead he pressed his
studies ever harder, reaching into further research on dreams and into
the biochemistry of traumas and their release. But his chief hope to be
helpful to patients at turning points, critical incidents when they needed
an extra vital boost to code the struggling energies within them—this
resource, he told the writer, came from the effort to keep his own life
straight, to walk in the way of the best he knew. As he managed to do
this, or to try again, under all the temptations or professional prestige,
wealth, women patients proclaiming love for him, and potential competition with colleagues, he found that he was "not against myself," that
he could reach for aid as far down as the center of his selfhood and find
there forces not wholly of his own making. Asked if he believed in spiritual healing, he always answered "yes" with a smile. While his questioner
might refer to a superior occult power from some other plane, he meant,
as he would explain when pressed, that spirituality was not violating
one's own foundations and was the basis of the healing he trusted most
in his consulting room. "If ye continue in my word," he once reminded
a group that Jesus had said of purity in behavior and understanding,
"then shall ye be my disciples; and ye shall know the truth, and the truth
shall make you free."

~ EIGHT ~
Out-of-Body Experiences

Edgar Cayce sat up and rubbed his eyes. He had finished a long trance session and awakened with a slight start, asking his wife, who sat beside him to give him instructions during the trance, "Did you get it?" Having been unconscious, he had no idea what he had said or whether he had said anything at all—for there had been times, when he was very tired, that he could not enter the trance state nor give a reading. After his wife nodded, he buttoned his collar and smiled. "I had a dream," he said to the writer and others in the room.

The idea of Cayce dreaming, while he was busy talking in deep trance about people scattered around the country, seemed absurd. Yet from time to time it happened. This time the dream was a little unusual.

"I went fishing with John, James, Andrew and the Master," he explained. "I asked where Peter was, 'Oh, you know Peter isn't here!' said James. Thomas said, 'Oh, yes, I was a fisherman—don't let them fool you, telling you to quit fishing. We are all eating fish.'" "All of us," Cayce added, "were in the nicest little boat on a lake."

Cayce had obviously enjoyed the dream. The center of his entire devotional life was the Master, and any sense of closeness to Him, even in dream or waking reverie, gave Cayce a lift as could nothing else.

In earlier days, when the pressure to give readings for those in pain and illness was not so great as this year—the year that proved the last of Cayce's life—he might well have taken a reading on the dream, to get an interpretation to match his waking judgment. But now he had to be content with what he could consciously make of the dream.

He knew it was important, for a dream of the Master was one that touched his very soul. He also knew it was not a warning, from the happy mood of the fishing. He also knew it was not literal, some sort of gathering of those particular souls in another plane, or at least he thought this unlikely. For his readings had told him that at least one of the disciples in the boat had already incarnated, and Cayce had met him—a man in England. Further, he had been assured that two others, including Peter, would incarnate during Cayce's lifetime, or soon after, to help in preparing the way for a new growth of spirituality across the earth. He took this to be the meaning of the comment in the dream that Peter would not be found with the other disciples, and it gave him a sense of promise. For Cayce was weary, and he welcomed every prompting that told him others would provide new kinds of leadership in a world at war.

More practically, he took the comments about fishing as encouragement from his own best self to get out on the dock behind his house, where there was a little freshwater lake, and to renew the fishing times he so loved. In the quiet at the water's edge, practicing a ritual as old as man on the earth, he had always found refreshment, balance, steadiness, assurance that "underneath are the everlasting Arms." But in the press of hundreds of pleading letters each day, since the publication of his biography, and in the demands of long-distance phone calls so numerous that the phone company limited the number of his incoming calls each day, in order to let others use the lines out of Virginia Beach, he had put his fishing aside. After this dream, he returned to it, at least for a while. He even ate more fish and seafood, in the light of his feelings about the dream, for he had long been convinced by his readings that dreams deserved to be examined for content at several different levels at once—physical, mental, spiritual.

But there was a puzzling element about the dream, as about many dreams. Was there, in addition to the various symbolic contents meant to give him aid and encouragement from his own best self, also a residue to suggest that he had moved somewhere in consciousness while having this dream? For it had the qualities of sunlight and beauty that he had learned to associate with dreams that his information said signaled a dreamer's entrance into another plane of consciousness. Had he for a flash been "caught up," as Paul said he had been so lifted into the "third heaven," and had Cayce retained only the sense that had been elaborated in the little dream? Did people actually leave the body in some way to be "present with God," as Paul had suggested?

The idea of leaving his body, or at least having part of his consciousness leave his body, was not strange to Cayce. He had learned from painful experience that nobody should pass his hand or an object over his solar plexus while he was in trance, for it would instantaneously stop his speaking. His source had warned him that carelessness in this matter could cost him his life, by separating an invisible connection between his sleeping–speaking body and that other part of him that was abroad seeking aid for someone through a reading.

He knew that he could be directed in trance to go anywhere and give such explicit detail about what he was watching that those who had listened, over the years, had become convinced that an important part of him was really on the distant scene. For example, early in his career, according to Mrs. Cayce, Cayce had been asked to "follow" several of his Kentucky townspeople each day, while they went about touring spots at the Paris Exposition. He had supplied such abundant detail that when his friends returned and examined the records, they made the case celebrated for years in that section of Kentucky. (Mrs. Cayce, however, had been unhappy with this use of Edgar's abilities, fearing that such a relatively pointless exhibition would not afford him the same vital energy and protection as when he sought to help the sick.)

Over the years, he had experienced a few dreams that in their form and content left him convinced that he had "been somewhere" out of his body during the dream. For example, there had been the dream when he found himself with Dwight L. Moody, a gifted preacher and evangelist who had given Cayce much encouragement at a chance meeting early in Cayce's manhood. Other ministers he had known were present in the dream, too, all of them by that time dead, as were the others in a great meeting hall that they entered from a dark hallway, where the light was dark blue and made people's faces look purple. In the meeting hall itself he noticed that all wore robes and were standing. They were waiting to hear the Master speak, as Cayce had been told He would, when invited to go to the meeting at the start of the dream. In the hall was somehow a light that Cayce couldn't see but realized it came from a Voice, which he knew to be "the Lord" speaking, though He could not be seen. The Voice asked, "Who will go to bring peace again on the earth?"—a fitting question in the midst of World War II. Then, Cayce reported of the dream, Jesus had stepped forward and said, "I will go. It is time for me to go again into the earth to strengthen my brethren, though I will not be born on the earth…" and the dream ended, leaving Cayce with a sense of joy and promise he could not put into words but that had often returned in his thoughts since the dream. The dream had left him with a sense that his work was worthwhile if in even the smallest way it helped to set men wondering and thinking, so that they might better recognize the closer Presence of the Master, when He came among them.

In reflecting on the possibility of being fully conscious yet out of his body, Cayce joined a long parade of those who made such claims in various cultures. It was the heart of the trance experience sought by the shaman among the Indians of the Pacific Northwest, and the essence of old Hindu claims that holy men could be seen in two places at once, miles apart. European folklore celebrated the claim in stories of the Doppelganger, or double who walks abroad, while men in battlefield experiences of World War II were currently reporting leaving their bodies after severe wounds, to travel over the terrain about them, seeing every detail with indelible clarity, while seeming to seek aid for their battered bodies.

Possible out-of-the-body experiences had been reported by investigators of hypnosis from its earliest days, when it was quaintly called "traveling clairvoyance." Hugh Lynn Cayce and other investigators such as Charles Tart and Andrija Puharich have reproduced the early hypnosis experiments with their own subjects in cases, for example, where subjects supplied such abundant detail of adjoining rooms unknown to them (rooms deliberately set to fall into disarray after the door was closed and all observers outside) that the hypothesis of some sort of "leaving the body" seemed worth considering. Under the influence of LSD or of sensory deprivation tanks, others who were not hypnotized sometimes also seemed to inspect their immediate surroundings as though from outside their bodies, while still other subjects reported similar experiences after surgery or in critical illness—when they seemed to look down on their bodies with detachment. Cases of people seen by others in an apparition miles from their bodies were studied and reported in considerable numbers by Muldoon and Tyrrell in England, as well as by Hart and Louisa Rhine in the U.S.

Can some portion of an individual's consciousness leave the body, split off and have its own perceptions? Could this be trained, as some of the earliest investigators had reported? Edgar Cayce in trance was asked a number of times, over the years, about such a possibility.

The Information responded that such experiences did occur, most often in dreams, when few were aware that they were abroad, although the careful study of anyone's dreams might reveal such incidents after a time. It was also reported that accident or injury, especially to endocrine gland areas and associated centers of the real physical body could bring about out-of-body experiences when they were not sought, usually with some peril to the subject. The attempt to induce such experiences while awake, rather than in dream or trance states, held considerable danger, and most people were advised by this trance source to "place self wholly in Christ, and let Him determine" when such experiences might be fruitful for the person. To be sure, the regular practice of meditation might keep free the channels within the personality and the body, along which such unusual experiences could occur, if there were the need to know another soul with the extraordinary vividness that such experiences made possible (as compared with the mental attunements of hunches and impressions), or if there were the need to make one's presence so felt by another living person that only an out-of-body experience would accomplish the goal.

Those who have kept records of their dream and fantasy experiences, in the effort to verify some of the claims of the Cayce source, have noted the relative rarity of material that would suggest the individual was detached from his body and looking back at it, while also inspecting in veridical detail some adjacent or distant area. Yet the experiences do seem to occur, sometimes with a suggestion of slipping out of the top of the head. A few have reported hesitation about whether to return to their bodies, and one psychic whom the writer has studied has for this reason vowed he would never again try to induce such an experience.

Several have reported wondering whether the Cayce material might be correct in suggesting that leaving the body for such experiences was not unlike the parting at death, and have wondered whether a lifetime of meditation would make it easier to undergo the transition of death when that time finally occurred.

Asking why extra-body trips have taken the dreaming or conscious person in one direction rather than another, investigators have raised the question of bonds with others. In psychic experience as in waking experience, do people take "trips" to see those upon whom their hearts are set? Does this account for the high proportion of out-of-body visits to loved ones by those who are ill or apparently have just died? Does like attract like in the psychic world as in the world of vacations, letters, phone calls, and dinner parties? If so, then it becomes important whom one chooses in his heart as his associates and perhaps even more important what one seeks from the meeting. When the spirit or force of an individual goes forth from that person, whether in a waking handshake or in an eerie dream, what kind of relationships does that individual seek with others? Does she or he exploit others for personal justification, convenience, power, position, advancement, or theories? Or can the individual meet people as subjects in themselves, as independent centers of reality, as points of becoming as cosmically significant to God and to her or his own soul as self? The thrust of the Cayce materials about meeting others out of the body was that attitudes toward others were critical in determining whether such experiences would be helpful or—more basic—take place at all.

Acceptance in Creativity

To the Edgar Cayce trance source, the question of radical acceptance of others was important enough to take sixth place in a graded set of foci for training in creativity. The chapter on this topic in *A Search for God* was entitled "Fellowship."

There are indications that while awake we all avoid those whom we have hurt or condemned; guilt is a barrier in the affairs of daily life. And those whom we have not rejected but treated by an opposite extreme, identifying and fusing with them, rather than accepting them as separate beings, find themselves rebelling against such assimilation to ourselves and often turning upon us with surprising force, as we may do with them when we do not feel appreciated. Further, while we may find the flow of fantasy heightened over an idol, such fantasy is rarely creative until it is tempered by full human relationships; "love is blind" especially in early stages. May it be as blind for ESP as for other perception? In a similar fashion we are bound to our enemies if we hate them, finding that "hate is blind," as well; while we may be fully aware of the faults of an individual whom we feel has outraged us, we are usually singularly ineffective in generating changes in the other while obsessed by him or her. It appears that people cannot function at maximum creativity in psychic ability or other relating, so long as they cannot approach others with an acceptance transcending both uncritical identification and unqualified rejection. As Martin Buber has so eloquently written, the "I" of an "I–thou" relation with another is a different "I" than the "I" of an "I–it" relation, when another becomes our thing, our abstraction, our convenience. We are whole and have access to our fullest selves, in Buber's terms, as we are able to stand, however fleetingly, in fully accepting relations with others. By contrast, when we stand in partial relations, necessary for the ordered affairs of daily life, we are but partly ourselves, for any kind of creative task.

Further evidence regarding possible laws by which we associate with others in psychic experiences, including those whereby we may leave our bodies behind and see them there, may lie in dream material. The interpreter of dreams so often finds the characters in them representing parts of the dreamer that interpretation usually begins on this assumption in clinical practice. However, one also finds those dreams in which individuals appear not so much as flags or signals of something as they appear in the knobby uniqueness felt in their living presence. Such dreams leave upon the dreamer a sense of the peculiar combination of promise and problem, presence and potential, biography and becoming, which lights the face–to–face meeting with someone well known. Such dreams produce more fitting, more authentic encounters with the dreamed–about one, if the person is living, or more apt memories and prayers for the dreamed one, if that individual is dead. Full encounters shatter stereotypes. Is it possible that dreamers leave their bodies to become present with others for just such full encounters?

Studies of the psychology of creativity have accented the factor of attitudes towards others, even though few others may be involved in the actual creative act. Self-justification before imagined others is a burden upon the flow of imagery and form, for a painter or a businessman alike. And self-justification is the typical concern where scorn has reduced the cast of respected associates on the stage of one's life. Likewise, belittling of others makes it more difficult to accept and use their contributions as valid for one's own creative work, while destructive efforts toward competitors or relatives alike tend to leave the actor afraid of himself being destroyed.

Taking up the issue of acceptance as a religious concern in creativity, the Cayce trance source turned to a religious question as widely distributed as men's faiths: Who is to be considered justified, worthy, before God? Ought the answer to be "the people of the Book," as it was for Moslems who did not slaughter those who had a written scripture, in the days of their early conquests? Ought the answer to be those of doctrinal conformity, as it was for the Inquisition? Ought the answer to be those untainted by visions, as it was for early American witch-hunters? Are the justified the upright saints or arhats of Southern Buddhism, or the penitent seekers for heavenly compassion in Northern Buddhism? Ought individuals emulate the ardent asceticism of John the Baptist, or the more relaxed city-trafficking ways of Jesus?

The Cayce source claimed that no one could properly be approached as a self-made product, either good or bad. Every individual had to be understood as sprung from a seed planted by God, a living soul. Since souls were of the nature of God himself, in their love and purity and vital creativity, they need not be justified and could not be; their very existence commanded respect, even when individual entities had to be avoided at times or struggled with unto physical death. Nobody could rely upon a political or religious grouping to dictate whom to take seriously in personal encounters, as Jesus had made clear in the parable of the Samaritan, where both distinctions were present. On the contrary, every one had to learn, sooner or later, that each must answer life with a consummate affirmation: "I am my brother's keeper." Who, then, was this brother or sister? Potentially every individual in the earth—anyone needing aid, a gift of personal talents, encouragement. Not some distant benighted savage for whom one might simply give missionary dollars, although such work had its place, but above all the one across the line of political right and political left—wherever someone stood or stumbled in need of aid that could be given.

· The Cayce information was explicit that the economically disadvantaged and the members of racial minorities were direct challenges to everyone; it asserted that these people must be given their rights, not only as individuals but as groups of people, for brother-sisterhood did not stop with personal kindliness. It also involved social responsibility, the taking of stands and the carrying of duties, even to the penalty that Jesus paid, if the individual had set the ideal "in Christ." Yet not martyrdom but creative service with the best of one's talents was the goal. To be one's brother's keeper was something more than cheering from a safe distance; the musician had better make music for him or her, the doctor healing, the manufacturer an opportunity for employment, the waitress an act of service, the psychic service by reading—or health was not in any of them, and they might one day hear from their own souls "Depart from me," instead of the words from the Throne so often cited by the Cayce readings for the end of the soul's journey, "Well done, thou good and faithful servant; enter into the joy of the Lord."

The service of one individual to another was not a deduction from something else, not a moral precept. It was a shadow of one's fellowship with the Father. Responding to an individual was not identical with responding to God as Father; one had still to pray in secret to the Father and to engage in meditation where all other beings but the One disappeared from view. But responding to any person was of the same order as responding to God, requiring no less than the elements of worship: thanksgiving, adoration, repentance, celebration, forgiveness of sins, dedication, and more. The nearest house of God to where one stood was the next human flesh. For this trance source the theme was never reduced to poetry or religious scruples; as one treated another, one was actually—not figuratively—treating God. In the other person burned always that spark of the divine, that celestial fire deep down, which the forces of another's soul could fan into flame. Even in dealing with the enemy, the reviler, the outcast, one could not settle for thinking positive thoughts but must come to a yearning for the other to fulfill the promise of his being. Such acceptance would not be sympathy, which was simply a sometimes-helpful emotion, but would be a total response of love to the enemy that could only properly be called adoration, in the sense of a turning toward another, much more complete than affection or liking or attraction. One had to pray actively for the One Force in another, not merely overlooking shortcomings but having a vision of something better emerging directly from the shortcomings, as the good in the other, which personal failings were blindly seeking to express. For such a purpose one might wholeheartedly call upon innate psychic ability, and ask the aid of Christ as well, that he or she might be shown how to pray and how to act with one who had erred.

If every individual were one's brother and sister, did one then merely wander about doing indiscriminate good deeds? Sometimes. But the first stage of creativity to be practiced was cooperating, covenanting. One had to enter into specific bonds, specific groups, specific traditions, in order to reach his or her own depths for the resources needed to fully love and accept others. Such associating would at times take precedence in activity, though not in attitude, over even the bonds of family life. As the Cayce source reminded, even Jesus had asked, "Who are my mother and brothers? They that do the will of the Father in heaven." One had to gather with the "sheep," mature individuals who consciously chose the Ideal, in order to be able to feed the "lambs" who would become sheep if they knew how. Every devout individual, as Peter in the Gospel of John, was called to feed both.

Could any individual by will alone choose fully to accept another in fellowship? Not in the view of the Cayce source. Such fellowship was ultimately found by alignment with God, Who alone could open one's eyes and soul to the other. In this vein, the Cayce source chose an appellation for Christ that differed from the terms most common in the surrounding culture, though it did not contradict them. More often perhaps than any other phrase, the designation given to Christ by the Cayce readings was "the Elder Brother." The phrase had about it the insistence that one dare not give honor to Christ that was not matched in principle in the way one looked at any other. The face of every individual would look different immediately after looking at the face of Christ, for in such a glance the destiny of souls could be known: to have again with the Father that "perfect fellowship which was in the beginning." Yet no trivializing of Christ, nor reduction of Him to religious leader rather than Messiah, was allowed by the phrase. For often the terms used were Lord, Master, Son and Light—to remind individuals of the gulf between their easy earth-trimmed ways and that transcendent creativity that someday, somehow they had also to make theirs. The ultimate destiny of every human was to become as Christ, no less. A soul might require eons to do it, and move through regions and planes unknown to those on earth, but the journey had to be made, and God had time that matched the size of His purpose.

How might one begin to practice the radical acceptance that marked true fellowship? As always, self-evaluation was one essential. One had to look at each day, each week, to find out whether in fact his or her life was bringing peace or contentiousness to others. One had to ask, with the aid of dreams and prayer, whether one would be willing to be represented in the very presence of the Almighty Father, solely by the way others were treated. One had to pry open the apertures of mind and heart to others, and it was as fitting to pray "help thou mine unbelief in my brother" as to pray "help thou mine unbelief in my God." At the same time, acceptance and rejoicing in oneself, one's own secret identity and soulship, would be linked with one's capacity to accept others. For the Cayce source, self-condemnation was a dangerous sin. One could repent, be sorry, set about changing. But one could not punish nor condemn and exile self, any more than one could another, for the soul had equally regal status in the Kingdom with all others who sought to "inherit the Kingdom." Needless self-doubt, self-castigation would be found to be a defense against responsibility for one's own life, and an unworthy attempt at placating God with a sacrifice not approved by Him. One who did not rejoice in the gift of his or her own life and personal opportunities rejected God as truly as the one who ignored a neighbor; indeed, the two attitudes were secretly linked within, for the loss of the sun of the soul, with its gift of love and vision, was the natural consequence of any eclipse of human dignity and worth. Every individual, oneself included, needed to be properly seen as striving to give form to her or his final understanding of God, for this was the force that set all souls and lives in motion and kept them on their journeys.

Specific disciplines might help to build the full acceptance that marked fitting fellowship of one individual with another. One could practice much at home, where it would be seen that no answer at all was better than an unkind one. There, where defenses were properly dropped, one could learn that a long face never glorified the God who spun the worlds and found the "good, good." In the daily walk of life, the beginning could ever be made, and the right direction made into a highway for the life, by being kind, considerate; more would be accomplished by little deeds wholeheartedly done than by great resolves honored more in speech than act. And again and again one would find the opportunity to risk a response to another soul, as one would want God to risk on him or her. "For if ye were judged by God as ye judge others, where would ye be?"

There was a bit of homey verse that the Cayce trance source often used, apparently taken from Edgar Cayce's own personal store of maxims, to sum up the challenge of fellowship, the dangerous and beautiful business of risking creation in partnership with another: "It is better to trust one soul, and that deceiving, than to doubt the one in whom believing would have blessed thy life with truer meaning." Yet the point of fellowship was greater than self-serving. It was no less than "glorifying God in the earth," a soul who was as unspeakably precious to God as any soul created, "be he black, white, gray, or grizzled."

Acceptance and Out-of-Body Experiences

Might the individual seeking helpful psychic experiences find that growing in the ability to truly accept others would at times free her or him to leave the body, in dream or in prayer, and stand close to another for sharing?

An able, elderly "sensitive" described to the writer an experience that followed shortly after painful chest surgery nearly cost him his life. Prior to the surgery, he had been involved in lecturing and demonstrations that took him across the country once or twice a year, as well as in counseling friends old and new who had come to rely on his aid. Often he was in trance, and he knew there were conditions of rest and diet and relaxation he would have to meet, to keep his physical resources intact under the strain of the trance work. Still, he pushed himself, responding to requests that in a year's time might include those of researchers, college professors, ministers, even government officials. Since he traveled so much, it was difficult for him to meet with the little study and growth group that had been the instrument of his healing once before and the vehicle for his helping people of many walks of life, over the years. He struggled to keep his balance with his own devotions, but his health failed, lung collapsed, and he required major surgery to remove part of his lung. During the painful convalescence, he had time to think, time to talk with people on the phone, time to greet visitors, some of whom came from long distances to see him. He began to be able to look deeply into faces, unhurried, to cherish those about him, rather than to feel he must lead them. To some of these visitors, as to the writer, he told the story of an experience that followed shortly after his surgery.

He had fallen asleep thinking of the one man in America whose healing prayer he most respected, a man he had not talked with or written to for years. The friend was hundreds of miles away in another city. He wanted his aid, for the pain was great, and often his spirits flagged, while doctors were not encouraging about his recovery, as a man in his seventies. But he hesitated to call his friend the healer, for he had long failed to write, and the barrier created by ignoring loved ones intruded itself. Then during the night he had a vivid dream. He found himself standing in the bedroom of his friend, hundreds of miles away. He saw his friend stir, noticed a score of little details in the room, felt the lift of love for his friend, and then was gone from the place. Even in his dream he found himself noting that he had been out of his body.

He slept soundly, unaware of pain for the first night since the surgery, and in the morning woke refreshed. His recovery grew more swift from that time on.

Two days later came a special delivery letter from his healing friend. "What were you doing in my room the other night?" it began. The letter told how clearly the friend had seen him, even to the extent of noting bandages on his chest, for just a moment. The friend had then stayed awake to pray and poured out earnest intercession for the psychic whom he had not seen for so long. "I know you were here," the letter continued, "and I only hope I understood the reason for your coming and was able to help a bit." He had helped. Or at least that was how the psychic saw it. He saw his out-of-body experience not as a psychic feat, put on like so many of his demonstrations, but as a cry for help from his own soul, leading him forth along lines of companionship strung anew in the quiet times of his illness.

Had he moved out from his body in a process foreshadowed long ago, when an empty tomb led to an out-of-body meeting with bewildered disciples, and the flesh refashioned itself for love?

∽ NINE ∽
Precognition

Edgar Cayce walked through the little workroom where the writer sat typing, preparing questions for the next day's readings.

Somebody had to read the correspondence with each application for a reading, in order to formulate questions for the end of the reading. Cayce was swamped with just sorting each day's mail to schedule appointments. Besides, he was not too interested in the fine details of a given person's need. His source had told him that one reason he did his work in trance was to keep some measure of distance between himself and all those problems and personalities with which he sought to work psychically. So he was content to glance at the first letter of inquiry or application and to let others study the correspondence to make up each day's readings and questions. Sometimes when the membership form in the little research association was in good order, he did not even see a note from an applicant. And sometimes people sent no information nor questions whatsoever, content to see what Cayce would get about them, or testing his ability. He did not seem to mind being tested, for he understood the doubts that people must have about his strange abilities. But Cayce's secretary had her hands full transcribing the many readings given each day, as well as supervising a busy office, which at one point employed ten additional typists and file clerks. So the present writer had volunteered to prepare the correspondence, instructions, and questions for each day's readings and was busy on this task when Edgar Cayce walked past to his lunch, saying nothing.

A moment later, Mrs. Cayce came from her kitchen, through the dining room and into the work area where the writer sat. "Edgar says you are leaving on the 11:40 a.m. Norfolk and Western train next Tuesday. Can we drive you to the train?" Her offer was spontaneous and genuine, quite like her. Indeed there was nothing unusual about the incident, except that she named a precise train time and day for the writer's forthcoming trip—a time and day that had not yet been settled.

To be sure, her husband may have been guessing when he gave her the information he "picked up" as he simply walked past the writer. There were only a few trains each day from Norfolk to Chicago, anyway, and only two railroads to consider, leaving from different terminals. Yet it was wartime and Norfolk was a busy seaport, so it was difficult to secure Pullman berths on short notice, as the writer had sought without success to do in his own lunchtime that day. He had been trying for one of three times, including the Tuesday departure that Cayce had quietly announced.

Not surprisingly, though not without humor, the writer and his wife began their packing and arrangements for their apartment, effective on the coming Tuesday. Cayce proved right. This was the day, the railroad, the time, when the departure occurred.

What had happened? The writer verified that he had left his home phone number with the railroad office, not his office number, and that no call had been made, which Cayce might have overheard. There seemed little reason to doubt that there had occurred yet another in the little forays into the future that had become second nature to Edgar Cayce. Whether Cayce had secured the correct train details by simultaneously piecing together the mind of the writer and the appropriate railroad officials, or whether some part of his psyche had simply constructed a whole event and felt it fit with the future, would be impossible to say. Cayce himself could not describe the elements of such events in his mind, except that he "knew," and knew he knew.

How far is it possible to know the future? Is such psychic experience the direct inspection of a future event that has not yet occurred—which seems impossible? Is it a computerlike assessment of a score of variables all swept into a glance and totaled up to reveal the future? Is it the inspection of a pattern element within the psyche, which may be similar to the pattern working itself out in the world beyond the psyche—so that a "fresh start in late morning" feeling in Cayce coincided with the elements working toward a "fresh start on a train trip on Tuesday morning"?

However it occurred, Edgar Cayce found the experience of certainty about the future familiar. Most of his detailed precognitive promptings had come in dreams. He had dreamed repeatedly of the founding and progress of his hospital, even while living in Dayton, before moving to Virginia Beach. He had dreamed of its medical staff, of its board, of its front steps, of the strains that would lead to its closing. He had dreamed of Atlantic University, founded on his work, and its personnel and back-ers. And his wife dreamed of the future even more often: she dreamed of a trip, of visitors, of a quarrel, of investment opportunities. Together they had learned to follow a piece of counsel from the readings about such dreaming: Man and wife, as well as close relatives and business associates, should learn to check their dreams together, for often one could dream more clearly of a coming event than another, or could supplement the dream of another with further pieces. (It was a kind of cross-correspondence between dream contents, similar to that which engaged parapsychologists in the study of messages from discarnates through mediums.)

But Cayce did not have to be asleep to be prompted about the future. If he were rested and in good spirits, he would know when he was about to receive a letter from one of his sons in the service overseas, or when a check from a donor to research was on its way in the mail, or when a relative of one of his employees was ill enough to die—though doctors had not yet diagnosed the case. He seemed to see at times the outcome of pregnancies, the prospects for a piece of real estate, the tendency to an auto breakdown.

His daily life experiences of precognition were not unlike those that had engaged soothsayers and diviners and prognosticators from time immemorial—except that he used no special divining equipment and most of the time did not seek information about the future. His dreams had in them a larger proportion of psychic material than the dreams of others his age studied by parapsychologists, but the range of subject matter and imagery was not essentially different from that in dreams of ancient times, where the story might say, "And they, being warned in a dream, departed by another way." As the writer has compared Cayce's dream experiences with those of other psychics, the content and symbolism has not seemed exceptional in Cayce's instance.

The question of how far an individual may accurately know the future has puzzled researchers from the beginning of modern work on psychic experience. What occurred in the case of seeming apparitions who appeared to warn against a train, which later wrecked? What led a dreamer like the Englishman, Dunne, to foresee catastrophes and the results of horse races? How could Soal's subjects, the photographer Shackleton and the housewife Mrs. Stewart, correctly call cards that had not yet been determined by the selection of a counter from a bowl of mixed counters? In the U.S., how were some of Dr. Rhine's best subjects on ESP tests able to score on a target sheet to be prepared in a few days or weeks, based on tables of random numbers selected in turn from newspaper figures on the weather?

No researcher today has the answer to these questions. What has become apparent is that individuals tend to have their own profiles in ESP touching the future; they seem to be interested in different kinds of events and people and in different spans of distance ahead. Further, their test scores on targets in the future tend to vary in much the same ways as their scores on targets in the present, under the influence of drugs, hypnosis, competition, encouragement, injury, or helpful partners; what seems to be one process of PSI confronts researchers, rather than a separate process for the perception of the present and the future.

People from many walks of life asked Edgar Cayce in trance how to become more effectively aware of the future. Mothers asked how to keep alerted for the danger of epidemics to their children. Businessmen asked how they might determine market trends. Inventors asked how they could safely get their devices to the patent office. Homeowners asked how they could be warned in advance of threatening earthquakes. A few eager students of mysteries asked how to foresee where they would be born in their next life on earth. Most of the seekers for the future were encouraged to study their dreams. But there was no magical divining screen offered in dreams; one could not usually expect to dream of the future of others, except his loved ones or close associates. Further, one could not usually expect to glimpse the future in areas outside his round of interests: A businessman would not be likely to dream of developments in Tin Pan Alley, nor an athlete of developments in theoretical physics. The subconscious, which accounted for most of the spontaneous psychic experiences in waking and dreaming life, was coded on what to expect of the future by exactly what the individual held and worked on in consciousness. The subconscious was not a ball of mirrors flashing aimlessly at the dreamer, correctly reflecting a bit of the vast future every now and then; it was a highly directional capacity, responsive to the conscious studies and work of daily life. To improve one's glimpses of the money market, one had to become a responsible banker, not attempt concentration on a dollar bill. If one worked creatively at his or her life, and with motives of integrity and service, he or she could expect glimpses of the future in the areas of life concern and responsibility as truly as one could expect to breathe, for natural psychic ability was constantly at work in a process the Cayce source described as "similar to self-preservation."

Of course there were things to learn about subconscious renderings of the future, both in dreams and waking hunches. One had to learn to distinguish between a signal to pay attention to something—an opportunity or a warning to be studied—and a signal to act now on something coming about. One had to learn to use reason, the deductive mind, in harmony with the raw data of psychic perception supplied by the subconscious, the inductive mind; better rational judgment supported and freed the psychic processes to function, rather than supplanting them. Further, one had to learn not to take too seriously all images of the future, even those that seemed notably psychic, for it was the way of the subconscious to depict things as present trends would bring them out if unchecked, in that strange inner landscape where time and space were ignored, and all things of the past and future tended to be set forth as now. A dream of the death of a loved one could mean many things, including the death of an unhealthy relationship with that person; if the dream were the warning of a future development, it might more likely be an indication of a serious concern that, unattended, would be grave, rather than impending extinction for the loved one. Yet the subconscious was not erratic in what it fed an individual of the future, for it would tend to give only what the individual could handle—if the nervous system and glandular system were not in some way damaged. One needed have no fear of being swamped in dire warnings if the desires to know the future were only to see that which could constructively be used without exploitation of others.

The quiet flow of assurances the Cayce source called *faith*, the evidence of things unseen, was the source of constant psychic impressions, even when not stimulated by great devotion or great need to reach an enhanced or elevated stage. Recognizing that such a flow would be there, one ought to pause briefly before making decisions involving the future, according to the Cayce information, and seek a "witness" from the "still, small voice." Before stepping into a stressful situation such as a quarrel or an accident or a delicate performance, one ought to pause and make conscious attunement with the good and godly spirit, which could prompt self to an awareness of what was ahead, and prepare for it. In an emergency, where one had to act but had no idea what to do despite one's best efforts at quiet and reflection, then one could pray for the answering Spirit of Christ to respond to the trembling of the soul, bringing him into touch with what he needed to know of the future. Cayce's source offered no magical trick nor claim that the effort to grapple with the future would be instantly effective. But on the other hand, this source gave the impression to those who sought counsel through many readings that individuals had more resources for knowing the future than were usually used, in an age when biblical accounts of guidance seemed more quaint than real.

In the years since Cayce's death, hundreds of people have used his suggestions for working with dreams of the future and have shared their dream content in small study groups and in intensive "project groups" held by the Association for Research and Enlightenment at Virginia Beach. Others have kept journal records for months, even years, of promptings of the future that occurred to them in waking life. There are many leads for research on precognition in all of this raw data. Varieties of temperament and interests are readily apparent in this material, as well as degrees of accuracy based on the use made of precognitive material. But one of the interesting variables that stands out appears to be the question of how much of the future can one handle. Fear, as the Cayce source suggested, may be a swift crippler of most kinds of psychic experiences. One who is afraid of a certain future, or afraid of personal adequacy and the trustworthiness of life itself, will not be a good candidate for the full range of psychic awareness of the future. It does not seem to work to seek awareness only of the pleasant that lies ahead; unless one can face the trying and frustrating as well, the unconscious appears to shut off most of the flow—as many people suffer spontaneous amnesia of dreams, while they are hiding from an unwelcome problem. Insofar as freedom from fear may be important for precognition, then the ability to handle stress may be critical in glimpsing the future.

Handling Stress in Creativity

As the Cayce source took up the next religious theme in its examination of the elements of creativity that man must work out in his pilgrimage with his Creator, it labeled the lesson "Patience." This was the word that summarized the essential capacity to handle stress, in working towards worthwhile goals.

Some of the earliest studies of creativity by psychologists have identified "endurance of unresolved tension" as the hallmark of the creative problem–solver. After an individual has defined a set of opposed values that she or he wants to reconcile in a productive solution, the creative person is notably the one who can wait without losing track of the problem. The individual may go on to something else, or sleep, or go to a movie, or pray, but the problem is always held onto. From time to time the individual may try out possible solutions, but he or she resists the temptation that seizes less able individuals, to simply take a solution and make it work as well as possible. At the same time, the person who scores well on tests of creativity is not a perfectionist, afraid to try a solution unless success is guaranteed. Characteristically, the individual will make an effort in due season, when the problem has ripened into solution stage.

Does such endurance affect not only the composing of music, the solving of equations in physics, the joining of wood in carpentry, the timing of an auto race, but also the accurate glimpsing of the future by psychic means? Does the ability to handle stress, including the stress of coming frustration and disappointment, color the capacity to stand in a larger present than is usually scanned to consciousness? It would not be surprising to researchers to find this the case. Most human beings handle stress by some combination of skill, defenses, and what is loosely called *ego strength*—capacity to endure tension and uncertainty, or insecurity. Where the defenses of rationalization, projection, repression, or other largely unconscious mechanisms predominate, the helpful flow of the unconscious seems impeded or distorted in the ordinary problem solving of daily life. It would seem reasonable to suspect that defensiveness might cripple the flow of helpful psychic promptings as readily as it cripples the flow of love, play, or study. Defensive postures of abandoning oneself to the unconscious in orgiastic bouts of emotion, or in hypochondria, or in paranoid fantasies might also impede precognition. Insofar as the psyche is a self-regulating system, it would seem likely that frantic efforts to solve problems would endanger the channels of precognition as readily as tendencies to avoid or deny problems. A steady posture of readiness to tackle what comes might prove to be most valuable, not only for marital success or business adroitness, but for opening the aperture of perception of the future.

In approaching patience as a religious question, the Cayce source appeared to be taking up the old religious question of how to correlate humanity's time and God's time, how to recognize the kairos, or moment of readiness in one's affairs, when the personal and the transpersonal meet. It was the question of the Kingdom of God, always here and always coming—how to stand in its shadow and face the future. It was the question of "storming the Kingdom," about which the prophets of Israel warned, as has the modern philosopher Martin Buber: Each person must find the line that defines the difference between one's readiness to act and one's willful seizure of affairs. It was a question similar to those in Chinese discussions of the silent way of the Tao, similar to the encouragement of the Hindu Bhagavad-Gita, that individuals could find a way to act without "attachment to the fruits" of the action, and like the question of living faith in Muslim references to the "will of Allah."

In the picture of patience developed by the Cayce source, what emerged was not passivity, but active alignment of the person with the timing that comes from God. Such alignment was not skill, though it might be perfected by experience and practice; in the last analysis it was a gift, the gift of the soul of man. Hearing the call of patience, which was more than dilatory waiting or restless pacing, and responding to the call in decisions of daily life, one might in time come to stand in steady relation with the soul, which is each person's mediator of God's wise time. "In patience possess ye your souls" was the biblical quote so often used by the Cayce trance source on this subject.

However, the Cayce information had one typical way of speaking of patience that was less biblical than metaphysical or philosophical. Over and over again this source spoke of growth to full personhood before God as occurring "in time, in space, in patience." Unmistakably, the Cayce readings were picturing patience as a third correlate of all events, beside time and space, when those events were seen—as Spinoza had long before suggested—under the aspect of eternity. But God's realm was not static and absolute, above all change, but the heart of all change, meaningful change; was not He the Creative Forces? Therefore, events could be described as occurring not only in time and space but also in a dimension that both the soul and God knew: patience. It was the biographical, historical dimension. It was the dimension where grace met law, for—said the Cayce source repeatedly—"ye grow in grace." An individual might like to leap into the Kingdom, to establish one's self as "saved" in a single decision or act. But the Cayce source kept asking people whether anything valued in nature behaved that way. Did plants leap into bloom, mountains leap into the air, babies leap into adulthood? God's way was slow, steady growth, in which the laws of becoming were both exemplified and learned. Hundreds of times the Cayce readings insisted that whatever was valuable for human beings developed "little by little, line upon line, precept upon precept." It was a perspective fully in keeping with a view of reincarnation, in which the opportunity to grow through many lives and grow in a fruitful direction was hinted as Jesus' intention when he said, "I am come that ye might have life, and life more abundant." Each life could be lived out to the full, in its own character, as one might value a jewel, a beautifully fashioned antique, an exquisitely bred blossom—for each life would prepare yet another part of the body of awareness and choices that grew upon and completed the very soul.

In the view of the Cayce source, creation was for keeps and need not be rushed nor anxious. Even movements and institutions and causes, revolutions and new worldviews should be approached in the patience that was God's own timing—a timing neither fatalistic nor frantic. Repeatedly the Cayce source insisted on one formula for effective and lasting social change: Each new idea or new way of living must come "first to the individual, then to the group, then to the classes, then to the masses." Individuals might like to jump at once to influencing the masses, as though to prove the rightness of his ideas by sheer number of converts. But such change was not durable. Minds and hearts had to be won, not just votes or shouts, and this required each individual's experiencing the change that was sought, as well as nurturing and celebrating it in small groups, out of which in time public leaders and larger institutional changes might emerge. The Cayce source was often tested on this formula by those who sought to publicize or promote Cayce's own work. One had to have a living experience not simply of Cayce but of a living process, of the Creative Forces helping him or her in life, before the individual had any business serving on the Board of the Cayce Association or helping in any such endeavors. In God's time, in the patience that only the soul rightly understood, there was time to discover about Cayce's work or any other: "Does it make you a better husband, a better wife, better in business, a better neighbor, a better artist, a better churchgoer? If so, cleave to it; if not, forget it!"

The opposite of patience was to be found when the person confused one's birthright from God with being God, when one tried to force the will upon affairs. The essence of sin, said the Cayce source, was "self-aggrandizement," the clutching to oneself of one form of power or another that should instead be held in partnership with God and one's fellows. Behind the violation of the call of patience would be found an attitude that sought to force the hand of God. As a soul, one could use his free will to so force events; but the consequences were always fear, fear that one might be so forced by others and by the universe. And of such fear the destiny was made, the anxious drawing to certain events and associations, which humans called karma—the reaping of what is sown. In living by grabbing, one might even find hell, which was described in one reading as becoming impatient with oneself.

The individual who lived in patience, seeking and trusting God's time, would one day see that in the long journey of the soul every trial had been of one's own making. Though it might not consciously be recalled what had been done to bring upon illness or failure or loneliness, these matters were not past finding out. Through prayer, introspection, analysis, and the cleansing of the channels of aid in meditation, one might come to understand what lesson she or he was undergoing. Though individuals were bound with others in families and teams and churches and other groupings, and shared in the struggles and guilts of all through "group karma," it would be found that in the important matters, each individual met only self. Christ had taken on the sins of all, in His unswerving journey to fulfill the will of God in His life; since Him, said the Cayce source repeatedly, "no man pays for the sins of others." Therefore, patience was enjoined—not railing at life.

Patience, said the Cayce source, would prove to be the watch at the gateway between body and soul. The soul had unspeakable force at its command, when used for good. Yet that same force could destroy an individual who was unprepared to handle it. Patience was the timing that screened one's promptings and shaped the calls of opportunity that would be heard or ignored. In this vein, every life reading—Cayce's best effort to characterize the fundamental character, weakness and promise of a soul—began with a phrase such as "Not all may be given at this time, but this we would give with the desire that this may be a helpful experience for the entity." It was made clear that not all of the urges, talents, past lives would be mentioned, but only those the person might then safely handle; months or years later, additions might be made—as was the case when Cayce was late in life given the supposed details of a lifetime never before mentioned in his readings—but only when his source felt he could handle it. There were many things in this view of which it might be said, as by the author of the Gospel of John, "Ye cannot bear them now." Patience would prove to be the key to the steady, safe unfolding of talents in the round of one's life—including psychic talents. These would begin to show themselves in dream, in vision, in times of prayer, in crisis, in quiet reflection, in helping others—but a little at a time so that the person would not "think more highly of himself than he ought," nor abandon good sense in favor of psychic flashes.

Was there a way to learn patience so that nothing ever went wrong in one's affairs? Emphatically not, according to the Cayce source. "When one is without crosses, one is no longer among the Sons"—among the children who knew their Father and chose Him. With patience was linked "longsuffering" and the other fruits of the Spirit. No one could expect to grow in patience without growing also in love, and love meant bearing the burdens of others—not being trapped by others, for they had not that power, but being ready to ease the pain of others, lighten their way, make their spirits glad. The goal of each individual was to serve others, but this was in fully creative ways that brought others to their feet and running; like Christ, each person was to be a "servant of servants"—not a doormat. Patience was not synonymous with indifference or detachment; it was apt response, in God's own timing.

How might one cultivate patience? Nothing less than steady prayer, seeking an aid greater than one's own to guard his impulses and defenses, could be trusted to nurture patience. And such prayer would be found no burden; for most people the time given to useless worry, spinning anxiety, could be better turned to quiet prayer—and then followed by creative action upon timely prompting. "Why worry, when ye may pray?" was a phrase frequently used in the readings, not as a churchly aphorism so much as an invitation to an experiment in problem-solving "Try Me," "Call upon Me," "Ask," "Seek" were bits of biblical admonition that sparkled through hundreds of readings, even the most prosaic medical diagnoses.

Yet prayer alone might seem moody and cloistered to some. Cultivating patience involved choosing a total way of being alive that embodied the trust that patience mirrored. So the Cayce source often repeated, "Keep the heart singing" or "He that would know the way must be oft in prayer, joyous prayer." Vital, delighted enjoyment of the journey of life would free the soul for its work or allow it to run up its kite for energies and wisdom beyond its own. A sunny way was not simply a social asset but an existential asset. The life lived in proper balance was marked by humming, whistling, teasing, playing, joking, seeing "the ridiculous, oft." "For if God be for us," the Cayce source often asked, "whom need we fear?" And as though to emphasize the point, the readings themselves sometimes parried questions with jaunty responses; a man who asked how much his childhood traumas were affecting his present responses might be told that the figure was "thirty-six and twenty-two hundredths percent."

While one might think that cultivating patience meant ever looking to the future, when things would be different, the Cayce source did not see patience that way. Instead, when asked to outline a prayer for someone to use as a model for his devotional life, this source usually focused at least part of the prayer upon the "this day" theme of the Lord's Prayer, by inserting the words, "today, now," or "just now." The effect could be electric, in its contrast with the traditional religious focus upon an unchanging vast heaven beyond the present vale. In the perspective of this source, the keener the focus on being alive and giving and being aware now, the more fully one exemplified patience. Indeed, said one reading, "Let us live each day as though the whole race depended on it"—in a variation on a biblical passage often quoted in readings: "Let us run with patience the race that is set before us." A steady jog, whose pace was set by a source within "not to be effaced," would bring the soul quietly closer each day to a conscious awareness of whose companion, whose partner in creation it truly was. How be patient? How handle stress? How face the fear of the unknown future? The phrase that sometimes appeared in the Cayce readings, as in Cayce's own letters to friends, was "Just keeping on keeping on."

Precognition and Handling Stress

Can the growing ability to handle stress affect the emergence of psychic experiences of the future?

A committee on which the writer served invested more than a thousand hours in redesigning a college curriculum and eventually in reevaluating the fundamental goals and character of the campus. Also on the committee was an eager and enthusiastic college teacher, anxious to get results in whatever he touched, whether it be his drama class or his friendships or his faculty duties. Young, he was determined to make his mark on campus.

He was also interested in developing psychic ability, which he was tempted to view as the hallmark of spirituality, although he also knew psychics of no little ability who were pretty vain and even dishonest. He joined an occult group that held training sessions in the dark, as well as practicing incantations and fasting, with the promise of developing psychic visions for each of its members. He saw much color and imagery, but little of it resembled outward affairs, and he worried about his spiritual health because he seemed so little psychic.

At the same time, he entered more and more deeply into the struggles for self-definition of his college, participating in systematic studies fostered by a regional accrediting association, and investigating with his committee the development matters of other campuses. In time he came to see that little would change in his school until the leaders were replaced, and he realized that such changes might be long in coming—though in fact they were not. Weighing the nature of institutional life, he came to see why so many checks and balances existed among faculty, administration, students, alumni, board, and philanthropic constituency, as well as with other colleges and learned societies. He matured a bit in his perspective and was given more and more responsibilities on his campus. His friends noticed some new notes of humility and finally even of patience.

Then one day he was watching a play where the hero was shot, the killing brought about in a circumstance in which many participated. It rang true to the sense of fateful but necessary slowness that he had discovered in his work at the school; it spoke of things ending out of their season but in patterns that, of themselves, were ultimately good. And at that moment he had a sinking sensation in the pit of his stomach, one which made him weak and ill. He went home and lay down, where it came to him with a certainty that gripped his whole consciousness that somebody he loved was about to die. He had never had such an experience before, but it was for him beyond mistaking. He could not place the person, though he prayed and thought about it long, except that it was not a member of his family.

The feeling stayed with him as a memory, a nagging reminder, until a few weeks later at a faculty retreat he was informed one morning that his best friend, the dean of the college, a man in his thirties, had died of a heart attack in the night. At that point the feeling left, but in its place came quiet assurance that the dean, who had worked so hard in college reforms, would not have held back his life energy from the task he had shared in so abundantly. The young drama teacher led in the memorial service for his friend, helping to keep it from needless sentiment, as the writer well remembers. Speaking of the death later, he was sure that his warning had been of this death, this loss. And he was almost equally sure that the factor responsible for opening the eyes of his perception to the event coming upon him was his newly won ability to be patient, to accept and begin to understand the cycles of the life and death of a college—or a friend.

When Jesus learned of the untimely death of John the Baptist and the collapse of John's movement, did his retiring to the mountains with his disciples allow him to find the perspective, the patience, the time beyond his own, which shortly would enable him to tell his disciples, without fear, of his own forthcoming death?

～ TEN ～
Retrocognition

Edgar Cayce was having a haircut. He looked over at the writer, waiting his turn, and said, "I'll tell you a story that happened right here." Nodding at his barber, he added, "He will confirm it."

The barbershop was modest, located on a business street a few blocks from Cayce's home. It was a place where Cayce knew he was among friends. Diagonally across the street was the railroad station, whose executive manager was on the board of the Association. Around the corner was the office of a long-time real estate agent at Virginia Beach, a member of his Tuesday night Bible class. Down the street a block was the drugstore whose pharmacist had for years mixed the compounds called for in his readings, and kept on hand the commercial products so often stipulated in those same readings: Atomodine, Glyco-Thymoline, Castoria, Black and White Cream, Patapar paper. Not much farther away was a photographic studio where Cayce sometimes stopped to chat about photographic equipment, or to order pictures of his grandson, in terms reminiscent of his own days as a photographer. Across Atlantic Avenue and down a ways was a gaunt frame hotel on the ocean, owned by another member of his Bible class. All of these solid citizens were frequent visitors at his home and office, or attended his Presbyterian Sunday school class, as did the printer who prepared forms for him, operating from his home not far away. Here Cayce was among friends who had come to like and trust him as a neighbor, as a figure of spiritual depth, accepting the contrast of his strange reputation as a psychic with his relaxed, open manner.

Cayce began his story.

He had been sitting in the same place, getting a haircut, while among those waiting was a man he did not know, who had brought along his small son. The boy was tired, yawning, and took out a peanut butter sandwich from a paper bag, apparently packed for a picnic later in the day. As he munched, he almost dozed. Then he walked over to Cayce's chair and without a word offered him part of the sandwich. The two had never seen each other before, yet the boy moved as surely and unaffectedly as to a relative. "Here," the father called, "he doesn't want your sandwich!" "Yes he does," the boy replied without moving. "He was very hungry on that raft. Weren't you?" he asked, looking up at Cayce in the barber chair.

Cayce stared the boy hard for a moment and then grinned and nodded. Like the boy, he had remembered something that linked them. He thanked the youngster and declined the sandwich, but with appreciation. The boy went back to the arms of his father and fell asleep, while his puzzled parent explained that he had never seen his son do anything of the sort.

Where was the raft on which the boy knew Cayce had been hungry? Cayce waited until he left the barbershop to finish the story. The raft that his own mind connected with an image of the youngster had been, he felt, part of another life. It had been on the Ohio River, in the early 1800s. There Cayce had finished what his own life readings described as a largely wasted and irresponsible life as a wanderer, a show-off, and even a bit of a rake, by fleeing from the Indians with others on a big raft floated down the Ohio River. The Indians were so hostile that the passengers on the raft could not land for food and became painfully hungry on their journey towards freedom. Here Cayce had lost his life, according to his own trance source. Sitting in the barber chair, he had seen the boy's face become that of a young man on the raft so long ago. Had the boy, drowsy and with the unconscious near the surface, also recognized Cayce? He thought perhaps so.

Over the nearly twenty years since his information had begun to discuss reincarnation, Cayce had slowly become accustomed to such seeming memory flashes in daily life, as to other forms of psychic experience. Receiving a letter from someone asking for medical aid but wondering about seeking a past-life reading as well, he would sometimes offer unusual encouragement, saying, "I think you will find there a Palestine experience" or "You may be surprised at the talents which the information will show." He was not promoting his own readings, for he never did that, but responding out of his own waking sense that seemed to place the person in a given epoch of history, with perhaps a special talent. As might be expected, his readings bore him out.

Occasionally someone who had secured a life reading would want what had come to be called a "check-life reading," following up in detail on a particular incarnation. When Cayce was asked which lifetime of several might be most fruitful to explore, he would sometimes pause and smile, adding, "The one in Early America, not the one in France," because of sensing what the person had been like in each place—or even momentarily seeing the face and form of the person before him change, as other psychics have reported.

Talking with his family about a distinguished person whose reading was scheduled for the day, he sometimes mused, "I wonder if he was one of the twelve judges." Over the years his information had tagged a number of individuals as having been involved with him as judges in a lifetime in ancient Egypt when he had been a priest. It was the lifetime when he reached, partly through exile and suffering, what he felt was perhaps his highest spiritual development and the one his trance source told him bore most significantly upon the present life. As a consequence, he was always more than a little interested when something inside himself seemed to place a person in his "memory" or retrocognition as an associate from ancient Egypt. He enjoyed more the associations that linked with Palestine in the time of Jesus and shortly afterwards, where he had lived in Asia Minor, he felt. But the Egyptian "memories" were the ones that bore upon the critical struggles for growth in this lifetime, affecting the growth and dissolution of his hospital and university, and he always approached them with alert interest. Visitors who saw a head of the ancient Egyptian Queen Nefertiti on his filing cabinet may have though it a quaint decoration, but friends knew it was an informal symbol of a stream of retrocognitive reflections that were always meaningful to Cayce.

In dealing so naturally with reincarnation, Edgar Cayce was handling the one phenomenon of his work that, more than any other, alienated him from responsible people in his times. Doctors were often keenly interested in his medical diagnoses and detailed prescriptions, as well as the theories of physiology that streamed through Cayce in thousands of readings—until they learned of the reincarnation material. Ministers and priests were fascinated by his detailed descriptions of biblical times, which included accurate accounts of clothing, coins, food, languages, customs, and even the correct distribution of names of the time in various languages familiar to scholars and archaeologists—until they learned of the reincarnation material from the same source. Scientists responded to the chemical analyses, psychologists to sophisticated descriptions of hypnosis, government officials to theories of social change in various nations—until they came across the reincarnation material

It did not help that details had been so often verified, by old court records or archaeological finds or history books—for this might only demonstrate that some part of Cayce's mind had access to factual sources about the past. Perhaps, as the writer surmised at times, the Cayce source was using all of this retrocognitive material in a reincarnation framework only to shock or interest people. Yet there was no interest in sensationalizing such material on the part of the Cayce source, and often warnings were given against stressing novelty to foster a "cult, schism, or ism." Those who were sure that the trance information must have unaccountably failed in accuracy whenever it took up reincarnation sought without success for evidence of such a failure or an explanation of it. The writer was fairly well convinced at one point that he had located a massive error in the Cayce materials, when he came across frequent references to the Essene group of Jews at the time of Jesus, or to similar groups of Covenanters, described in the Cayce life readings as significant precursors of Christianity. During the 1920s to 1940s when Cayce was supplying abundant materials about this sectarian movement in Judaism, alongside of convincing material on Jewish temple leadership and other purist or Hassidic groups, there was not a responsible biblical scholar in the world who would have endorsed Cayce's picture. Yet not long after his death, the Dead Sea Scrolls were found, and confirmation poured in of many of Cayce's reports on sites, practices, and even the presence of women in the retreat centers—so long denied by scholars.

How representative of the psychic experiences of others were Cayce's seeming experiences of retrocognition of the past, which occurred to him in daily life? He dreamed at times of ancient Egypt or Greece or some other area where he had been told by his source that he had lived; the dreams were vivid and always presented an issue that needed facing in his present life—they were not simply colorful excursions in the night. But while such material seems to appear in the dreams of others his age and with his interests, it is rare in the experiences of dream researchers to find as much of it as Cayce's dream records show. To be sure, Cayce also dreamed often about photography, more often than most people— perhaps because he was much involved in photography, as he was much involved in reincarnation.

In the writer's experience, most of the best-known psychics in the U.S. and Europe today take reincarnation as a matter of course and report their waking experience of retrocognitive glimpses as naturally as they report imagery from out of the past coming into consciousness when they hold a token object—a wrist watch or medallion—for psychom-etrizing. But such agreement proves nothing, for it may be a tradition, a stereotype among psychics; one seeking a census of psychic experiences in India finds an even larger proportion of "sensitive" reporting of such past-life material. Retrocognition has long been a part of the thought world of much of the Orient, where a Buddhist monk may expect as a natural part of his growth and training to recover in detail material from his past lives and will ascribe a ready meaning to the promise of Jesus that the Holy Spirit "will make known to you all things from all times."

Parapsychologists have tackled the question of whether such direct inspection of the past is possible. Much examined has been the case of the two English ladies who reported a waking journey through French palace gardens, in which everyone they met seemed dressed as though from a past time. And two other British women reported hearing the full noise of a long-ago battle, one night when they stayed at an inn located where such a battle had in fact occurred. But such instances might be chains of coincidence. Hypnotists have sought to tackle the problem of retrocognition by the bold method of age regression, which psychiatrists had used effectively to take patients back to detailed memories of child-

hood. Why not, the hypnotists asked, take people back beyond childhood, to previous lifetimes? The results in the case of a supposed Bridey
Murphy (*The Search for Bridey Murphy*) made newspaper headlines during
the 1950s and were carefully examined by Professor Ducasse of Brown
University; even better cases were reported by Ruth Montgomery in *Here
and Hereafter*. Most notably, Professor Ian Stevenson of the University of
Virginia Medical School set out to interview people around the world
who thought they could remember and prove details from past lives.
With the aid of a research grant, Stevenson explored subjects young and
old in India, in the U.S., in the Pacific Northwest, and elsewhere, producing the first carefully researched volume on this topic in the modern
West: *Twenty Cases Suggestive of Reincarnation*. Still other investigators have
probed the ancient phenomena of seemingly haunted buildings, trying
to develop theories of how a living person might perceive appropriate details from the past in such buildings, while Hettinger, Karagula,
Puharich and others, such as the present writer, tested seemingly able
psychics on the stretch of the past, including even ancient cultures and
languages, which they seemed to bring to consciousness by touching
objects from those times.

No consensus has emerged from these investigations, except perhaps
an interest in keeping open the possibility of retrocognition—direct
inspection of past events by psychic means, whether in personal "soul
memory" or some other process free in time. Too little is firmly established about the nature of any kind of psychic ability to allow speci-
fication of when it is used in viewing the unknown past—for such an
unknown past must always be represented by present records or facts
to be verified, and nobody knows whether a psychic is viewing the past
or the present verifying records.

Edgar Cayce's trance source was, of course, questioned repeatedly on
how one might have psychic experience of the past. Such knowledge was
not particularly stressed by the Cayce information, for this source gave
detailed medical, vocational and spiritual aid to thousands of people
without ever mentioning the subject. Yet those who sought to understand their own makeup, and the forces that drive men, were encouraged to explore the realm of reincarnation as matter-of-factly as they
were encouraged to explore childhood memories, or ideals, or hidden

defenses. Most commonly, the Cayce source encouraged the exploration of retrocognition through dreams, where one might find he or she was already recalling bits of an unknown language, or scenes of an ancient place, or artifacts that bore directly on present problems and opportunities; one could expect retrocognition as well as precognition. It did not help the individual enough to see in advance a crisis that might be met the next day; one also could profit from discovering why certain kinds of people were disliked, or why one feared authority, or why one made sure decisions about textile marketing, based on past-life experiences that might come back in dreams.

Not all retrocognitive dreams would be pleasant, according to this source. The writer heard two Cayce readings that interpreted the battle nightmares of young children as memories of having been killed as children in early days of World War II; here the solution, according to the Cayce trance source, was quietly calming the child as he fell asleep, when he would be most open to helpful suggestion from a parent. But in general, when the body was not injured, the unconscious would supply only retrocognitive dream material that the dreamer could safely use and handle.

Might the doorway to psychic perception of the past be opened by sustained effort? Many who have been interested in the Cayce theories have recorded their dream and waking perceptions, which might be of the past, and studied the possible accuracy of these perceptions. Abundant evidence has emerged that the mind can fool itself, for an individual seeking to establish his importance can produce fantasy—chains, which any psychiatrist can recognize. The writer heard one person interested in the Cayce materials sententiously pronounce that he was Peter, reincarnated, only to be told by an alarmed associate, "You can't be! I'm Peter!" But others in less need of ego-supportive imagery have recorded suggestive experiences—including those of perceiving awake the face and character of an associate or loved one in exactly the same details that the entranced Cayce saw. But none has yet duplicated Cayce's ability to take a newborn baby and sketch past-life influences, as he saw them, an entire personality structure of talents and urges and weaknesses and interests—often borne out in astonishing detail in later years (though possibly by conscious or unconscious imitation of the reading).

Some have found unusual quickenings occurring to them in reading historical novels, or visiting museum wings of ancient cultures, or wearing costumes of a certain period. All of this material is difficult to verify as retrocognitive and for the present can usually be studied only for the depth of response in the percipient (as indicated, for example, in her or his dream responses to the stimulating exposures), and for the general usefulness of the experience in the life of the percipient (producing better self-insight that enables him or her to operate, for example, less defensively). If any one factor stands out in the tentative explorations of those who have sought to open their minds' eye to the unknown past by retrocognition, it may be the importance of approaching such material for its usefulness in the present, rather than for verification of philosophical theories of human destiny. For the key to psychic experience of the past may be one often noted as important in psychic experience in the present: how far the individual is prepared to make productive use of what is received.

Productiveness in Creativity

The Cayce trance source rated productiveness as such a basic religious issue in the development of creativity that it focused upon the question in the seventh lesson suggested for the little book, A Search for God. The chapter on this concern was entitled "The Open Door"; in the chapter was emphasized the helpful resource of the Christ Spirit, standing at the door of every individual's life and ready to enter, if only the individual sought to employ such aid in practical, productive service of others.

The American psychologist William Sheldon, developer of somatotyping theory and methods, has suggested that adults can be usefully divided into the wasters and the productive—with the distinction revealing much about all kinds of creativity in the person. Writing from Mexico City, the psychologist and analyst Erich Fromm has defined productivity as one of the two ways in which a mature person can make meaningful closure with life and other persons, alongside of loving. Distilling what he believes an important contribution from among the irrelevances of Marxist thought, he also emphasizes how cooperation in productivity affords a more promising framework for the development of all kinds of human creativity than can ruthless competition.

Is it possible that the degree and kind of services rendered, forms created, work turned in may contribute not only to artistic quality and business progress but to ESP workings as well? Can the use to which one seeks to put his psychic cognition affect its flow, whether in revealing the present, the future, or the past?

It seems likely that the person who has not found a productive way to live, whether in employment or in the duties of household and family life, would be particularly vulnerable to the cheap satisfaction of fantasy, especially fantasies of contacts with the dead or fantasies of having been someone important in a past life. On the other hand, lacking useful circuits in which to channel psychic material might have the effect of closing off some of the flow of material from the unconscious, as well as distorting it. Both developments would seem to be potentially harmful to the function of ESP. To be sure, laboratory experiments on ESP have shown many subjects able to score briefly when they are doing no meaningful work except guessing—and yet guessing in the context of research may prove to be exhilarating work indeed.

A barrier to creativity sometimes discussed by artists, scientists, and inventors lies in talking too much and too soon about one's work. The effect of such verbalizing at times appears to be the dispersal of creative energies and imagery; some scholars have even speculated that this was the process seen by Jesus when he warned many whom he healed to tell no man about it. Those who can, do; those who can't, teach—so runs an aphorism warning against overtalk in creativity. It would seem possible that the effort to secure retrocognition into one's personal "past" or into some period of history or chain of events might be frustrated by doing so for the sake of talk, rather than for the sake of making a difference in some creative, productive act.

Psychiatrically, adult living is marked by willingness to take the responsibility for one's own life, to develop a way to be for something, rather than merely against grievances; to come alive in shared effort, rather than wait for a parental figure or lover to "turn me on." Is the same requirement of responsible productivity to be found guarding the way to retrocognition? Is one more likely to have useful glimpses of the unknown past to heighten his labors, rather than to charm him into beginning long–postponed labor and loving?

In taking up productivity as a religious issue, the Cayce source touched upon an old theological riddle. Much of religiousness, as seen for example in early Buddhism, has been focused on getting out of a predicament, on God's work in what theologians call "the order of re-demption." Man is often seen first of all as a sinner, as a sufferer, as a prisoner, in which the agency of the divine is needed to redeem, heal, or free. On the other hand, there have been strands in religious history and thought where the focus has been upon each individual reaching for her or his full stature as a builder, as a lover, as an artist, through the aid of the divine. Taoism, Confucianism, and some of the devotional Hinduism have at times stressed this approach, as have robust forms of Judaism. Here the individual is seen first of all as a creator, a gardener, a fashioner of cultures charged to "multiply and subdue the earth"; one is viewed in "the order of creation."

The Cayce source in its essays on religious themes was never far from touching upon each individual's sinfulness: selfishness, pride, lust or self–will. No prayer suggested by this source omitted such reference, and no encouragement to positive thought suggested that human evil might be ignored. Yet there could be little doubt that the Cayce source placed radical emphasis on humankind's role in the "order of creation," ahead of the "order of redemption." Creation was each individual's birthright, for the human creature was made in the image of the Creator and destined to become a conscious co–creator with God. Redemption occurred to get humankind back on to this track, rather than creativity being a far–off reward for faithful participation in redemption now. As the Cayce source asked many a sick person, "Why do you want to get well? What do you seek to do when you are well?" so it seemed to take a similar approach to the broader predicaments of sickness of soul. One had to keep an eye on the potential for good, for beauty, for love, for truth, or a sufficient motivation to change could not be achieved. In this context, psychic ability was simply one more area for seeing that God's ways toward hu-mankind were ways of promise, of astonishing creativity and goodness. If someone could find by psychic ability the cure for a disease, then this was only part of the work of the Creative Forces, which ever sought each individual's health and joy. And if someone by psychic ability learned to make a good living or grow prosperous, this was no affront to the Creative Forces, which sought humanity's material welfare just as truly as any other end. To be sure, the human journey would be found in the long run to be a "crucifying of the carnal," where one would learn to live in an animal body without identifying with it, or "seeking the flesh." But creation was not first of all punishment, nor testing, nor temptation, nor torment. When these things occurred, they were of one's own doing and always remediable by a return to the Source for guidance.

The emphasis on God's incredible helpfulness was a major part of the religious thrust of the Cayce information. The emphasis was not merely verbal but seemed acted out by Cayce's own helpful work, as well as by the rich guidance appearing in dreams and prayer life of those who were coached by readings. A God who has chosen to "give the Kingdom" to his children was the God the Cayce trance source unfailingly communicated. Such a God could not successfully be identified with religious scruples or taboos, although individuals could quickly learn the value of restraints. But in this perspective it was clear that religion was made for humankind, not humankind for religion; the Sabbath was to be kept that one might prosper in the journey Godward, not as a duty but as an opportunity.

In the perspective of the Cayce readings, it did not make sense to speak of miracles. The Creative Forces did not now and then break through the lowering skies to give individuals a helping hand, even in the startling phenomena associated with figures such as Edgar Cayce. The Creative Forces were always at work, showering their blessings on individuals, seeking each individual's full becoming as co-creator, but in lawful ways. The very law was itself God's mercy. The regularity of grace—its dependability—was the assurance that it was grace, not a passing marvel.

In the approach of the Cayce readings, God was to be found ever at hand, helping, through "the open door." That door was the readiness of the flesh to respond to the divine, if one sought aid for the right purpose, for service rather than for selfishness. As one reading put it, "spirituality must be expressed in materiality." There was no room in this picture for a Gnostic devaluation of flesh. Although flesh was neither the soul's ultimate home nor one's best creativity, it was a present opportunity that dared not be ignored. The flesh was a cloud, a barrier to full psychic perception, and probably to full awareness of beauty and truth as well, for the soul had donned earth-consciousness as a diversion, in the long journey toward wholeness. But once the individual had entered into this realm of creation, into the ways and laws of the earth, one would never find the pathway out by pretending he or she wasn't there. One could not "rise above" the human condition. Rather, one must "lift up" the very flesh itself, in its concrete life of glands and nerves, by using material existence as a channel for helping others. When the body was spent in sweat that another might find life sweeter, then God Himself stood at the open door, and a body was a treasure to wear, to use—it was even the temple of the Most High.

There was, in the view of the Cayce source, a law that an individual could have only by giving. What one sought to share with others—this was what grew in one's ideals and talents, until it became a lasting resource throughout other lifetimes. No scheme of self-development, self-perfection alone would work for long, for it was out of harmony with the soul, with the Creative Forces. No one should seek simply to be saved in some private journey of justification, for this was not the pattern of the Christ, Who freely gave Himself to others.

The precise mechanisms of worship would be found to be the same as those of all other truly creative efforts—in this the Cayce theory of kundalini energies rising within man found a parallel to the old Latin saying that to work is to pray: *Laborare est orare.* One could not separate religiousness from daily loving and manufacturing, for these acts occurred along the selfsame channels of creativity. There were only whole acts of giving, where the thanksgiving was intertwined with willingness to carry, to push, to heal, to teach. One might step aside for times of quiet alone with his Maker but never aside from the intent to make the way brighter for someone else, or the prayer itself would falter, betraying the character of the soul that sought to present the petitioner before the Throne. Although the Cayce source enjoined daily meditation upon everyone who truly sought to walk with God, and regular intercession for others, it matched this almost athletic program of piety with insistence upon creative action. "Do, do, do," or "Try, try again," or "Ye only learn the laws of action," or "True understanding comes in application" were notes at which the Cayce information hammered away over the years. The

Christ Spirit could be found knocking at everyone's door, but it would not enter until asked, and the asking must be for more than self. It might be easy to say, "The Son of Man came not to be ministered unto, but to minister," but the fact was that all souls came into being for the same destiny—a destiny that they could not fulfill by ritually celebrating the self-giving of Jesus.

Yet the open door that one might find within, ready to welcome a Christ who would give one aid for another, was not to be swung by blind activism in productiveness. The very revelation of God to an individual occurred through the same door. Insight into the workings of the Creative Forces, vivid imagery of the structures of the soul and its Lord, might be found in dream and vision as one sought to serve. Truth and judgment would be given as readily as energy and love, if one sought to be fully productive in life. It was not wrong for one to seek to know God Himself, if the desire were motivated, as Paul had said, by love. Each time one earnestly chose to do the will of the Father and consciously sought the aid of the Christ, one would discover that she or he had attained a new concept of the Father, however difficult this might be to verbalize. Knowledge would come as well as good will, through the open door that God Himself had fixed in each soul.

How might one begin to cultivate, to train in self, the productivity that could find an open door for aid beyond his or her own? One might begin with expectancy. It could make all the difference in the affairs of one's life whether one really expected healing, solutions to problems, a better world, or whether one only sought to endure, grieving his lot. The Essenes were characterized by the Cayce source as a model of an expectant community, as were the early Christians, who literally expected the coming of the Holy Spirit to their aid. Yet expectancy was not a dwelling on some unknown religious future or upon a past biblical age to be restored. Expectancy was a matter of how one might approach each present task, each present relationship, ready for the most valuable outcome to emerge from the play of all the factors involved. Expectancy was exemplified in the growing trust that "All things work together for good to them that love the Lord," for having all things work together for good was the true business of the Creative Forces, the very character of God at work in each situation, however unseen. The formula was an exact picture of true creativity. One who knocked at the open door would find a way to reconcile quarreling lovers, to match prices with costs, to combine chemicals into new compounds, to embed worship in the day's work, to fight leukemia with special transfusions—for the Lord of the Universe was the Lord of all this becoming and not the God of shrines and structures alone. So one might show forth expectancy by a process as concrete as choosing a truth each day and living it out, inviting the partnership of that endlessly creative mind below the surface, which was the builder in each individual.

As one worked at productivity, at partnership with God through the open door where extra energy and wisdom flowed, it would be found that increasing one's own usefulness went hand in hand with increasing that of others. One had to stop before each individual whom one truly engaged and find for self the way in which that person was trying to build his or her image of God, however haltingly or perversely. This was not kindness, good manners, but a law as fixed as any in electricity or chemistry. There was no way to be more loving without helping others to love, no way to work longer hours without enabling others to enjoy their work, no way to build a better world except upon the talents of others. For one's own soul, the source of an individual's every talent and prompting, the mirror for the Everlasting Creator, shone like the evening sun upon the face of another as upon oneself; it was of the same Force as God.

Finding productivity meant studying the conditions under which one could become rapt, caught up in a task, swiftly and surely responsive in a situation. One of these conditions would be balance, in every level of one's life. To keep the mind and body alert for productivity, one had to eat what was best, in one's personal experience. One had to discover a personal balance of quiet and activity, of solitude and companionship, of work and play, of study and application. Each who sought to find more and more easily that open door would need to work out one's own guidelines, one's own regimes, not as burdens but as good sense for greater aliveness. Part of such a regime would be found to be the choosing of a household of faith, a church or a synagogue or whatever it might be called, where one might truly serve—not just attend services. This kind of association was not a mere accident of history but an expression of elements of the soul's journey that could not be fulfilled without covenanting. Each different faith, each sect, would be found to have its special functions—for none would survive without meeting some human need. Yet each would also have its own temptations, weaknesses, and perils, so that the servant who joined with others to find the open door to true productivity would need always to remind self Whose were the kingdom, power, glory.

Productivity and Retrocognition

Might one find that working to give away talents released a capacity for seeing things helpful out of the past? Does productivity, along with other elements, genuinely affect retrocognition?

A young mother found herself swamped in the duties of childrearing and homemaking, shortly after leaving college. She had never been an especially good student, although she also knew she had never tried very hard, preferring instead to concentrate on her drama roles in her extra-curricular theater work. She was interested in psychic things and once had a reading from Edgar Cayce. With her husband, she attended lectures on parapsychology and sought out demonstrations by a medium.

But she could find little time for study, and precious little time for prayer and quiet, with four young children. Still, she kept a sunny spirit, doing what she could to enrich the life of her church, especially by guiding a play–reading and discussion group. Years went by in which she occasionally had dreams that seemed to her linked with what Cayce had described as her past lives, and she had a few experiences of warnings that helped her protect her children. But she could hardly think of herself as psychic.

Then—it seemed almost overnight—her children were grown. What was she to do now? With much hesitation she agreed to share in the leadership of a discussion group on a retreat weekend. She did better than she had ever thought she might. Those in the group felt the steady flow of love that had become second nature to her as a mother and a wife, and they began to relax, to speak deeply of their lives, their failures, their hopes. She took the responsibility for guiding a weekly study group and again did well. To her surprise, she now began to be keenly interested in reading, especially in history, and sought every chance she could find, at the beauty parlor or on a bus or waiting in line at a shopping center, to snatch some reading time about the development of myth and ritual in ancient cultures. She found her sense of the drama helping her to feel her way into long–ago materials, and her sense of family life helping her to understand social structures of other times. Now she began to teach a more formal class and to lead people in workshops, where the writer saw her at work, comparing dreams with historic myths and symbols.

She was becoming a productive person in her second life, in the career she had once put aside to rear her children and serve her husband. She was using her mind thoughtfully, carefully, systematically, and beginning a new program of graduate studies. At the same time, she began to notice a striking development as she worked with people in small groups. She would see, when someone leaned forward to disclose something personal to others, that for her the features of the person's face changed somehow before her eyes. At first she saw the images of the person's childhood, the point at which there had been a hurt, or where the individual had lost trust in life. But then there began to be other images, quietly superimposing themselves. Here was something Chinese—and it led her to perceive better the other person's sense of courtliness. There was something Hungarian, in this case military and aggressive, to be tamed and redirected. Another might present a Greek countenance, with a love of rationality and dialectic exchanges that made others impatient yet always clarified discussions. Was this imagery entirely from her own mind, a fantasy projected onto others to facilitate her better response to them? Perhaps so. She could not prove what she saw. She could and did share her impressions, which she rarely mentioned to anyone, with two different psychics who felt they could see past lives as they saw other things about individuals; to her surprise, they corroborated her judgment. When she learned that one of her group members had received life readings from Cayce, she was again surprised to learn that she was hitting the same themes he had struck, though not as fully nor as many. Slowly she began to wonder whether her psyche had, in her efforts to become fully productive and helpful as a teacher and group worker, opened the door to retrocognition. But the question had to remain a question, for there was no way to prove the accuracy of what she saw. It did leave her wondering about certain biblical materials.

What had Jesus seen, when he looked over Jerusalem and wept, speaking of how that city had stoned the prophets? Had he known only a poetic reminder of its long history as a center of faith and a center of idolatry? Or had his vision opened for a moment into a living impression of the city's whole history, rolled out before him, so that he could only weep for its betrayed promise? Perhaps it did not matter whether his vision that day was poetic or retrocognitive. What mattered was that he went on into the city to do his job, sharing every ounce of his being with his fellows, on a journey sometimes lonely but finally resolved in the events of the resurrection that still stagger individuals' imaginations and point to a productivity that does not fail.

~ ELEVEN ~
Prophesying

Edgar Cayce lay in quiet trance on the couch in his library. It was a sunny June afternoon, and his wife had just given him the hypnotic suggestion to speak on world affairs to the forty or so persons packed into the library. This was Congress weekend, when his friends and well-wishers came from all over the country for several days of lectures led by Cayce and other speakers. Now was the time for the Cayce information to give counsel on a subject of general interest, as had become the custom each year. Past subjects had included the times of Jesus, the nature of psychic ability, the nature of sleep, and prehistoric peoples. In this war year of 1944, it was to be the affairs of the major powers and their destinies.

Among those present were the writer and others who had heard readings tersely predicting the end of the war in 1945, with the end coming suddenly once it began. The room was hushed, for all longed to hear some assurance that the war would soon be over. But when Cayce began to speak in his state of altered consciousness, he did not speak as a political or military commentator, though he had shown many times that he could provide accurate analyses of economic, political and military affairs of specific nations. Indeed, he had done so well recently in briefing a diplomat on China that interest in Cayce's work had grown in Washington, and the writer had answered the phone one day to hear "This is the office of the Vice President of the United States"—requesting three days of readings from Cayce (though Cayce's death intervened before they could be given). But here at the Congress, the entranced man spoke not of strategies but of morality. He spoke little of the Axis nations and much of the Allies, and he addressed himself not to their righteousness but to their national sins.

Cayce's emphasis might have been predicted. Whenever earnest seekers came together with serious and high-minded intent, his trance discourse tended to become elevated, tended to turn to questions of humanity's relations with God. What so often was practical counsel, factual information, would take on a note of urgency, as listeners were offered choices. The man who functioned most of the time as a seer, concerned with the problems of individuals, now functioned as a prophet and addressed himself to the concerns of the group. His speech as a prophet was not merely prediction, for there were bits of prediction all through his readings, as through his dreams and waking hunches. It was speech that was not so much *foretelling* as *forthtelling*—speaking the truth of the human situation as he saw it. Prediction was incidental; a direct encounter with his listeners was the intent.

He began by speaking of spiritual laws and indicating that each nation over the centuries had developed its understanding of these laws and their applications. "There are, then, in the hearts, the minds of men, various concepts of these laws, and as to where and to what they are applicable . . ." The weakness of each nation would be found to be its own form of gratification, as it attempted to use these laws.

The trance voice took up America. Although it was wartime, and most Americans were inclined to make comparisons with others nations to the disadvantage of foreigners, the Cayce source reminded listeners of themes developed in many other readings, where it was warned that the American people had to face racial problems, problems of poverty, problems of indifference to minorities. "What is the spirit of America? Most individuals proudly boast 'freedom.' Freedom of what? When ye bind men's hearts and minds through various ways and manners, does it give them freedom of speech? Freedom of worship? Freedom from want? Not unless these basic principles [of each individual's relationship to God] are applied. For God meant man to be free . . ."

"What, then of the nations?" The voice of the unconscious man was measured, firm. It began the roll call.

"In Russia there comes the hope of the world. Not as that sometimes termed of the communistic, of the Bolshevik, no. But freedom, freedom! That each man will live for his fellow man! The principle has been born. It will take years for it to be crystallized, but out of Russia comes again the hope of the world." Listeners stopped breathing for a moment. This was a hard teaching. As middle–class Americans, they had been trained by a generation of newspaper articles and political speeches to despise Russia. While they might celebrate Russian idealism in novels, it was alien to them to consider that Russia's Marxist dream might have a good core, an ideal that could one day break off the husk of bureaucratic Communism and become the seed of a new type of cooperative society around the world. Yet here was the Cayce source insisting that they pay attention. Russia might be atheist, but it was, as other readings had insisted, touching a pattern well pleasing to the Creative Forces insofar as it strove to build a society where each individual would be his brother's keeper.

Yet the Russian momentum would need guidance, and that guidance should have religious depth, of the sort that could come from America, if America lived up to her dream rather than selling out to a materialism that only masqueraded as holiness. The voice continued, asking how Russia's future should be guided: "Guided by what? The friendship with the nation that hath even set on its present monetary unit, 'In God we trust.'"

Here the Cayce source stopped to place a challenge squarely before the listeners, as was often the case in readings of a prophetic character, which insisted that all lasting social change must begin with the individual. Taking the image of the slogan on the coin as an emblem of American ambivalence, the voice asked of the motto "In God we trust": "Do ye use that in thine own heart when you pay your just debts? Do ye use that in thy prayer when ye send thy missionaries to other lands—'I give it, for in God we trust'? Not for the other fifty cents, either!" The sarcasm was pointed. People laughed, but nervously. Caught up in the soul–searching of the occasion, they were flicking back in memory to ask what indeed they trusted in their lives, how much in God, justice and kindness, and how much in financial canniness.

Then the voice went on to charge America with the sin of self–righteousness. "In the application of these [spiritual] principles, in those forms and manners in which the nations of the earth have and do measure to those [American dreams of freedom, brotherhood, trust in God], in their activities, yea, to be sure. America may boast." The American dream of self-determination of peoples, of a society of shared plenty, of not treading on the rights of minorities, of religious concern framed in religious freedom—this was a valid dream for all peoples, as Americans were quick to insist. Yet America boasting in itself violated the spirit of true brotherhood; chauvinism was no substitute for respect for the unique contribution of others. "But rather is the principle [of freedom based on a spiritual ideal] being forgotten when this is the case, and that is the sin of America."

The quiet voice continued, turning to the land from which America had drawn language and law; it spoke of the temptation to snobbery, to imperialism, in both politics and culture. "So in England, from whence have come the ideas—not the ideals—ideas of being just a little bit better than the other fellow. Ye must grow to that in which ye will deserve to be known, deserve to receive. That has been, that is, the sin of England."

Moving to the Continent, the voice of the entranced man contrasted the birth of modern France in ideals of freedom, equality and fraternity with France's more recent focus on sensate values. "As in France, to which this principle [of freedom in shared responsibility] first appealed—and to which then came that which was the gratifying of the desires of the body. That is the sin of France." Was the entranced Cayce merely expressing American middle-class disapproval of Parisian mores? Or was he striking at real decadence in France, which would one day have to be met in the struggles of colonials, students, strikers?

"In that nation which was first Rome," the voice continued, bringing into focus the heritage of Roman law and Roman right, which was the foundation of all Western social structure, "when there was that unfolding of those principles [of freedom in shared responsibility], and its rise, its fall [as a people], what were they that caused the fall? The same as at Babel. The dissensions. The activities that would enforce upon these, in this or that sphere, servitude—so that a few might just agree [politically], or that a few might even declare their oneness with the Higher Forces [religiously]." Here the sleeping man spoke sternly of the human temptation to bring about social and religious conformity by force, by empire, by ecclesiastical power. "For theirs was the way that seemeth right to a man but the end is death. That is the sin of Italy." Nobody listening could have foreseen the changes toward permissiveness and internal freedom that were to come in the Italian church within two decades.

The trance source moved to the other side of the world. It spoke of Chinese isolationism as its sin yet warned that all had best be alert for what would come from China. "The sin of China? Yea, there is that quietude that will not be turned aside, saving itself by slow growth." But then the Cayce source went on to speak of the strength of China. "There has been a growth, a stream through the land in ages, which asks to be left alone, to be just satisfied with that within itself. It awoke one day and cut its hair off! This, here [in China], will be one day the cradle of Christianity, as applied in the lives of men. Yea, it is far off as man counts time, but only a day in the heart of God—for tomorrow China will awake." It was a promise the Cayce source had made before, and not especially flattering to American listeners, who prided themselves on providing political and religious leadership for the future. The insistence here was on something different than the political and economic justice that one day would be distilled from Russian experiment; the Chinese contribution would specifically be to the rebirth of Christianity—not to the Christendom of missionaries and church empires but to the real faith that might draw men together "in Christ."

Typically, the Cayce source paused in its flow to challenge listeners to examine their own lives, to determine whether they were individually ready to share in such a rebirth of faith from out of China. "Let each and every soul, as they come to their understandings, do something, then, in his or her own heart."

Finally the voice took up India. Here the Cayce source showed clearly how its fundamental outlook differed from much of historic Hinduism, by its insistence on service toward others ahead even of self-development—although the Cayce framework contained strong teachings on individual disciplines and self-understanding. "Just as in India—the cradle of knowledge not applied except within self. What is the sin of India? *Self*. And leave the 'ish' off, just self"—not greed, not imperialism, not taking from others by being selfish yet stopping short of full giving to others, in a path of development too often limited to the self.

The reading was soon over, and people spoke quietly around the room as Cayce sat up and rubbed his eyes. What had they listened to? Had it been a collection of meaningless generalities of platitudes and prejudices? Or had they heard an incisive judgment of the trends of nations and peoples, warning them of their own temptations to narrow vision? And how were they to take the little exchange that had occurred in the question period, when a question was asked as to how Germany might be taught democracy after the Allies had conquered her. The answer had come back sternly: "Raise not democracy nor any other name above the Fatherhood of God and the brotherhood of man." This had been a shock. Were not American-style democracy and the laws of God practically synonymous, as any American could testify? Or would it be necessary to try to fully understand separate peoples when the war was over, helping each to develop its own government, ideals and dreams—whether or not these copied American ways?

Nobody in the room felt he had taken part in something sensational. If this was prophecy, it was certainly not very entertaining. Instead, there was over the group an air of soberness, a sense of having been judged and warned.

Readings on such broad subjects had been slow in developing in the history of the Cayce information. Most of his readings had been strictly medical, and most for individuals, until one day in Selma, Alabama, when Cayce's Sunday school class gathered on a Sunday evening to see whether they could secure a different kind of material, just at the end of World War I. To everyone's astonishment, they did. One of those who heard about it was a Selma relative of Woodrow Wilson, who arranged then, in great secrecy, for Cayce to go twice to the White House, giving readings on the famous Fourteen Points and insisting that the League of Nations was the right direction for America at that time. The Cayce family was sworn to secrecy and to this day will not discuss this material, though old records have brought it to light for investigators.

Over the years there had been many occasions when the Cayce information slipped into an enhanced or elevated state and offered its firm challenges on human affairs. To be sure, these occasions numbered only in dozens, out of thousands of readings; but they were memorable. It was insisted that there had been an ancient civilization called Atlantis, as Plato had said, and that this civilization had destroyed itself by the misuse of inventions. Today, said the Cayce source, the same souls who had once before obliterated a civilization were back on earth again, either to learn a lesson or to repeat their mistake. Great numbers of children were being born who understood electronics and atomic power, as well as other forms of energy; they would grow into the scientists and engineers of a new age that had the power to destroy civilization, unless this time they learned spiritual law as well.

Looking at the American racial turmoil, the Cayce source quietly observed that many who were today born black had been white slave owners and importers before; now they were having an opportunity to build the very people and heritage they had destroyed—or again misuse their power.

Describing changes in the crust of the earth, oftentimes with startling geological accuracy as to fault lines and minor quakes, the Cayce information warned that human activities (nuclear bombs? Draining oil fields?) were affecting the crust of the earth. In terms reminiscent of Noah's time, the Cayce source insisted that the activities of nature were not impersonal forces but responsive to the same order that governed moral affairs; men could so live as to bring on their own destruction—this time by fire, not water, as the New Testament warning had correctly envisioned. In particular, the coastal cities of California could be destroyed, the farmlands of Alabama and neighboring states inundated, and a crippling breakdown of the American economy could follow, so that each man who wanted to eat would need a plot of ground on which to raise his own food. Yet these predictions were not offered for the newspapers but quietly given to individuals who sought aid in planning their lives and their service to their fellows. And always the Cayce source insisted that some of these changes were reversible. At the very least, men who lived good lives would be warned of catastrophes. And there was still, as to Abraham of old, the assurance that even a few godly individuals working together could save a city, or a religion, if they prayed—and worked as they prayed.

How typical of the psychic experiences of others were the Cayce prophetic materials, where his information spoke to groups of people?

Each year prognosticators with varying degrees of psychic ability announce lists of coming events. However, it is not always typical of them to couch these warnings in terms of national ideals nor to set existential choices before their fellows. For parallels, one would need to turn more to philosophers, theologians, poets, playwrights—those of impassioned vision. For this was the quality of the Cayce material that could rightly be called prophetic; it was elevated, shot full of an earnest sense of each individual's opportunities with God. In this material the factual element that drew Cayce admirers fell into the background, and the heart of the exchange was one man speaking with all the force of his being to his fellows. The subjects were not all religious, such as the work of Christ or the nature of the church; neither were they all political, such as the systems of government and the economics of nations. Some were psychological, calling individuals to better self-understanding through dreams. Some were sociological, urging a better understanding and keeping of marital bonds. Some were esthetic, reminding of the opportunities that individuals had for creating beauty and loveliness for their fellows, through the arts. But whatever the topic, the language was strongly biblical, and the thrust was the soul's opportunity to become a co-creator with God—now, today, in this present walk of life. Though the language was biblical, the sense was not one of returning to hometown religiousness; there was no magic about answering the prophetic challenge, nothing to be gained by empty chanting of "In God we trust."

Parapsychologists have tended to ignore the prophetic type of psychic material because it is relatively unusual and because it carries an aura of dogmatism from which science has been only recently rescued, itself. However, anthropologists studying primitive leaders with psychic endowments have noted among them unusual states of ecstasy and impassioned address, while researchers of LSD have wondered at the gripping sense of certitude that appears to accompany certain types of personal and social insights of those who take the drug and remain permanently changed afterwards. On the other hand, biblical scholars, classicists and Orientalists have often tended to study the endowments of religious leaders of ancient times as though nothing of the sort could ever occur in the present; exceptions have been the French scholar Guillaume and the German scholar Wach.

Unfortunate confusions in the study of psychic experience might begin to disappear if the phenomena were looked at as a whole. Those who have only experienced little promptings or auras, even from the dead, often tend to trivialize all psychic experience, while those who have had some experience of astonishing "opening," where they saw and heard more than they could ever put into words, tend to ignore the physiological and psychological mechanisms studied by parapsychologists.

The Cayce source was asked about the operation of psychic ability in those experiences here called prophetic; it always ascribed the action to the superconscious—that portion of the human unconscious which could place one in direct relation to the Creative Forces of the Holy Spirit. This kind of attunement was to be distinguished from the normal promptings of the soul, for it far transcended them in scope of awareness and capacity to formulate issues. To be sure, such enlarged awareness did not come at the expense of the soul or in violation of his ideals but in amplification of its daily work and commitments. A small-minded person could not expect to have large visions—unless the individual had sought and won and shared these in some former life, so that they might flash back again as a challenge to become awakened. But even where the capacity for attunement through the superconscious was available, the actual occasions of operation were affected by many things: the needs of listeners, their readiness to act on what they heard, the longing in the heart of the psychic, the helping presence of those on other planes, impending crisis or trials. For the gifts of higher attunement were each individual's to seek but God's to dispose according to a Wisdom that saw all the needs and intentions in a given situation.

Those who have been interested in the Cayce materials for several decades have sought to cultivate with some care the conditions of what is here called elevated psychic experience, such as prophesying. Most often they have noted it as coming in a vision associated with prayer or meditation, sometimes in a dream. Occasionally they have found that words came to their minds and lips in a steady, helpful flow while making a speech, and a quiet and peace settling over them and their audience, which have led them to think of attunement with the superconscious. Individuals have sometimes found they could "speak the truth in love" to spouses, or children, or business associates, and do so caring as deeply as they spoke helpfully. Like many who have worked at their sharing in groups of Alcoholics Anonymous, some in their study groups and project groups have been surprised at how penetrating could be the address of one to another, when supported by a loving, praying group field. But the one discipline critical in opening the way for psychic ability of a higher order has seemed to many to be meditation.

Meditation in Creativity

The Cayce source considered the place of meditation in training for creativity to be so significant that it instructed the compilers of *A Search for God* to place a chapter on meditation as a preface to each volume of that work. Then it returned to the subject, in a broader context of living in conscious awareness of communion with God, in a chapter entitled "In His Presence."

The term *meditation* has come to stand for a variety of practices, from introspection to concentration, from visualization to emptying the mind. The Cayce source used the term in a strict technical sense, to refer to a specific discipline and process that, when properly practiced, would move through a series of stages, completing itself in the gaining of deep subjective quiet and a sense of holiness, often accompanied by having the field of consciousness filled with light.

To associate a specific discipline of emptying consciousness with creative activity might seem far-fetched. Creativity by itself sounds like action, the bringing about of something new or appropriate in a given form. What could silence have to do with action? How would one fill the mind with a needed solution by emptying it?

In the view of the Cayce information, meditation was the twin sister of prayer. By specific acts of prayer, one might bring the consciousness to focus on the divine, might enter into attunement with the super-conscious realm of the self and into relation with the Creative Forces. Through thanksgiving, praise, adoration, penitence, contrition, dedication, and the others acts of prayer, one might become humble before the Throne, might bring the wayward psyche into a plastic state where a Source greater than itself might affect it. But getting ready for change and accomplishing it were two different things. Meditation ought to follow prayer, as the time for a movement in consciousness, a shift in values, a quickening of some needed center within. After meditation one might find a problem spontaneously resolving itself, or a helpful image presenting itself to the mind. But meditation was not to be entered into for the sake of some special goal; this was the business of prayer. Yet it was the nature of meditation to free the channels of the person to receive guidance, and if one did not receive it shortly after meditation, one could count on the action of such guidance when next faced with a decision or a need for invention. Through the channels cleared and kept fresh by meditation could come more swiftly the flow of imagery and assurances that made up faith, "the evidence of things unseen," including helpful psychic promptings of all sorts.

Researchers into creativity have studied the process of "incubation," during which an individual codes the mind with a problem and then waits for a solution to present itself, often after sleep. But they have rarely studied the specific religious processes of prayer and meditation, in part because these make assumptions about the nature of God and humankind, which remind scientists of an unwanted medieval world view and smack of magic. Nevertheless, there are hints that prayer and meditation might be highly effective in freeing creativity. These processes may serve to confirm an individual in identity and ego—strength, so necessary to face a difficult problem and endure the strain of waiting for an answer. Further, they may serve to lower defenses that impede the flow of helpful unconscious material into consciousness, and they may bring to bear powerful motivation on the solution of a problem, by turning the individual toward his or her highest values.

If ESP is a reality, then the seemingly pointless process of focusing the mind to empty consciousness may foster a flow of ESP signals into the psyche and out of the psyche in a state of rapt attention that has often appeared in effective psychic functioning in the laboratory. Moreover, prayer and meditation may have some place in fostering that elusive changeover from normal to elevated psychic activity, which can be observed in any highly gifted sensitive from time to time. Prayer and meditation might make the difference between an individual's helpful promptings, largely for self and loved ones, and those larger openings—one's group, one's people, one's times—in ways so abundant and effective as to merit the terms of *prophecy, wonderworking, guidance,* and *healing.*

Might prayer and meditation be critical for development not only of higher forms of psychic ability but for other types of creativity as well? Could the handling of political conflict, the marketing of products, the fashioning of symphonies, the solving of medical problems, the teaching of children all be made more sensitive by such processes? A hallmark of the highest creativity appears to be that the solutions presented take account of the needs of all who are involved, not just of the primary creator. The best leader often leads people to arrive at needed decisions by themselves, out of their own resources. The best artist requires that the viewer become invested in the painting, and the artist extends the invitation to do so. Do prayer and meditation add to creativity the extra dimension of how the other person can respond, what he or she can see, how she or he would put it? If so, they do in fact offer a larger dimension to every creative act, which can become an event with several centers, instead of a purely personal expression.

In taking up meditation as a key process in creativity, the Cayce source raised the question as old as any form of religion—the meaning of devotional acts. It turned its attention to the common base of the whirling of Muslim dervishes, the human sacrifice of ancient cultures, the totem meals of primitives, the handclapping of Shinto, the flower offerings of Hinduism, the swinging of the resonating bull roarer by Australian bushmen, the Hebraic practice of circumcision, the Catholic mass, the Quaker devout silence. Insofar as some aspect of prayer and meditation could be found at work in all worship, what was happening? And in particular was there a process of wordless meditation such as that long practiced under the Hindu term *dhyana*, the Chinese term *Ch'an*, and the Japanese term *Zen*, which ought to interest Westerners, as well?

The Cayce trance source began its treatment of the theme "In His Presence" by insisting that there was no way to glorify God in worship or devotion that set Him apart from His creation. His presence would be found "in, with, under" all of His creation; any effort to limit God's presence to sacred things, times, places would quench the spirit. Unless He were the One Force sought in play, in study, in belonging, in work, He would not be found in worship; for exactly the same channels of energy were called upon in the physical body, in the action of the autonomic nervous system upon endocrine glands, under the stimulus of conscious thought in the cerebrospinal system, and with an impact from unseen sources, for all of human creative activity of any type. Indeed, meditation was itself a very high order of creative act, in which something real and new was brought about, released in physical consciousness, however little perceived at first; it was its own form of conception and birth in consciousness. What happened in meditation was some form of raising of the ideal into consciousness, some movement of emphasis and quality in the very center of the human being. An ideal would be activated in the imagination and begin to do its work throughout the life, if the ideal were of a high enough order to draw from the soul a full burst of energy and meaning in meditation.

Prayer, according to this source, was "a concerted effort of physical consciousness to become attuned to the Creator," while meditation was "an emptying of self of anything that might hinder the Creative Forces from rising along natural channels to sensitive spiritual centers in the body and psyche." As William James had said of prayer, real work was done by it. But because real energies, real patterns were handled in prayer and meditation, these also held dangers. So strong were the currents, once they were trained, that as Paul had said of taking communion, one who did these things without the proper preparation of body and mind did them "to his own destruction." So the Cayce source warned that there should be cleansing in connection with regular devotional times—cleansing of the body, cleansing of the thoughts from all distractions and worries (even if one had to stop and dispose of these before continuing, as Jesus had warned about placing a gift at the altar while hostile towards one's neighbor). There needed to be balance in diet, rest, recreation, and work in order for the natural processes in prayer and meditation to move smoothly.

Exactly what needed to be done in meditation, as it was presented by the Cayce source as a way to stand "in His Presence"? The process was one of first freeing the body to enter into a delicate act of concentration and focus of energies. One needed to sit up straight (or lie straight) in a poised and unforced state. There needed to be a time of prayer, sharing with the divine both one's sins to be forgiven and one's honest gratitude, as well as the longings of the heart; the essence of the prayer would be found to be communion, however, more than anxious instruction of

God. One could stand before the divine as an individual might stand with the sun at her or his back, sure of eternal support and action from realms one had not created. Then the body would need to be quieted for meditation—and each person could find what worked best. Cayce took seriously ancient traditions of breathing procedures, even to tracing their physiology and the delicate pressures these placed upon endocrine gland areas. This source also treated chanting, incense, gongs and bells, instrumental music, candles, light—each of which might work for some according to what they may have effectively used in some past life.

But there were no mechanics of meditation that would force it, only that which in its own way spoke of the divine as a real Presence to the individual. Meditation was not a focusing upon aids, for meditation had but one purpose, "the coming of the Lord" into an individual life. To make certain that this was the focus, the Cayce source offered a series of affirmations that might be held in the mind as microcosms of God's coming to human consciousness, and each individual's responding. Biblical in their phrasing, they evoked the whole sense of the pilgrimage of the people of God, seeking to understand and glorify Him. Each affirmation contained some note of service; each contained some note of human shortcoming. The tone was warm, strong, earnest. The person seeking to meditate was invited to reflect on the force of the affirmation at some other time, perhaps in a study group, or when working on ideals. But at the time of the meditation, reflection, reasoning and analysis were to be laid aside. One was to hold the action, the movement, the total thrust of the affirmation gently before the mind, until all other thought and sensation dropped away. Where prayer was a deliberate filling of consciousness with high resolve and awareness, meditation was a stilling of consciousness. Practicing meditation daily, one ought to be able to keep only the Presence before the mind, drawing attention back from the rippling play of thoughts, until unaffected by outward sounds and sights. In this deep abstraction, a number of events would occur to signal that real inward action was taking place. Currents would seem to move along the spine, or dizziness would take over consciousness, or swaying from side to side or back and forth would become evident. None of these was in itself important, nor were sensations in particular parts of the body, from the gonads to the head, where the sensitive centers of the real body were located. In patience and in steady waiting, one should be at peace with the Lord. In time there would come those moments when the whole arc of meditation was completed, and consciousness was filled by an indescribable stillness and peace, as well as often by a flowing, melting stream of light that filled the entire field of awareness.

These were merely accompaniments. What was really happening in meditation? The aftermath might tell. Often one would find such abounding good stirring within to perhaps call this the most blessed of human experiences, consummated in the next generous handshake or helpful word or work on a committee. For one fruit of meditation could be the release of ancient guilts and defenses, the stilling of fears and compulsive drives. Problems could slip into perspective as challenges and opportunities; one might look upon one's whole life as God looked upon creation and call it good. For hours, or even days, after meditation had done its proper work, one would find that the answers needed would come—not in some strange occult way but in a heightening of the flow of ideas and impulses that had always been there. An individual could go to bed at night aware of being more truly alive than ever before, and more truly one's self.

Sometimes meditation would bring tears, tears of parting from old ways that no longer seemed worthy, or tears of rejoicing at the incredible goodness of God to so give Himself to humankind. Sometimes it would bring a heightening of sexual energies or a quickening of other emotions and drives, which then needed to be faced and given constructive expression. For this process was calling forth the total life force in an individual. Worship of this kind could be dangerous to the person if it were not anchored in loving service to others, in energetic self-giving. There was no way to seek to be "in His Presence" in meditation, if one did not strive to find self "in His Presence" as one stood before another person or before the realm of Nature—buying groceries, pruning plants, making a speech, reading a book, repairing a vacuum cleaner, struggling with an enemy, supporting a drunk. God was either a Presence with all of His Creation or He would be found in none of it.

The Cayce trance source never wearied of encouraging people to meditate. It was not, in this view, a luxury for those with time on their hands. It was a necessity for the human being to be human, as essential for the total growth of the individual, and for health and balance, as breathing was for the body. One could survive for long periods without it, perhaps for a lifetime, but only by developing halfway substitutes—various rituals of the arts or crowd gatherings or sexuality or Nature worship. Better to do that which was the way appointed in the human frame and heart, as a way to meet God. Then what was good in private and corporate rituals would thrive from the ground supplied by this primary devotional process, while that which was unworthy would fall away.

In the view of the Cayce information, meditation, accompanied by prayer, was no less than an individual's meeting God in body and consciousness here on earth, not waiting for some other plane. It was "Good News" that "He walks and talks with thee"; it was a promise not reserved for holy men, prophets, and saints but for all who would accept it and act on it.

What was necessary to cultivate meditation? One had to set before one's consciousness some concept of God, the best that could be conceived, and let it be prepared to grow. In the view of this source there was no way to dare God to present Himself, to reach Him at the conclusion of an argument. One had to make the initial gamble of setting such a possibility before the mind and allowing experience to stretch and enrich it.

Further, one had to set one's house in order. If there were practices contrary to one's true ideals, however little these might be voiced, then these practices—whether of cheating, of boasting, of belittling, of cruelty, of using others—would make the individual afraid within. And fear could block meditation, as it blocked the flow of so much else that might be helpful from the unconscious. "When there is fear, know that sin lieth at the door" was frequently said by this source. Not the reasonable fear from a momentary danger but the anxious fear that nagged at the back of the mind, that daunted the spirit of a person. One had to set his paths straight in order for meditation to work.

It was needful to be regular, for at least fifteen to thirty minutes a day. Most would find that an early morning time was best, although some could begin at a period in the middle of the night, when distractions would be at a minimum. But as in prizefighting or singing or any other complex skill, regularity was essential, for the mind and especially the body to find the way into meditation. Moreover, once the flow had begun, one ought to seek to touch it in moments of quiet during the day, by memory and focus. The much discussed "still, small voice" would be found to work, to answer, to supply helpful nudges all day long, if one opened the channel and kept it open through meditation. Yet even as meditation began to yield its treasure, its indescribable honey, one had to make it the basis for special claims before one's fellows; Jesus' parable of the Pharisee and the Publican at prayer was to the point, for boasting could stop the delicate process by distorting it

What would be found the greatest reward of meditation? Special skills and gifts? Remarkable powers? Fortuitous events? All of these might occur, for God was a Creator God and sought His children to be creative. But the greatest gift in meditation was the self-giving of God, the bringing to human consciousness of greater and greater awareness of One who was not a person yet intimately personal, and the bringing of a way of life meant by "abiding in Him." There could come a sense of partnership with the Nameless One, which made every day an adventure, and the long journey of the soul a pilgrimage into active joy that defied description.

Meditation and Prophesying

Probably many factors affect the emergence of that rare experience that might be called *prophesying*—speaking the truth to a group of people in terms they can hear and receive, with a wisdom and love and helpfulness beyond one's own. The entire force of a life may be involved, as well as the need of others, and one's readiness to be strange, to be a fool for God, while yet to be ordinary and keep all the commandments. Yet it may be that meditation has a special way of quickening a realization that all one's days are lived "in His Presence," so that when a Presence beyond one's own is needed, it can be found.

An able psychic once visited the same New England campus the writer often visited. He had shown in many settings that he could at times give readings of striking accuracy, by having individuals write their names on a piece of paper that he then held in his hand. Details of their health, their marital status, their religious life, their vocation, their homes and clothing—all came easily to him. His accuracy varied with his good spirits and the general good mood of those he sought to help. Standing before the entire faculty at a special meeting, he dazzled them with his undeniable virtuosity. Then he visited some classes and spoke of his experiences. At first his presence was merely an adventure and a campus challenge. Professors who had been sure there was nothing to ESP were shaken by his performances as they observed him at work, not only in groups but in the quiet and privacy of their homes. Then the atmosphere on the campus grew serious.

Students and faculty alike began to look at their own lives. What might an able psychic see if he really looked at them? They sought him out for conversation where they did most of the talking—conversations that became confessionals. The psychic in turn felt the force of the stirring about him and took himself off for long walks in the woods. He stayed on campus longer than he had planned, and night after night he met with small groups, speaking ever more deeply to one person after another. He recalled days as a young adult when he had studied the Bible more than of recent years, and he reexamined his own life, to see where it was going and what kinds of associates he had drawn. He spent time in quiet, and he touched a flow within him that he had learned to trust in times of meditation, which he had too often allowed to be squeezed out of his life.

Then he turned back to trying to aid one person after another, offering new directions in vocation, new hope for worn-out marriages, new promise to alcoholics, compulsive gamblers and the confused—each represented in some small way on the campus. He worked so hard that more than once his face grew pale and his nose began to bleed; often he went back to his room utterly exhausted. Something more than phenomena was astir on that campus, and he knew it. A few times he spoke fiercely to a whole room of people. Difficult days were coming to America, he said, and this campus had to be making its contribution to understanding, to good will, to research, to community built on love of truth. He found himself speaking, as he rarely did, of God's impatience with those who forever turned their backs on Him. Students and faculty heard him without affront and without indifference.

When he left the campus, students and faculty continued to talk, but not of his striking psychic accuracy, so abundantly shown to so many of them. They talked of their lives, of their times, of their worldview. So many made plans to begin a new life that, by the next fall, over a third of the faculty had sought new positions and found them, while the school itself began an entirely new chapter in its self-definition and service to its constituency.

Had his psychic tidbits slipped into prophecy? Had the Word of the Lord been spoken, not so much by the psychic, who spoke much and earnestly, but by those who answered him in their hearts and with their lives? Was this possible both because of the openness of the campus and the readiness of the psychic to find his way back to a quiet spot within, to that flow of meditation he knew how to trust? Had he, in his groping and well-meaning way, found his way to the kind of consciousness that had enabled Nathan to speak the truth in love to wayward, wife-stealing David, saying "Thou art the man"? And in his efforts to help people find and trust their best selves, had he touched some part of what came upon Samuel when he took Saul, seeking lost farm animals, and anointed him as the future king of Israel? He made no claims, and in later years he often wished he might get back to the sharing he had found at that college, when things came to him straight and deep, and he knew it was right that he should be given to shake up a whole campus.

~ TWELVE ~
Wonderworking

The reading for the afternoon was to be a strange one. Instead of being given the exact location of his subject, Cayce would be given only his name and the designation, "missing in action in the South Pacific," together with the base post designation used by the Post Office. The effort would be to locate the man from his birth date and place in a life reading.

In the reading room, which was Cayce's small office filled with mementos and photographs and his desk piled high with letters to be attached beside his portable typewriter, sat the parents of the missing Navy airman. Frantic with worry since their son had been reported missing in action, they had decided to risk all their resources on a trip to seek Edgar Cayce's aid in locating their son.

Cayce had given them little encouragement, explaining in letters and phone calls that his gift required having the location of a person, in order to give a reading about his present circumstances. He knew that in the past he had been able to locate criminals by first being directed to the scene of the crime, but he also knew that becoming immersed in a crime, even while unconscious, tended to upset him. He had found that he might be caught up in the emotion of watching a murder, with his voice rising to an unaccustomed shout of warning, in the midst of a reading, and with a disturbed feeling for days afterwards. More than once he had located embezzlers, thieves, murderers in the past; but his information had warned him that while he could do it, the process was dangerous to his own balance and was like using a razor blade to chop down a tree. He knew that on occasion his information had been able to locate one person out of millions in a given city, when an address supplied proved faulty and the need was critical to get a medical reading; only recently he had done this in locating an individual in Los Angeles, after a period of silence and seemingly intense effort, accompanied by a quiet aside: "Pretty big place to have to look." He knew, too, that his trance source had once located the lost aviatrix, Amelia Earhart, in a location that sounded reasonable to her relatives and associates but that the exact instructions given had not been followed out by search planes. What good would it do to locate someone if nothing were to be done about it? Why locate the Navy officer if the Navy were unable or unlikely to act on the information? If the man were dead, why give his parents—and his wife back home—the end of hope earlier than necessary?

But the parents had pleaded, and perhaps Cayce had touched within himself some sense of the probable outcome, for he finally agreed to try to locate the officer, and the writer and Cayce's secretary sat down with the parents to work out the instructions and questions that might bring results in the reading.

The room was quiet and everyone in keen expectancy when the reading began. Perhaps the expectancy, as well as the presence of the relatives, added to the attunement involved, for the voice of the sleeping man had hardly begun by locating the officer from his birth date and record (those strange Akashic records in time and space, which the Cayce source seemed to turn to for life readings), when it went right to the question at hand. The airman was alive but wounded, it said, and was being cared for by natives. He was ill yet should recover within a few weeks, if all went well, and be rescued by American forces. Meantime, all that might be done by the parents and others who loved him was to pray for him. And in a quiet way the assurance was given that the prayers would have effect, being met by the same forces that made possible Cayce's giving of readings—these forces would also aid. The location itself would not be given, except that it was on an island in the area where his plane had been reported downed. Then, with one more admonition to pray, the reading was over.

The parents left carrying hope, even though disappointed at not being given the location of their son. Something of the quiet authority of the voice giving the reading had reassured them that their son was really alive and might make it back to them. Several months later, they sent word that their son had indeed been found as promised, after having been wounded and cared for just as the reading had described.

Why had not the entranced man given the rest of the details? Was it a part of the usual restriction that people would only be given information they might act upon, in their own round of life? Did he foresee the awkward struggle that might occur in persuading the Navy to institute a search on the word of an ex-photographer speaking while unconscious in Virginia Beach, Virginia? Did he fail to locate the boy and only imagine the details that later happened to coincide with events? Or had the Source been protecting Edgar Cayce from the flood of inquiries that would swamp him if he located even one flier by his unusual ability—or protecting Cayce from his own inflation over such a feat? It had been made clear over the years that final details on locating buried treasure, or collecting rewards in the Lindbergh kidnapping, for example, had to come from some other person—usually in dream—which the Cayce source could then verify. But Cayce himself could not be asked to perform feats that would turn him into a side-show marvel, stopping the quiet flow of helpful medical, vocational, and religious counsel.

And what had been the substance of the process hinted at, that the aid normally given through Cayce would this time be given in the form of a helpful force reaching out to affect the wounded man and his helpers—both native and American rescuers? Was Cayce's gift, whatever it was, capable of being used not simply as ESP but as some form of psychokinesis as well, impressing itself upon people and perhaps even upon the tangle of signals that made up the work of a search party? Once before, there had been such indications in the readings, when relatives sought to locate a businessman who had left home under mental and emotional strain caused by financial collapses of the Depression. They were given the answer that he was alive and well, but not given his location, for this would violate his freedom. They were urged to pray for him, and encouraged also to secure some of the strangest readings on record, when for about two weeks the sleeping Cayce was simply silent during the reading time, lending the presence of a helpful, loving force to the runaway man. In time the man returned, and his account of the lifts he experienced during his agony of decision—whether to return home or even whether to go on living—made striking parallels with the times of the readings taken.

In general, Edgar Cayce was not inclined to use his ability as a direct force to affect objects or people. As he told the writer, he believed he had previously developed such a psychokinetic ability, when he had healing force and the capacity for moving objects, or materializing objects psychically. But in a recent lifetime he felt he had misused the ability by showing off in a carnival setting, as well as attracting attention to himself rather than helping others with their needs. So he had come into this life without the ability to work wonders or to influence flesh by direct flow of healing energy, except as he would be able to link the desires of his heart with the Spirit of Christ, who could indeed do any such thing that was needful. Accordingly, he was inclined not to experiment with physical manifestation, although he gave the impression that if he were ever in desperate need for aid for some member of his family, he would probably try to serve as an instrument through heartfelt prayer.

Often those close to him sought his aid in those little crises when psychic guidance or psychic outreach might seem to help. But his answer, typically, was prayer. For example, the writer and his wife once lost a beloved dog, when a car drove up at the end of the block and strangers scooped the dog into the car, driving off. Three men were in the car, and the indications were that they might want the dog to train as a hunting animal. Asking Cayce about this event, the writer was told that he and his wife should release the dog completely, "blessing it to the use" of the men, if the abductors needed it more than the present owners. It was a hard teaching, and Cayce was not dogmatic about it yet obviously sincere. With considerable effort, the writer and his wife made the attempt, and nothing less than prayer would have made it possible. Cayce grinned, when he saw that the effort had been made, and said only, "Watch." He refused to make any comment, when a few days later the same car with the three men drove up and let the dog out where they had picked him up. It was clear that he took no credit but also that he felt that the prayers of each who offered them could help to make the best outcome for everyone in such a situation.

Cayce's limited experiences with the possibility of *wonderworking*, performing the movement of objects, the changing of storms and climate, the affecting of events, placed him in distant touch with the most controversial aspect of the history of psychic phenomena. In every culture of the Orient and the Near East, as well as in primitive tribes from opposite ends of the earth, there have been tales of men and women who could make things happen. Biblical accounts would be representative of those from India and elsewhere: a jar that would not empty, a plague of locusts, bringing water from a rock, bringing victory in battle by an upheld arm and staff, quieting the sea, evoking an eclipse, walking on water, feeding a multitude out of little food, changing water to wine, and even raising the dead.

In modern times there were parallels to investigate in the astonishing mediumship of D. D. Home, who performed without fees for some of the best minds of the nineteenth century in Europe and seemed to have levitated out a window and back, as well as moved chairs and tables so forcefully that strong men could not hold them, and changed the temperature of a room in a few minutes. Indian rainmakers challenged the observation of anthropologists, while Carl Jung and others studied the ways in which alchemists had sought to invest psychic energy in the action of metals upon one another. What set these processes apart as wonderworking from the more commonly studied psychokinesis with dice was their performance in a setting where they were a sign, where they were used to convey to a group, rather than only to an individual, a force that would show forth the Grace of God. Drawing this line was not easy, but the distinction so often mentioned in these chapters between ordinary psychic experience of daily life and elevated psychic experience seemed to be a valid one in the manipulation of objects, as with perception of the unknown. Jung's suggestions that the symbolisms of alchemy were meant more to influence the deep reaches of the unconscious than to influence metals alone would be representative of the psychology under investigation in wonderworking as a phenomenon. What was it that, in classic biblical cases, allowed a prophet to say, "The Lord will do a thing at which every ear shall tingle," and even as he spoke to have it happen? Was he merely predicting, or was the prophet given power to bring it about, in the very act of speaking—as Guillaume has suggested in his study of "the acted sign"? Something of this process seems to have been at work in the activity of an able psychic whom the writer observed trying to heal a little girl from seizures. The psychic said one day, "Something has been shown to me, which I will show you to study. She will never again have a seizure when I am in the same town with her—although when I am away, I will have to pray to prevent or stop one. This will be true whether she knows I am in town or not—and I do not know why. But I know it is important to study, to understand, to see how we all need and help each other." Over a five-year period, his prediction was proven correct, as far as her family can determine. The events were small, compared to biblical wonderworking—small, that is, to everyone but the suffering girl and her family. But they may have operated along the lines of wonderworking, which needs further study, for the psychic seemed clearly in an elevated state when he grasped the promise for the girl and for those who were trying to learn and grow with him.

From time to time, the Cayce source spoke of biblical incidents of wonderworking as though they had actually occurred. Sometimes the Source corrected details, as in telling that Jesus had touched a man presumed dead on the forehead, to raise him from the dead—not taking his arm, which was bound according to the custom of the time for corpses. At other times the Information gave supportive details on how Moses used his staff, or how sheep were bred to bear different markings, or how the multitudes were fed by Jesus, or how Mary had conceived without being given to a man. This material was given spontaneously and in a vein of helping listeners to understand laws that they might study—in patience—to employ helpfully in some measure in their own lives; it led those familiar with the Cayce materials to view the Bible much less as the "religious fairy tale" it seemed to many of their contemporaries.

In the view of the Cayce source, specific energies were involved in wonderworking, operating through the delicate seven spiritual centers of the real physical body. Because of the notoriety involved in such phenomena, inquirers were repeatedly told that these were the most dangerous of psychic phenomena to attempt. Yet they were also assured in a few cases when dream material specifically showed a person that she or he could develop such ability for others, that the force to move objects or materialize and dematerialize objects could be brought to work under the terms that Jesus had stipulated for difficult healing: prayer and fasting. However, only those should make the attempt who had the prompting that Jesus had also mentioned, namely faith—not simply blind confidence but the quiet springing up from within that promised them such ability as part of their lives and work. One who had the necessary faith to move mountains would then be the one who sincerely listened to the stream of assurances and promptings from the soul and answered with all the force of being; if such a stream included a call to move mountains, then one might move mountains, in time—and patience.

Some have been drawn to an interest in the Cayce materials on wonderworking in the hope of developing a psychokinetic force that might be used either for personal gain or public service—perhaps in the field of electronics or photochemicals. But as they have experimented with the laws suggested in the Cayce materials, they have repeatedly found that beyond little bursts of happenings—such as seeming to dislodge a picture, or to break a glass, or to open a book repeatedly at a desired passage, or to affect the preservation of food—they have been unable to sustain such a force as an independent gift. Their observation has usually been that much more development of prayer, especially group prayer, would probably need to be developed. And that something in their own purposes probably needed to be cleansed and strengthened before they could handle such a force if they succeeded in developing it in a stable, public way. Studying dream material accompanying such efforts, they have reported that central to the achievement of physical phenomena that might be used openly with others would appear to be complete purification of the will—sacrifice of all striving for attention and power over others. Seeking to cultivate this end, they have often been led into quite different avenues of creativity than they intended—including child guidance, the making of music, and the developing of medical appliances.

Sacrifice in Creativity

Martin Buber has written that two forces stride as twins down the centuries wherever individuals have practiced their religions: prayer and sacrifice. Having turned to the focus on prayer and meditation in the previous lesson in religious dimensions of creativity, the Cayce source turned to sacrifice in its lesson entitled "The Cross and the Crown," as part of *A Search for God.*

Linking sacrifice with the psychic phenomena of wonderworking would be strange only to those who have not studied the correlation between asceticism and wonders in the lives of the saints of West and East—whether those wonders were the moving of objects or the more practical manifestations of driving individuals to build churches and hospitals. Gerald Heard has suggested, following Hindu traditions about the building up of vital force and energy, that the intense religious focus of holy men, matched by strenuous athleticism and the narrowing of bodily expression, under the impulse to sacrifice one's will go God's, could indeed produce the phenomena described, though little accredited by the modern world. While such sacrifice might at times have about it elements of masochism, it need not but might be of the order of idealism that motivates a monk to lay aside sexuality for generalized tenderness— even if the goal is not always reached. Whether such asceticism reached all the way to abandonment of identity, as the Buddha had tried and rejected, or included only the sacrifice of self-will and idolatrous urges symbolized in the Hebrew tradition of an empty Holy of Holies at the center of the temple of Jerusalem, would have to be explored. But the content of many ancient accounts, including that of Samson's vows and accompanying strength as a Nazirite, would suggest a linkage between sacrifice and wonderworking.

If, as the Jewish analyst Neumann has suggested, there is at work in every individual a tendency that can be called *centroversion*, in comparison with *introversion* and *extroversion*, as a tendency to orient the ego to a superordinate Self below the surface of consciousness, then sacrifice of self-will, of complete ego autonomy, might affect the flow of all kinds of creativity. Not only psychic phenomena but all artistic creating— invention of machines, building the United Nations, development of new forms of culture—all might be affected by whether the necessary inward promptings were organized to support a faltering ego or to link together a strong and capable ego with another center of the person, his specific point of contact with the divine. Such a person might indeed act, as the Hindu Bhagavad–Gita pleaded, without concern for the personal benefits of one's actions: acting without self–justification or self–defense. But to arrive at such a new structuring of the psyche, one might have to undertake a veritable "journey to the underworld," meeting the tests and developing the abilities suggested in ancient myths or dramatized for Christians in the life and work of Christ, where the cross was followed by the crown of free companionship with the Father.

In taking up the theme of the cross and the crown, the Cayce source was touching not only on the problem of voluntary sacrifice, as in all forms of asceticism, but also on the problem of involuntary sacrifice— that theme which in Catholic tradition has allowed baptism to the unbaptized, and therefore salvation, through the blood of martyrdom. What indeed is the human creature to make of suffering? How is one to understand God's action with self in pain and death, and how is one to respond to trials? Why is the sacrifice of human life upon an altar wrong, or what is the error in impassioned suicide with the hope of reaching a better world? How is an individual to distinguish between the sacrifice of giving something up and that sacrifice which Erich Fromm has called "giving out" as the truer form of sacrifice?

In the Cayce view, the historic symbol of the cross represented individuals having to make right their relation with matter. The action encountered in each person having to bend the will through what seemed like the ultimate test to flesh—pain and death—had begun when souls first entered the earth and "reversed law" by seeking to find gratification in "lower vibrations" than their proper realm of being. As a consequence, they had to find not simply an exit—which of course death provided in itself—but a transformation, a way of working and living with matter that would give to them an understanding of its laws and a way of sharing with one another through the right use of matter. Bodies had to be tamed, to be tuned, to be "lifted" until they were developed channels of grace from God, and from one individual to another. In this process, by many lifetimes of learning and giving, one could revise the original "fall of souls," and in fact make the whole journey worthwhile, a glorification of God.

But one would have to undo certain attachments in the process, and insofar as an individual identified with animal creation, that person would experience the loosening of these attachments as pain and humiliation or even as punishment. Yet the crosses in an individual's life were not punishment but focused opportunity. They allowed one to learn the laws of whatever ideals were chosen, however falteringly. If one chose earthly possessions as an ideal, one would have to learn the place of things. If one chose and used power, the lesson would entail learning how power was affected by the purpose for which it was used. If one chose love, then the laws of love would have to be learned, perhaps even of incest and loneliness, if necessary, until the soul stood free in the capacity for Godlike love. In the long journey, each would find that the crosses were also the crowns. One would also find that none but self determined the crosses, that she or he brought upon self each trial that came her or his way. Individuals would, however, find that they could draw aid unfailingly from the One who had walked the way of the cross before, in all things tempted like others, the One who "though He were the Son, yet learned He obedience through suffering." In the Cayce view, the soul who was the Christ was fashioned at creation as were all souls but given special charge over His fellows, who sought their way into the earth, and given the opportunity to show His fellows the way to new life in the flesh, until it might truly be said that "the Word was made flesh and dwelt among us, full of grace and truth," and "from Him we each re- . ceived, grace upon grace," to become with Him true sons of the Father.

The concept of the necessary cross was a hard teaching, not congruent with the usual cheery optimism in psychic circles, which asserted that man could have whatever he wanted by mastering occult powers or by securing the marvelous aid of the departed. In the Cayce view, individuals could have all of creation, all of the Creative Forces of God Himself; but each person had to earn these through growth and proper use—and growth could often mean release of lower forms of creativity in order to achieve higher forms. One might have to give up the beating of sticks and logs, one day, to play the piano. One might have to give up military drill with its pomp and killing, to teach others the full art of dance that celebrated a national heritage. Each giving up would at times seem a cross and require a genuine sacrifice. But the sacrifice would in fact be no greater than that made by a fetus upon leaving its lovely womb—a shock, not destruction. The cross was always also the crown, if chosen not "for narrow mindedness" but "for freedom."

The beginning of right understanding of cross and crown, then, would be to know oneself and every other soul on earth, even newborn babies, as sinners. No other view would be realistic or even helpful. Here the Cayce source presented a view that closely paralleled ancient doctrines of original sin, even to linkage with sexual gratification in the "fall of man;" yet the sin had been not of one man such as Adam but of every soul, and not a taint imparted by birth, but a problem brought upon each soul in its own past choices. Such as sin would be known and found in every soul's efforts to play God over its fellows—in a fashion that made the Cayce view not dissimilar to Freudian views of the university of the child's Oedipal strivings to use the parents. But understanding oneself and others as sinners did not define human destiny; it only enhanced the understanding of present choices. For the promise seen in Christ was every soul's promise, "to be able to live a perfect, blameless life on earth," truly overcoming the flesh without deserting it nor belittling it. To find this promise, each soul had sooner or later to choose "to know only Christ and Him crucified" as his ideal. By any other choice, one made self "a thief and a robber" to one's best self. Such a choice was not a religious choice, not merely a matter of church membership and ascent to creeds or rites. It was acceptance of a pattern that would be presented spontaneously in the soul of each individual, in its own way and time.

Furthermore, the pattern would have its representation, for those who answered to the best within them and around them, in other religions than Christianity. The Cayce readings were adamant that wherever individuals had sought the One God in true faith and love, there the Christ Spirit had led, "in every age and clime." It was no handicap to be a Buddhist, a Moslem, a Jew, even a primitive sun worshipper, provided one followed out the highest ideal known; in time each soul would find that the path led to the same Father as Christ had proclaimed. And that journey would be found not simply waiting, not punishment, not exile, but fulfillment, becoming, true creativity. For "He will withhold no good things from those who seek His Presence"; the tales of the mighty works of God among humankind were not deceptions. He chose to give them no less than the Kingdom, no less than Himself as their birthright, if only they would use their energies to bless one another, in every concrete way their talents afforded. The Cayce picture of crosses, then, was not of hard gem-like souls being polished by abrasion, but of living branches and vines, finding always new shoots put forth precisely where the hurts were—and bearing fruits on every branch in a kingdom of becoming, which was not dying to life but awakening to it.

If one's crosses were ultimately one's own, then was life to be lived to meet one's own trials and not those of others? By no means. There was in fact no way to meet a cross but to turn it into a crown. Each curse had to be made a course of blessing for others. Blindness allowed one to help others to see, poverty to give treasures not for sale, tyranny to open the door to freedom; for each, "stumbling blocks must be turned into stepping stones." The Cayce source was definite about this, in pointing to the process that, for example, has made Alcoholics Anonymous such a success. Each person would learn that where he or she could most effectively aid others was likely to be where self had to struggle the most; one's weaknesses were not simply to be overcome, but made slowly into wonders, the points of one's greatest strength and love and understanding. In this process the swiftest growth would be found to be "joyfully taking on the cares of others," wherever these might be found and rightly approached "in our own little world." For truly helping others should be seen as an opportunity, a privilege of helping none other than Christ Himself to bear the burdens of the world. Each individual could make the force of her or his life-field available to that larger, purer and infinitely creative Field, which individuals called "the Christ," and in so doing one could come under the law of mercy rather than of karma. For the destiny of souls was for them to become "heirs and joint heirs" with Christ, and leaving out the "joint heirs" would block the entire inheritance, however dutiful the life—as Jesus had shown in the image of the elder brother of the Prodigal Son.

Were there not accidents, blind happenings that punished and destroyed an individual? Asked about this, the Cayce source replied that indeed there had been accidents, "even in creation," but that no one should use this as a justification for blaming others for what came upon self. Far more than people realized, they drew upon them, in infinitely subtle ways that included psychic manifestations, exactly the predicaments in which they found themselves. This process extended even to lifetimes as mentally retarded or defective—which Cayce's source added then indicated that such people should be worked with in definite ways, not abandoned to strangers. The process extended to sudden death or to the soul withdrawing quickly from life at any age, when the task that it entered to accomplish was fulfilled or blocked. The picture drawn by the Cayce source was one of staggering wisdom in the spinning universe, operating under laws of justice and soul-development that both transcended and harmonized with what is called "natural law." If the picture of this source were taken literally, the universe was not only friendly, as philosophers often asked, but unspeakably loving, fired with love from God Himself.

How might one begin to meet personal crosses, personal trials, so as to find them crowns? How might one undertake sacrifice of one's own willfulness without abandoning the creative will as an instrument for glorifying God? A beginning would need to be made in attitudes. Resentment at strains would unfailingly block the transformative process, as would blaming others. When pain and frustration came, and the temptation to flee to safety or to thrills, or to try to corner life within some human power, one should stop and say in his heart, "Lord, to whom shall we go?" Slowly, the fear in each crisis would begin to diminish, as one found that she or he had been protecting things, images of self, which did not need to be protected. Turmoils would lessen and consternation depart, as one sought to be conscious of the force of the divine in and with every important action and decision. One did not always have to solve problems correctly nor expect to do so, as much as expect increasing capacity to try and try again.

And if one wanted to know whether progress was being made in the realm of sacrifice, the answer was not to be found in psychic feats alone. For signs and wonders and miracles were not God's way, as Jesus had showed in handling His own temptations. Remarkable things could come about lawfully as an individual grew and worked with others who together sought the will of God. Indeed, the Cayce source insisted, nothing in the biblical record, even the raising of the dead, was impossible for those who sought to train for such things for the right purpose—especially because they could count on an aid that the man Jesus had not known, the aid of the Risen Christ, to guide and resonate and focus their creative energies. But the right measuring sticks for people of good will and humble spirits would be found much simpler than miracles.

Were they entering each new trial with a little more joy, a little more good nature, a little more spirit of adventure? Then all was well with them, whether they were moving objects by hidden powers or simply moving dirt with shovels as ditch diggers. And yet better as an indicator of growth, were they taking up the burdens of others where they rightly could, and in good spirits that forbade martyrdom or boasting? This was the final way in which they or anyone else might know for sure whether they were becoming disciples of the Master: "that ye love one another"— and not only the ones who loved them back, or even thought like them, or responded to kindness. What was the sign that could be trusted? Not sacrifice that was a slaughter of oneself and others in the name of a fixed righteousness. Not sacrifice that turned good energies aside for feats and made stones into bread instead of bread into vehicles of feasting and communion. But the sacrifice that was service, imaginative and people–building service, wherever a trouble could be turned into a talent, and a crippling into a clap of insight, a cross into a crown.

Sacrifice and Wonderworking

Might sacrifice have anything to do with capacity to work wonders upon people and things? Cases are difficult to find, but hints are there to raise the questions.

A European psychic who had made a reputation at solving crimes came to the U.S. for a series of demonstrations and to participate in some modest research projects. During his visit he drew good–sized crowds at his demonstrations of seeming mind–reading and clairvoyance, and not surprisingly he was called upon by the police force of several cities to help solve crimes—sometimes in their good faith and sometimes in suspicious tests. In one case in a large Eastern metropolis, he correctly found a young man who had committed several murders, and had himself placed in a cell with the psychotic lad. After talking many hours with the suspect, he had suddenly broken into a painful memory of the young man's past—his parents had tortured him—and he was able to get the boy talking of this and start him toward rehabilitation. He was given an honorary police badge by the city for his work, and it was a source of much pride to him. He carried it in his wallet and often showed it.

Then one day he was in a city on the West Coast, when he was called by a frantic doctor, seeking help in reaching the mind and spirit of his troubled son, who had repeatedly tried to commit suicide. He went and talked with the boy, establishing a rapport by reference to the lad's inner thoughts and hopes and fears, which several psychiatrists had failed to achieve. He saw the lad several times and helped him, but he knew he would soon have to leave to return to his native country. In one touching visit, he heard the boy plead with him for some means of remembering him, some way of recalling what their relationship had meant. And the psychic knew instinctively he should give the boy something of his own, some object that was stamped with his own identity. He had done this with others before. It was not enough to assure the lad that he might telephone him at any time, nor to promise him that he could slowly gain his balance through psychotherapy. What should he give him? His pen? His watch? He knew in an instant it would have to be the police badge, the object that had caught the boy's imagination when first they talked. It was part of him, part of his very self-image, his sense of worth in a strange land, and therefore the right thing to give.

The psychic was not surprised when the months that followed turned into years, without the doctor's son again trying suicide. Nor was he surprised that he did not really miss the badge, nor surprised that his work from that time more and more turned to work with doctors and less with police and the stage. He was beginning to find that he could muster a force that read x-rays without seeing them, that located strange roots to be used in medication, and that could even guide a surgeon's hand and timing in a delicate brain operation. Some sort of wonderworking was coming into his reach, and though it frightened him with its responsibilities and often made him want to turn back, it also opened up for him the meaning of the Old Testament as he had never felt or understood it before. He began to understand that one could make many mistakes, have many failures, yet if he were willing to share his real being with others, something promising would keep occurring. He saw at times that he might one day be more than a psychic—a man. Like Daniel of old he might cease one day to bow before wealth and power, trusting his abilities even to the point of discarding the love of others' lionizing, which was his own lions' den.

~ THIRTEEN ~
Guiding

The little boy was screaming. It was time for Edgar Cayce to start the afternoon reading, but it seemed impossible to get the necessary quiet. How was Cayce to pray and go into trance in his study, when right outside his door, in the library, a three–year–old was crying at the top of his lungs in pain and fear?

The child's parents had brought him all the way from a Midwestern suburb to make a personal contact with Cayce and to be for a physical or medical reading. The young Army officer and his wife knew their youngster's case was virtually hopeless; the boy had cancer of the eyes and had already been operated on eight times. He was now blind and in constant pain. With the aid of sedation and loving care, they could keep his crying to a whimper much of the time, but now they were not certain they could get him quiet enough to leave him for the hour and a half they would be in the reading room.

One of the secretaries in the office took the lad in her arms and began to talk to him, to rock him. Then she carried him into the next room where there was a parrot in a cage, an old sea salt of a parrot retrieved from a German submarine, who swore and who whistled at girls. As the boy quieted down to little gasps and coughs of crying, she described the parrot to him and explained that the parrot always knew exactly when readings were to begin, though nobody told him. As soon as the door to Cayce's study closed, the parrot would fall silent and stay that way until the reading was over, when he would begin once more with "Whatcha want?" or "Who's there?" or something a bit less refined. The boy caught the spirit of the comparison with the parrot he could not see, and snuggled into the girl's arms. He, too, it turned out, would stay quiet while the readings were given, including one on him.

The writer sat across the room from the unconscious Cayce, watching the boy's parents as the reading began. "Yes we have the body, present in this building." The parents were tense, earnest, obviously never far from prayer. The entranced voice traced the history of the ailment, examining contributing factors in the circulation, in the nervous system, in endocrine function. The history of the surgery was reviewed and a sketch given of exactly how the boy felt and how his cycles of pain developed through each day. At this last, the parents turned to each other open-mouthed in astonishment. How did Cayce know about the timing of the pain peaks? For that matter, how did he know what medication they were using and the name of their doctor? Their faces were flushed as they leaned forward to listen to the steady voice explain what should be done, and explain whether there was hope.

Indeed there was hope, said the firm voice. Recovery would take a long time, but if the beginning were made at once, relief would be found before long, and in time healing. The boy would even regain his sight.

The mother wept, and the father bit his lip. It was evident that the assurance had struck home to them, touching their own inner spring of faith. In that moment they, too, were sure that their boy could be helped, in spite of all the negative medical judgments that had been given. How could Cayce be so right about the boy's history, his behavior, his care, and be wrong about his prospects? As the secretary took down the full medical regime of electrotherapy, chemotherapy, physiotherapy, and even diet, they listened as though to burn the instructions into their minds. They were surprised to hear the name of a doctor in Philadelphia recommended—someone far from their home and of whom they had never heard.

After the readings were over for that period—four of them—they went into the other room to get their son, who clutched at them. They thanked Cayce with evident feeling, and the young wife hugged him. Making arrangements for a copy of the reading to be dropped off at their hotel that night, they left.

It was nearly a year later when the writer had the opportunity to interview at length the Philadelphia doctor, a woman who taught medicine as well as conducted her private practice. She reviewed her doubts about the hope that Cayce had offered when the parents had come to her, and her hesitation to use the Cayce treatments. However, the essence of the Cayce approach was similar to her own, placing heavy reliance on stimulating better circulation to the cancerous area, and she decided to take the case. She described how frantically the boy had cried each time he was brought to her waiting room, his little mind filled with memories of visits to doctors and of painful surgery and shots. It tugged at her heart when he fought to get away from her, groping in his blindness. But she made a friend of him in time and even began to look forward to his visits for treatment, as she knew the boy did. Then came the day when she looked into the waiting room and noted with astonishment that the boy seemed to be reaching for a hat on a chair next to him. Quickly she took the mother aside to ask whether the youngster was seeing, however dimly. The mother responded that she had been wondering, too, though it seemed too much to hope.

But sight had begun again for the boy. And the time came, months later, when the doctor had one of the happiest moments in her long and busy practice. She stepped into the waiting room and saw the lad across the room catch sight of her. Without a word he slipped from his mother's arms and ran to the arms of the doctor. Though she was a professional person, she was also a woman. She wept and scooped him up in her arms.

Was she able, the writer asked, to definitely establish that the Cayce treatments had stopped the course of the cancer and aided in the restoration of the vision? She could not. There were too many unknowns involved. And in fact, cancer—like other diseases—sometimes showed spontaneous remission of symptoms, when the growth would stop of its own accord or by some process not initiated by physicians. All she could say was that if she had it to do over again, she would follow exactly the same regime of treatments, until research—on which she and her colleagues were making a beginning—could establish which part of the Cayce treatments, if any, had been effective, and how. Further, she responded, she was going to make a trip to Virginia Beach that year to study the Cayce medical materials and hoped to be able to return for the same purpose regularly, though without publicity.

What had Edgar Cayce done, what had changed and moved in his consciousness, when he began to speak, saying "Yes we have the body, present in this building"? Had he really inspected the very tissues of the boy's body and examined associated events of surgery and medical care carried in the boy's own unconscious and aura (the process described by his own information as the source for such readings)? Or had he developed fantasy material that happened by sheer coincidence to fit exactly with the facts of the case—as he had by similar coincidence in thousands and thousands of readings before this one? And where did he get the name of the doctor, whom he had not known previously? Not to mention the details of a therapy for a particular kind of cancer, which was by general medical knowledge not yet susceptible to therapy. It had all gone by so swiftly in the reading room; he had done it so many times before, for so many sick people and for so many doctors, even doing it twice a day for years in a hospital devoted entirely to treating people on the basis of his readings. His capacity could be accepted as some sort of a natural wonder, a sort of Grand Canyon of the mind, when one was right there looking at it. But when one stepped back and asked what might possibly have gone on, the mind boggled. Tales of traveling clair-voyance under hypnosis only made the phenomenon of such guidance more tantalizing, for such hypnotic phenomena had proven impossible to duplicate at will, and far less accurate medically than the usual Cayce performance, as well as lacking Cayce's precise medical terminology. In-stances of medical counsel from supposedly discarnate doctors speaking through mediums offered certain parallels, sometimes even exceeding Cayce's medical fluency; yet the best of such mediumistic work had not yet proven under research investigation to be as stable as the Cayce phenomenon. Even hard-boiled university investigators, interviewed by the writer on their personal experiences with the Cayce readings, tended to lean to interpretations not far from Cayce's own, positing some sort of universal intelligence that Cayce might be in touch with, through his own procedure of prayer and trance.

The kind of guidance given to the parents of the cancer-ridden boy could hardly be called prophecy, for there had been no attempt to link the factual counseling with any group trend or commitment, nor with any immediate character concerns. There was no mention of the affairs of nations, of churches, of movements and causes and leaders—just definite, detailed medical aid for a family that desperately needed it. Yet the aid given was clearly of a different order from the little helpless flashes and promptings that had become a natural part of Cayce's waking life—far more detailed than he would be likely to see in an aura. And even though Cayce's dreams showed him capable of grasping the needs of a situation or individual in considerable psychic detail, they were never as rich in detail of aid for others as was such a reading. Compared to these other phenomena, the guidance that came in readings would seem to require description as enhanced or elevated psychic experience.

Cayce's speech in giving readings would become measured, rhythmic, stately. In spite of its grammatical omissions, based on an oral rather than written style, the discourse of the readings could often be scanned as free verse. At their best, these readings had little of the turgid personal style so familiar in the records of automatic writing, and little of the snips and snatches that sometimes characterized mediumistic or psychometric material. A complete creative form seemed to be instantly fashioned—at times reminding a listener of Japanese haiku poetry. Yet the form varied in completeness and polish from day to day, and from period to period in Cayce's life, just as did the amount and precision of detail in the content of the readings. Enhanced or not, some readings offered only the bare minimum of factual material and recommendations, while others flowed and sparkled with both facts and value judgments. Some were awkward in grammar, while others were smooth.

Was Cayce in his readings conforming to the type of the seer in the history of religions, as that encyclopedic scholar Joachim Wach suggested on the basis of his comparisons with Greek, Hebraic, Peruvian, Hindu, and Chinese figures? Unlike the more striking figure of the prophet in various traditions, Cayce was limited in healing and wonderworking gifts, limited in administrative and organizing gifts as a reformer. But when it came to gifts of vision, his limits were difficult to determine.

Indeed, it sometimes appeared that the only limits on the scope of the Cayce counsel were (a) those of proper instructions given to Cayce, at a time when he was sufficiently rested, peaceful of mind, and in a certain state of health (not too soon after a meal), and (b) those of the seeker's capacity to use information in his own life, in constructive service of others, without unfair advantage of any man, nor damage to the seeker or Cayce in personal and social functionings. Within these broad limits, many factors appeared to affect the quality and scope of each day's readings—factors in Cayce, in those around him, in the seeker, and perhaps in the times as history or part of God's "plan of redemption." But the range of targets demonstrated over the years had been staggering.

There were readings in the files on buried treasure and buried talents, on investment opportunities and on opportunities with the Infinite, on leukemia and on loving, on child rearing and on crime control, on Egyptian architecture and on endocrinology, on fluoridation and on the fields of stars, on ancient gods and on airplane design, on chemical compounds and on Christ, on stock markets and stock-taking of ideals, on angels and on anger, on movie scripts and on motions below the crust of the earth, on marital covenanting and on merriment, on death and on dentures, on visions and on viscera, on the Bible and on bile. The list of material in this guidance process was evidently of about the same size as the material in human affairs, past, present, and—less sweepingly—future. The writer once undertook a study of what subjects were not dealt with at any length in the readings, and then indexed and came up with agriculture as somewhat under-represented—probably in part because Cayce's work seemed to draw relatively few farmers over the years. The list could be lengthened, but because of the range of the life readings, which claimed to offer snapshots of people in all sorts of occupations and stations in life from many periods of history, the list of fields of human interest not at least suggestively touched on in the Cayce readings would be surprisingly short.

But as might be expected of a phenomenon that might truly be called guidance, rather than mere supplying of information in a kind of psychic computer service, the range of human value questions dealt with was as great as that of the factual material and equally a hallmark of the Cayce phenomenon, though not as widely celebrated in his lifetime nor since his death. In the field of ethics and morality were issues of war and peace, family living and the character of corporations, race relations and sexual relations, taboos and trade practices, penology and panaceas, biblical norms and basic cosmology of the soul and God. In the field of aesthetics were more limited treatments of norms and masters in each of the major art media, as well as studies of symbols and signs, of periods and pressures in art history, of the relation of beauty to love and truth and godliness ("For music alone may span the distance from the sublime to the ridiculous"). In the field of logic and the search for truth were treatments of perception and cognition, of hunches and hypotheses, of conscious logic and unconscious logic, of syllogisms and of statistics, of archetypes and analysis, of thought processes in half a dozen different states of consciousness besides waking attention, and of revelation and reason, theology and theorizing, myth and mindfulness. In the realm of values called the holy, there were materials on rite and on resurrection, on sin and on God's secularity, on penitence and on praise, on creation and on caring, on faith and on Fatherliness, on Jesus and on judgment, on healing and on happiness, on brotherhood and on borrowing Grace. While there were essay-like passages on each of these topics, the general treatment was situational, personal, existential. People were not given maxims alone, but choices. They were not fed teachings so much as met where they were and taken seriously in their own value thrusts. In the handling of what mattered in the quality of people's lives, both ultimately and proximately, the method of the Cayce source was to work with what was given in the seeker, either in his consciousness or just below the surface in the working of an ideal. For it was the perspective of this source that the relation of evil to good was not poles apart, in a given individual, but evil was "just under good." Evil was good energy and values misapplied, misunderstood, misused, misfocused in the blind willfulness of souls; but evil was not so much to be exterminated as raised to the good that it could be. Psychosis was not far from prophecy, cruelty not far from carrying another, withdrawal not far from wisdom in silence—if only people could see the gap and make the effort. The gap between right and wrong was a cosmic gulf in the eyes of God, and yet right and wrong were as close as seed and shell in God's view of each man's growth.

These were perspectives that questioning drew, when the Cayce source was asked how a high form of psychic or seerlike guidance was possible among human beings. Characteristically, the Cayce source insisted that individuals could use the same processes Cayce used, to secure the guidance they needed for their own lives, in dreams and prayer and meditation, with waking hunches and judgment. The difference between most people and Cayce was only that most people could secure guidance for themselves and their loved ones, while Cayce was able to make his psyche available—through long training and dedication in past lives—for anyone to seek the guidance he needed. But others would be found to have natural endowments similar to and greater than Cayce's, his source insisted right up to the end of his life. Such souls could be "drawn into the earth" by parents who lived upright lives and prayed to be given the treasure—and to bear the trial—of a soul with such special talents for service and guidance of others.

During Cayce's lifetime, especially from 1932 until his death in 1945, his close associates and his family sought to cultivate their own gifts of guidance along lines suggested by the Information. Usually they were most successful in giving aid to family members, on a wide variety of topics that included medical information, vocational guidance, business judgment, childrearing, and psychotherapy. But at times they could give similar guidance, and even secure insights and visions of genuine theological depth, for members of their prayer and study groups. They found that many factors affected their ability, which seemed to have a different profile for each person; some were able to offer health hints to others, some able to counsel on marital relationships, some able to touch hidden value springs of a life, some able to interpret biblical or other material to make a meaningful world view. But among these factors, one that stood out was care not to divide the universe too far into realms of sacred and secular, of holy and unholy, of God and Nature, of religion and business. Unless they could find themselves working with the same springs of creativity, the same Source, in the same Spirit, in whatever they undertook, they would not be likely to secure effective guidance in any realm for long. God was either to be God of their whole lives or hidden from their view. It made a difference how they polarized their universe.

Polarizing in Creativity

After dealing with prayer and with sacrifice, the Cayce source turned to the question of religious understanding, religious belief, for its next area of focus among the religious conditions of creativity. Characteristically, it took up a perspective in which both idea and act were united, by using a phrase from biblical history that was both a proposition and the heart of the Jewish prayer of faith, the Shema. The chapter on polarizing, on conceiving the fundamental structure of religious thought and action, was entitled "The Lord Thy God Is One" in *A Search for God.*

Psychic ability of every sort seems so irrational, so unpredictable, so much at the mercy of controls outside of consciousness, that linking guidance with any particular convictions may seem arbitrary. Yet every approach to the depths of the unconscious, where psychic ability seems clearly to take its origin, as viewed by modern research, shows how responsive the unconscious is to conscious thought and plan and stance. Dream material is full of commentary not only upon the activities of the previous day's consciousness, as Freud so well showed, but upon the conscious formulas and trends of the life style—as contemporary research in dream laboratories suggests. Psychotherapy in all its forms is based on the conviction that the unconscious material in certain neuroses and psychoses can be changed by changing the work of consciousness—its names, plans, claims, poses, formulas, convictions, abdications. Inventors correlate their flow of new material with conscious coding done by studying a problem, while most artists come to expect their inspiration to need matching and stimulus by conscious technique. It would not be surprising if the flow of helpful unconscious material called *psychic* were also responsive to the basic structures of thought and conviction, held in consciousness.

However, the choice of the ancient formula "The Lord Thy God Is One" as a focus for the polarizing of the mind by understanding and conceptualizing would seem a difficult one. Is the Oneness the transcendent holiness of Hebraic tradition, or the immanent One behind all things in Hindu tradition, or a One Mind of philosophical idealists, or a One Energy of philosophical vitalists? Is the God under discussion a personal or an impersonal being or reality? What kind of thought is implied in the use of the phrase "The Lord"—how far devotional and within a covenant, and how far philosophical and objective?

Behind all of these questions, it was at least clear that the Cayce source was struggling against all kinds of dualism, all efforts to make the split between matter and spirit, between God and creation, between reason and revelation, into cosmic splits rather than conveniences of thought. How might dualism affect creativity, whether psychic creativity or any other? The Swiss psychiatrist Carl Jung has suggested that most dualisms are rooted in an unhealthy separation of spheres of the psyche, of consciousness from the unconscious, of ego from a deeper Self. Insofar as Jung may be correct, then any ardent dualism tends to break up the effective harmony of surface and deeper layers of the psyche, which appear in creativity to stimulate and fructify one another. Insofar as such dualism is a defense against something felt unworthy and dangerous within oneself, then that part of the mind will be isolated, exiled, restricted in its production of both negative and positive material. Freud's mission—as Fromm has called it—may be seen as a heroic struggle against one form of dualism that splits the mind by repression of primitive urges, rather than by large-minded acceptance of human motivation and controls.

In the area of high-level or enhanced psychic ability, such as offering effective guidance and helpful information for others, the peril of dualism of attitudes towards the psyche—however projected outwards onto the cosmos—would seem to be the peril of invasion of spirituality by material from unrecognized personal conflicts. Something of this process may be seen at work in some lonely female automatic-writers whose discarnate controls appear to be dominantly masculine, bent upon serving the every wish of the medium—including unconscious erotic desires and power drives. The danger is no different from that encountered where people interpret dreams of normal psychological function and balancing as oracles from a higher self or from a divine spirit. That many dream symbols, including sexual symbols, may be interpreted on both personal and transpersonal levels is hardly to be denied; what may be symbolic of incest for one may mean rebirth for another and both for a third. But the peril in banishing part of human experience as unworthy in a scheme of grand dualism need hardly be labored. Amputation will never replace transformation, in the things of the human mind and spirit.

In taking up the question of dualism and monism, the Cayce source turned—surprisingly late in its progression of topics—to the question of religious belief and conviction, which is as old as faith. When the Buddhist takes refuge in the Dharma, when the Hindu seeks direct knowledge showing "That art thou," when the Jew seeks to become bar mitzvah, "son of the commandments," when the Christian struggles for a creed, when the Muslim chooses to set Allah above the logical necessity, when the Australian aborigine sets apart the circumcised male youth for instruction in men's truths—the question of religious belief and conviction is to the fore.

Characteristically, the Cayce source refused to separate knowledge from action. The right approach to God would be found in a combination of reflection and hard study with action that was at once attunement and service. Out of such an approach understanding would come. While the Cayce source often spoke philosophically of "the Oneness of All Force" and spoke psychologically of "turning within to the Christ consciousness which is One with the Christ," its characteristic formula was the devotional formula of ancient Judaism, "Hear O Israel, the Lord Thy God is One"—for here was a way of approaching non-dualism that was set in the living experience of a people, rather than in the armchair of the philosopher or the laboratory of the psychologist. The caution of the Cayce source regarding purely rational formulations of the nature of God and creation, of God and human, was in part grounded on a view of humankind by which truth could only be found through transformation; the consciousness of an individual could grasp and use only what had been lived out and activated in the soul. One could understand with wisdom, more than with learning, only as much of the Creative Forces as had become one's own through choosing and enacting an ideal. Concept and life-trajectory went hand in hand; concept not girded by experience could be a plaything or a snare. Even the most delicate interplay of senses and reason was not an adequate guide unless formed, quickened, prompted by unseen patterns coming into the background of consciousness from the soul and its superconscious awareness of the way things really were.

In the approach of the Cayce information, it was necessary that the human mind be correctly polarized toward the divine at work, in order for the mind to achieve its maximum creative function. Such polarizing was of the order of tropism, as a plant turns toward the sun, rather than of the order of electricity, with positive and negative poles. The opposite of God was not some structured anti–God nor devil, though evil had its structures and some human patterns were assuredly devilish even to the extent of becoming autonomous thought forms. The opposite of God was that which was not yet fully in harmony with Him and conscious of its nature and destiny. If one could talk about another direction from the One Force, it would have to be disorganized force, misused force, compulsive force—exactly what distracted souls showed in their spinnings, turnings, hidings, and masqueradings. But even the force to be selfish, to do wrong, was God's force—there was no other force in creation. And because it was God's force, it would ever be transforming, turning into other modes, suggesting other meanings, calling forth new predicaments and results, turning man—and all creation—Godward. For even the creatures and things of the earth, said the Cayce information in one passage reminiscent of Mahayana Buddhism, must reach the consciousness of their Creator some day, and individuals could, in their journey in the earth, render this service to brother animal and sister stream. It was not a small canvas on which the Cayce source painted its sketches of creation and destiny.

To get at the conception of the universe that would free the soul to be itself, each person had to learn that "dualism confuses and mystifies," that "all material things are spiritual," that "the Father doeth the works" and stands behind and with all His creation. From time to time one might even glimpse, as did Job, that "all things work together for good," that "God gets himself glory even out of men's evil." But this sense of the ultimate unity of the cosmos and Creator would be found to be the most difficult truth for human consciousness to fully attain and in some sense would never fully be grasped except by metamorphosis, by the person's becoming more than was supposed. Likewise, each individual had to learn that God was not to be found in special times and places called religious or holy. One who could not find God in the face and heart of a brother or sister could not find Him in a temple or grove; one who could not find Him and share His presence in cooking and serving a meal would not find Him in serving communion. It was One Force at work in every aspect of human life, and the point of elevating some segments to the status of holy things was only to emphasize that God was always there, in even the most ordinary things and events—like one day of the week, or bread and wine, or auras glistening out of sweat.

Yet to call God *One* and turn one's face towards Him might well require thinking meaningfully in Trinitarian terms or some other symbolism that made the One luminous in its spectrum of Creative Forces. The Cayce source never wearied of saying that the formula of "Father, Son, and Holy Spirit" had come to the human mind and stayed there because it so well corresponded to three-dimensional existence—while on other planes perhaps six- or seven-dimensional existence would require different types of symbolism. On earth the primal symbolism of the Trinity was parallel with human three-ness: The Father was like the body; the Son—ever the Builder and Helper—was like the mind, while the Spirit was like the spiritual or soul realm of experience, ever tugging at self. So long as one had to contend with these three overlapping realms of reality, all drawn from the One, the individual would find Trinitarian thought helpful.

But there were limits in thinking of God in terms of substances, even metaphysical ones, for the primary category of the Cayce source was "force," in speaking of the divine. Not substance but process ran all through the readings. Even organs of the body were described as "those forces of the liver" more often than as "the liver." Mental tendencies and unconscious complexes were "forces of the mental." In the perspective of the Cayce information, the cosmos was seemingly an indescribably rich flow of interpenetrating fields and fluxes, of vortices and events, of vibrations and waves and harmonics, rather than of fixed things and structures that the conscious mind so liked to postulate. At times the Cayce source would be impatient with the neat structuralism that would incline a seeker to ask whether or not she had arthritis or asthma or some other partly labeled condition; the voice would indicate that the total condition of the body had been described, organ system by organ system, and the individual might call it whatever was wished, just so she set about treating those conditions. The Oneness, then, might better be grasped in a schema of forces and processes, of events and relationships, than in a schema of substances and structures, places and hierarchies.

The Cayce source moved freely back and forth between philosophical language and devotional language in dealing with questions of polarizing thought and action about the divine. At times the concepts used were of laws, while at other times the same laws were described as the promises of God. Both ways of thinking were used as though they had value, even in intricate questions of karma, where matters of justice and law were discussed as freely in terms of souls and universal forces as in terms of "meeting self, with the help of Christ." There was no clear priority given either to rational reflection, quickened by a life of commitment to ideals and the One Lord, or to inspiration welling up from the unconscious but requiring conscious interpretation and decision. There was, however, an insistence that no great vision or experience was needed to begin to live within the polarizing awareness, "The Lord thy God is One." Even though the Cayce source insisted that Jesus had demonstrated the reality of direct, personal relations between humankind and God, so that every individual could set as his or her destiny being able to say in the now, "I and the Father are one," there was no insistence that each person go through a conversion experience or turning-point revelation to find the Oneness. Like everything else of value in creation, this discovery of Oneness would come a little at a time. But entering into meditation on the assumption that the divine would really be there, touching the human field in some authentic way, would guide and speed the growth.

If not by seeking or waiting for some blinding invasion of God into consciousness, how might one begin to cultivate the polarizing of life to the affirmation that "The Lord they God is One"? The beginning might come in self-analysis to discover just what sort of God one showed forth in life. Was it a God of Sundays and public pronouncements, of religiousness? Or was it a God of love and work and play, as well as of worship, a God of dailyness? Was one's God the God of good behavior or of the whole person? Was it a God able to handle human evil as well as goodness, to turn crosses into crowns, for one who was "hid with Christ"—who had found a fully human Lord over "the imagination of the heart"? Each individual was representing a personal concept of God by daily life as surely as if she or he were a sculptor carving it, or a singer intoning it, or a theologian explaining it.

But activity alone would not provide the index of one's polarizing towards that final One. There would have to be turning to the still, small voice and toward the crowning Light and nectar of stillness that could be found in meditation. Only by entering into the "holy of holies" in one's own inmost being, through prayerful intent, could one find guidance as to whether one's life was properly glorifying the One in the most creative way. For one could become easily confused and attempt without such guidance to live out spiritual laws on the physical plane, or mental laws on the spiritual plane. One might confuse sacrifice of the will to God with sacrifice of one's identity to parents or country. One might confuse trusting the constructive powers of the mind with an outlook where God Himself could be made to do the bidding of the mind through concentration. One might confuse the real physical laws of death with spiritual death and separation from God. There were laws for each realm, within the whole creation straining and dancing its way Godward, and only attunement could sort out the laws into their proper spheres, polarized around the One.

Polarizing and Guiding

The phenomenon of effective guidance, including psychic information for another person, may be rarer than the prominence of fortune tellers and soothsayers in human history might suggest. Yet some measure of it may go on all the time for those whom we find bound in the bundle of life with us, whether by love or fear. Of the many factors that may quicken and enrich such guidance, how much does the achievement of understanding about the non-dual relation of God and His creation make a contribution?

A nun in her thirties sat in her place in a sensitivity training group, which the writer observed. Like many another of her sisters in these times, she was feeling the need to reunite the worlds of the secular and sacred, so divided in popular piety, however they may have been unified in the best of theology. She was wondering aloud again, before the group members whom she had grown to love and trust in a relatively short time, whether she ought to leave her habit and her community and take up a place in wholly secular life, bringing to those around her a sense that the gifts of God are for everyone and not alone or especially for the religious.

The group members, all lay men and women, were finding it difficult to respond to her question and were surprised at how strongly they projected on her. Some wanted to see in her the purity they felt they had lost in their own lives; some wanted to see her choose the way of love and sex to justify their own life courses. Some saw in her the opportunity to be helpful to others without the burdens of family and children—burdens they had always said kept them from real service to others (or had they?). Some saw in her work as a nun the possibility of a contemplative life in which long hours might be put in searching out a direct relation with God. One after another, the group members contributed their subjective awareness that they could not see the nun for herself, in her own pilgrimage, because they were allowing her garments and office and vows to make her into a thing rather than a person—a religious thing, either great or small as the case might be, but a thing.

Further meetings came back to the nun's question, which she did not force upon the group during the week of close sharing but which she addressed as honestly as the others were expected to address their own life questions. Finally, after the group had gone for a long walk together and settled down before the fire for a quiet time of prayer and talking with one another, one man spoke to her. "I think," he said, "you can have whatever you want, so long as it is within your capacity to handle, and you want it to share with others, and you are willing to pay the price of growth that is involved. You seem to want to love more deeply and personally than you have ever done as a very effective teacher and nun. My guess is that you may have this loving in or out of your Order, as you wish. For as I have looked at you this week, I have seen less and less a representative of the church, and less and less a woman. I have started to think more in terms of life's possibilities and less in terms of its restrictions. If you want to love deeply and closely within the bonds of your vows, you can pray for this and I think you'll get it, though you may have to spend more and more time with children and with trainees who really need you. But if you ask to love a man and have his children, that God may be glorified in this fashion, I think you'll get that. For the God we have been talking about this week is one Who we have said withholds no good thing from those who love His coming. If it is true that He offers Himself unceasingly to us, then He is not first asking, 'What are you doing for My church and My traditions?' He is first asking, 'How alive are you, how whole and how happy?' For nobody can peddle joy who hasn't got it, can he?"

He spoke slowly, looking straight into the face of the nun seated on the floor before the fire near him. She began to weep as he spoke, although she was smiling as the tears ran down her face. Something in the way he had caught hold of her struggle, the way he had put it, had answered to her deepest self. As he finished, she reached over and seized his arm, and for a moment they locked arms, as wrestlers might, or companions on a long journey showing that each would hold the other from fainting or falling. The group was quiet, before the fire. Then a guitarist in the group strummed a little and began to sing, "Puff, the magic dragon, lived by the sea . . ." The song made no sense for the moment at hand, but people laughed and sang it, while somebody passed cokes and potato chips, and the group settled down for the rest of the sharing at hand.

The nun went home and talked her heart out with a fellow Sister, one who was also considering leaving her role as a nun, though also remaining devout and active in the Church. Central for each of them was the man's perspective that God was a God who wanted to give Himself and His fullness of being to His children, in whatever way they sought it, in order to share it with others. The thought became guidance to them in the fullest sense, and they worked out their answers in terms of it. As events unfolded, one stayed in the life of a nun and the other left; when last the writer talked to each, they were both more fully alive and happy than ever before, growing into new ways in their respective spheres.

Had the man by the fire merely given advice? Was he simply projecting his own problems onto the nun? Or was he really looking at her as a person for the first time, free of the hidden spectacles that had divided his world into the things of God and the things not of God? Had his polarizing toward a God who streams into all creation and seeks man's fulfillment over institutional offices, though not apart from them, given him the opening to speak the truth in love to the nun? He was not sure, when he described the tape-recorded event later to the writer, but he noted that he had trembled as he spoke. "Funny," he said, "but although I am a Presbyterian, I think I know where people got the name Quaker, from the quaking and trembling that I felt; it was good, it was great, and

I don't know where it came from, but I felt clean and right and sure of myself, for once."

Had he found an attunement that led him to the surety with which Paul had spoken, when he said so many centuries ago, "Circumcision or uncircumcision, it availeth nothing" unless a man be in Christ? Had he found the direction in which to turn, the polarizing Jerusalem for his soul, so that he could stand secure and offer to a fellow pilgrim guidance as rich as it was simple?

~ FOURTEEN ~
Healing

Edgar Cayce was not following instructions. He had finished the readings sought from him that morning, and now it was time for him to awaken from trance. The phrase he should have used after the last reading was "We are through, for the present." Instead, he had said, "We are through with this reading," which was the usual signal for his wife to give him the instructions for the next one. She leaned over her quietly breathing husband to say, "That is all." He did not respond.

She was eager to give the suggestion for his body to reestablish normal waking patterns of circulation and "nerve forces," and to give the final instruction, "Now, perfectly balanced and perfectly rested, you will wake up." She knew that he had been giving more readings per session than before, spending between three and four hours each day unconscious, instead of the familiar total of an hour to an hour and a half. She feared for his health. He had recently been ill, and he showed the strain of the hundreds of requests for aid arriving daily—requests that had filled his appointment calendar two years ahead. She worried about him, aware that he had predicted he would never see his sons again.

The unconscious man cleared his throat and began to speak. "Now we have the body of M– D–." Mrs. Cayce was startled and looked hastily at the secretary, who was beginning to transcribe the words. They both knew the girl in question, as the daughter of a long-time friend and member of the study group working on *A Search for God*. But neither knew of a request for a reading for the girl, nor did the writer, who also sat there listening.

In the past a reading had been volunteered, on rare occasions, for someone not scheduled for the day, the reason always a crisis. A few times, a reading had even been given before the application arrived but after it had been sent, when medical aid for someone meant life or death. Now here was a reading beginning for a college girl, who they were sure was in good health.

The voice of the unconscious man spoke swiftly, locating the girl in the dormitory room of her college, not far away in Virginia. She had just fallen from the upper bunk in her room and injured her spine. She needed expert medical care of a specified type. Outlining which vertebrae had been inured, and how, the Information went on to recommend exact treatments. Offering assurance that with the proper care the girl would recover without lasting effects, the reading closed, and the voice now came to its accustomed phrase, "We are through for the present."

The secretary hurried out to telephone the girl's mother, who lived nearby in Norfolk. To her surprise, she learned that the mother knew nothing of an accident. Concerned, the mother took down the essential details of the reading and in turn telephoned the college. She found exactly what Cayce had described; her daughter had fallen from a bunk in her room and was in great pain. College health authorities had not yet decided where to take her for hospitalization, and the mother was thankful to be able to give them instructions. Then she packed and drove to the hospital herself, armed with a reading on her daughter's care. Meantime, the Cayces alerted the prayer group of friends and associates, which kept regular times each day for a list of people in need, and the members of the group began at once to intercede for the girl in their prayers.

In time, the girl recovered completely, avoiding the paralysis that was feared.

As happens among good friends, all thoughts were on the girl's recovery. Little attention was given to the role of Edgar Cayce's information in bringing her aid. Given the nature of Cayce's work, as they saw it, why should she not have received a spontaneous reading?

But how had it happened? In what kind of psychic field did Cayce operate, where he could be examining the bodies of others in points as diverse as Alaska and Florida, prescribing medications and physicians from anywhere in the country, and yet simultaneously keeping track of the emergency needs of those close to him? The only explanation offered by his family, who took the unusual reading in stride, was that at some level of his being Cayce was joined to the girl through her mother, who was close to him through her sharing in their search–and–study group. The family had seen before that the bonds of love formed invisible con- nections, over which aid flowed spontaneously when it was critical. If Cayce did not produce a spontaneous reading needed for someone close to him, he might instead dream of the person's need and the answer to it. His own readings had said that everyone keeps track of his loved ones, below the surface, and receives helpful warnings or alertings in dreams or hunches.

Through his medical and psychological readings, Cayce had always been involved in some aspect of healing. This had been the central force of his work since it began years ago in the office of a physician named Al Layne, who had used him for diagnosis of cases under hypnosis. While the final purpose of his work might be felt by Cayce to be something like arousing people to a memory of their true identity as souls before God, as his dreams showed, his means had most often been the relieving of pain. Over the years he had been asked for readings on all sorts of physical suf- fering; each day was marked for him by the hope of helping someone's hurt. It was the focus that Cayce felt kept his feet on the ground, kept his purposes good, and enabled him to handle temptations to notoriety or wealth. Far back in his boyhood, when his unusual experiences first began at age thirteen and he found he could know the content of books by sleeping on them, he had first prayed to be of use like those he had been studying in the Bible—and "especially to children." He had then received an assurance that became the touchstone of his life, a promise that he could help people with their pain.

Yet his abilities in healing were sharply limited. He could diagnose, he could inspect like an x–ray to secure needed medical facts. He could present an entire medical history, including injuries long forgotten by a patient, and he could describe symptoms exactly as they felt to the sick person. He could explain an ailment and its development, step by step, in exact medical terms for an attending physician, if need be. And he could, through his readings, prescribe a complete regimen of treatment, seeming to draw on every major type of resource for healing: drugs, surgery, electrotherapy, diet, exercise, hydrotherapy, manipulative therapy, hypnotherapy, psychotherapy, serums and vaccines, and more. When asked by the proper person, he found that his source was able to describe microorganisms as they appeared under magnification by a microscope, could point to where researchers should seek a new cure for a dreaded disease, could report on cures as swiftly as they were developed anywhere in the medical world, and could lay out a complete theory of physiology. Yet the point at which Edgar Cayce's participation in healing stopped was the actual exchange of energy in what is often called *spiritual healing* or *prayer healing*.

Others had to carry out the medical instructions of the readings. And if someone was called upon to aid another's healing by the laying on of hands or by round-the-clock prayer, it might have to be someone other than Edgar Cayce. He felt that he was not completely without such ability and joined his prayers with others in his little group for healing prayer. But beyond that, his psychic ability to engage in direct healing was limited.

To be sure, he often noted that some energy of his appeared to reach out helpfully to others. He could feel it when he counseled friends and strangers in his study and could even see the changes in their auras. He could feel it when he spoke with all his heart to a lecture audience and sensed their warm response coming back to him. And he could see for himself that his love and care made a difference when a spontaneous reading like the one for the college girl initiated the healing that someone else would finish.

By his sharing in the events of healing, through his voluntary and involuntary psychic abilities, Cayce was touching a stream of claims of healings as old as humankind. From every ancient culture, from every primitive culture have come reports that certain individuals could contribute a special force to aid the recovery of others from disability of body and mind. Some did it by virtue of their office, as was the case with the supposed healing powers of "the emperor's touch" in the days of Rome or the healing aid of anointed priests in Greece, Egypt, and elsewhere. Others made their contribution as a personal gift, perhaps from a vision such as that made famous at Lourdes, or from biographical developments of figures such as Ambrose Worrall, who found their endowment thrust upon them as Cayce had his. The biblical record offered evidence of both types, from the admonition for elders to pray for the sick person and lay their hands upon a person's head, to the startling stories of healing that followed every step of the ministry of Jesus and appeared in the work of his apostles and followers.

What have modern investigators discovered about the question of paranormal ability to affect healing? The subject turns out to be immensely difficult for research. Because nobody yet clearly understands more than broad outlines of how the mind affects the body, all the processes of psychotherapy must be weighed in the search. Dramatic results obtained by hypnosis require that every form of suggestion be considered. Work with LSD and other chemicals affecting consciousness suggests that even small amounts of trigger chemicals or hormones may have large effects, if the individual is properly prepared in her or his attitudes and is helped in a constructive and appealing setting. More promising than working with sick individuals, for careful research purposes, have been attempts to influence the behavior of bacteria or to affect the growth of plants, because the range of variables to study is more limited than in a walking, talking, groaning patient. Yet this research effort to catch specific psychokinetic forces of the mind appears to have its own limitations; for the energies of love—whatever these may be—are likely to be mobilized and released differently toward plants than they are towards humans.

Interest in healing through some form of prayer activity appears to be growing, both of those churches that allow intense emotion in worship and suspend a certain amount of learned doubt, and in the traditional churches of the religious establishment in both the U.S. and Europe. In groups such as the Order of St. Luke and Spiritual Frontiers Fellowship, the interest of clergymen in healing has served as an ecumenical overpass across historic sectarian barriers. Around the world, comparable interests in religious dimensions of healing, especially through prayer, periodically came to the surface in Hassidic Judaism, in Sufi piety, in Bhakti Hinduism. But interest and stable knowledge are not the same, and the day of quality research on such healing seems yet far off.

Especially during the later years of Cayce's work, individuals sought readings on the processes of indirect healing, or healing with nonmedical energies. A group to study and conduct healing was formed as the result of a dream vision, and this group sought and received a long series of technical readings of the processes in healing. Consistently, the Cayce source affirmed that aid could be brought to the normal processes of healing by the resources in prayer and meditation, especially of a group. This aid was not designated as more spiritual in God's eyes than the work of a physician, and no encouragement was given to ignore sound medical practice and counsel—the very business in which most of Cayce's readings were engaged. Yet those who sought to understand nonmedical healing through prayer were told that definite energies and laws were involved, and that there would be times when such aid would be critical in the recovery of a suffering person.

Not every ill person would get well through paranormal healing. Some would die, and that would be their healing, as they came into a state of mind and body where they could enter death without fear. Others would be helped only to face some point within themselves where the distresses of mind and body originated—such as resentment that affected the respiratory system, or anger that affected the liver or stomach, or fear that constricted circulation to the limbs. At that point the individual would have to make choices, take hold of her or his own healing, and even God would not take this privilege away. But always it would be found helpful to surround those in pain with the force that flowed out in honest prayer. The insights and decisions of the sick might be better reached against a prayer background, and at times the very life in the cells would respond where conscious thought could not.

An interest in healing that involved psychic and prayer energies has persisted over the decades among those informed of the Cayce ideas. Seekers after gifts of healing have fasted, meditated, joined hands, tried different times of day and night for intercession, followed the guidance of dreams on how to pray, created a healing field of force through group meditation, kept prayer lists, and tried to correlate beneficial medical procedures with nonmedical procedures. Results have been promising enough to keep the interest alive and growing, especially an interest in the Cayce theory of kundalini and spiritual centers. Yet it has also become clear that many who seek to affect healing do so as a substitute for productive living in some other areas of their lives. People who view themselves as failures may sometimes nominate themselves for special talents in healing, without first undertaking the discipline of bringing their own lives of loving and work into order. But the experiences of suffering has proven no disqualification for healing, for it may sensitize an individual to the point of one choosing the relief of others' pain as an ideal, and out of this ideal talents in healing may grow. Whatever else appears to be critical to the development of effective healing gifts, and meditation would surely be high on the list of relevant factors, the simple matter of caring would seem to some of these seekers to be basic. There has been no sign of a technique that could by-pass real concern for the ill. Healing may rest on loving, as it appeared to do in Cayce's aid to the college girl, and appears to do in effective groups of Alcoholics Anonymous, not to mention groups studying *A Search for God*.

Loving in Creativity

If asked to name the elements of fully human creativity, many would begin by naming loving. Yet the Cayce trance source placed this subject twelfth and last in the first volume of *A Search for God*, in a chapter simply entitled "Love." Only after prosaic beginnings in cooperation, self-study, and other disciplines, accompanied by prayer and meditation and growth in patience and sacrifice, would the full topic of love be taken up. By that time no mere attraction, nor vague good will, nor habitual association, nor mutual exploitation would pass unexamined as love.

Approaching love as a precondition for effective psychic function, and especially for healing, would seem strange only if psychic ability is viewed on a mechanical model. If ESP and PK are merely the response of certain stimulated organs, rather than the matching of complex body-mental states with complex outer events through intermediary forces, then asking about love would be as irrelevant for psychic ability as for asking how a finger perceives or radiates heat. If psychokinesis in particular is merely the focusing of a beam of invisible energy, as one might concentrate sun rays with a magnifying glass, instead of a complex triggering and releasing of healing energies by a strengthening of existent fields of force, then asking about love in healing would be as irrelevant as for asking how an arm pushes. But healing may prove in fact to involve the synchronizing of fields, not only the fields of the healer and the healed, but fields of a divine force and at times of cooperating agents both living and dead. If all these centers of being are involved in healing, then asking about the loving quality of their relationship may be highly pertinent.

Some of the most striking ESP research has shown that people in mutual bonds of affection and respect may make the ideal participants in experiments, even though they are not acting as sender and receiver. Experiments suggest that the presence of a loved schoolteacher acts as some sort of catalyst for the results of certain children on tests, and it is possible that the widely noted differences in results achieved by different ESP experimenters may also be traced to their capacity for genuine mutuality with subjects.

In many fields of creativity the question of the quality of bonds among participants holds the central attention of investigators. Why does the painter fail to transcend mere technical competence so long as the love for his or her teacher is idolatrous love, rather than the regard that frees self to use talents as the teacher used them? Certainly the love needed for a symphony conductor to wring the most from the performers is more than sentimental identification; conductors often have to be fierce and to struggle with musicians to bring forth a creation worthy of their talents. Leadership studies circle around the question of the kind of regard and support that constitute effective, activated love, breeding confidence among participants and trust in their own talents, whether the leader be a football coach, master of a ship, a political reformer, or a salesperson. Each leader must find some way to exert upon others the full force of personal energy and talents and imagination, so that the others respond from their own creativity rather than with simple conformity or rebellion.

When the place of love is examined in the creative problem-solving of marriage and child rearing, the problem grows more difficult to study. Here talent and position count little, and people must find the way to bring out the best in each other without benefit of spotlights and cheering. Battles must often be fought over breakfast tables or in the dead of night, if the divorce court and the juvenile court are to be avoided. Beyond the emotion in loving, beyond the cherished pairings and groupings, beyond the loyalties and identifications, there may lie a fundamental stance that unlocks all sorts of creativity. Martin Buber has suggested such an approach in his postulation of "I-thou" relations as over against "I-it" relations, in humankind's dealings with nature and with created forms, just as in one's dealing with others.

Taking up the question of loving, then, the Cayce source addressed a question central to viewing each individual as co-creator with God and all others. In so doing, the trance source grappled with religious questions centuries old, as individuals have tried to find what is the "apt force" (Gerald Heard's phrase) that they might bring to bear on one another and even on nonhuman creation. It is the question behind the Confucian ideal of uprightness and gentlemanliness, the question in the ecstasies of devotional mystics of India and medieval Catholicism, the question of whole-souled answering to the divine call in Judaism, the question of respect for orderly becoming in Apollonian Greek faith, the question of compassion for all sentient beings in Northern Buddhism, and the question of life-defining totem bonds of African primitives. How can individuals stand with one another so that life will flow between them, spilling over into their works and even into the Nature that supports them?

The Cayce information described love as "the healing, cleansing, blessing force." It was not a social invention, a convenience of relationships, but first of all an attribute of the soul. Indeed it was a force so truly of God that the Cayce source could say of Genesis, "the earth looked good to Love" at creation. As a soul attribute, love was that which enabled humans to "give without asking in return," just as God gives, "pressed down and overflowing" in the vessels of His love.

Such love was not merely emotion, nor interest, nor attachment, but a vital force, capable of changing the energy fields in oneself and other people by "raising the vibrations." It acted as directly as a musical instrument might set another instrument to resounding. This was why group fields of love, whether families or work groups or study groups or even cities and nations, had such potential for good; they could build up a group field of the force of love that was as great as the musical force of a symphony orchestra in perfect tune and rhythm. Those who sought to make love an active, helpful force in the lives of others for their healing, strengthening, or transformation, would not reach their ends by solitary efforts alone, although solitude had its place.

Yet love was not mass enthusiasm, either, for one had to overcome in self whatever one sought to help another overcome, or the individual would simply broadcast personal troubles to another by native ESP under the name of love. The Cayce source was firm that healing of every sort, physical and mental, social and financial, spiritual and aesthetic, had to come about in the one who sought to be helpful, before it could reach its maximum force for another. One had to choose the Creative Forces before finding the key to unlocking these in others. One who sought in love to free others from inward terrors had to work through personal panics; one who sought in love to help another fight disease had to overcome indulgences that lowered disease resistance. Love would be found a powerful force, bringing psychic energies and other energies to bear where they were needed. But love was no magical substitute for growth.

Truly loving others would be linked with one's love and regard for her or his own soul, as a gift from God. While "no man should love himself more highly that he ought," it was also true that false self-effacement or self-belittling or self-condemnation was crippling to the healing and blessing force of love. One had to learn to give thanks as for the fruits of the spirit in the life of another: "Thou shalt love thy neighbor as thyself."

But the key to loving of both the neighbor and the self was not to be found in praise or favors. It was right where Jesus had put it, in the loving of God with all one's mind, heart, strength, and soul. Because love sprang as a force and pattern-giving element from the very Godhead, it was there that each individual must turn to learn how to love. In the view of the Cayce source, this meant "putting on the mind of Christ," turning the whole psyche by sustained choice to attune itself to the ideal found in Christ. Along the channel formed by such attunement, as surely as radio signals on a given frequency, there would come assurances, quickenings, promptings, and even strength and energy, to make love real in one situation after another.

The mind was not to be left out, and there were laws of love, such as forgiveness, just as there were laws of everything else in creation; these laws were to be studied and learned by experimentation and practice. But love was that which could make law effective, make it helpful, make it relevant. Even karma, that seemingly impersonal process of visiting upon an individual exactly what was needed to round out one's understanding of what self had chosen by actions, would be found to reach its maximum effectiveness in love. For "love is law," said the Cayce source, as "law is love." The orderliness of the universe was God's loving gift to man. Part of that very orderliness was that all law moved and swayed under the force of love, becoming an individual's living helper as the impersonal and threatening sea could bear up a craft, properly sailed.

Some souls mistakenly turned away from love toward an artificial righteousness, in the fear that the Creator did not mean for individuals to be happy. But, said the Cayce source, happiness was the very intention of God towards humankind, as seen in the use of the word *blessed* by Jesus. Even *blissful* would not be too strong, as one would find if he or she set about a life of love focused on others. The joy and peace that would follow would not arrive overnight, but as they came, they would be known by the person as transcending all other pleasures. There would be failures; there would be times when love did not reach the one intended; there would be crosses. But even as people knew in their hearts that love given in families was never lost, neither was love lost, which was given anywhere in the family of God, to one's brother (or sister). As the Cayce readings often reminded, "A cup of cold water given in His name will in no wise be forgotten"; this was meant literally enough to indicate that one could risk loving when the cup might be rejected. The love intended was not an ethic of fairness but of God-sized risks that another's soul would respond; such effort was never wasted, though it might take eons to bear full fruit, for fields invisible to senses were built up by true loving, and the very shape of thought forms was permanently changed. The concept of *nation* would mean one thing as a thought form in one age and something else in the next generation, if love were brought to bear as the light of the nation's art.

There was a treasure to be found and shared in love, according to the Cayce source, which would not easily be found elsewhere. In the love of one individual for another, one might discover no less than a clue of the love of God for each soul. To be sure, God's love was there in Nature, as one would find if it was sought. But in becoming a "channel of blessings" each day, one was opening the way for others to find the pearl of great price: the One not far off, and ever ready to respond, even to be known. So the ways of love could afford to be simple, "just being kind," just turning aside to laugh and weep and work with others in the daily walk. Love was like light, ready to slip through the tiniest crack in the day's affairs, and the little things were its home. Celebrated and chosen in the washing of dishes, in the "preferring of another" in auto traffic, in playing with a neighbor's children, in the extra time given to a customer, in a chantey lifted among flagging spirits, love would one day be found strong enough for the test of difficult forgiveness. For "offenses must need come" in the human situation, but "woe unto him who brings them." The One who sought to love, to let her his light shine in the sunlight of a larger purpose where one's light might hardly be noticed, would find an ability to forgive and forgive—seventy times seven. Not because the individual was wise, although wisdom might make forgiving easier. Not because the person was without flaw, "for all have sinned and fallen short of the glory of God." But because forgiveness, the healing of doubt and fear and condemnation, was God's way, and the way in which the soul sang.

Honestly sought, as one might dig a well in a dry land, the flow of love would be found within anyone, for it was there as a fact from the soul. Nothing could separate an individual from it, as the Cayce source often reminded in repeating a telling passage of Paul's in Romans: nothing of principalities or powers, of heights and depths, of life or death—nothing except one's self. Only the choice to turn away, to gamble on lesser creativity rather than the greater, would eclipse the inner sun of love. An individual could choose to build barns and heap up a harvest, or choose to build a kingdom of vassals, or choose harems to satisfy personal appetites, or choose to withdraw from responsibility and to drift. Yet death would quietly end each such solution and set the soul free for a further journey, even as the merciful karmic deaths of ambitions or property or prowess would allow fresh beginnings in this life. The love of God was never far away, ready to help any who sought to make it one's own; it could be found in dreams, it could be found in prayer and meditation, it could be found in dancing and play. It was the birthright of the soul.

What was involved in learning to love, training to carry the golden flow? "Let us consecrate ourselves," began one reading—not tricks of remembering the names of others, no flattery, no gimmicks of manners. One who set out to love was setting out to adore and glorify God, for that was exactly Who dwelt in another, however hidden or covered over. The hearty confessions, the purifying of body and mind, the shared dedications that individuals reserved for their altars were no less proper for the approach to one's fellows, in the little things of daily life—not in pomp but in sincerity; not in rite but in responsiveness; not in dogma but in delight at the very being of another—these were how every one was a priest to another.

Prayer and meditation could keep love's channel open through attunement, while encouraging others and "magnifying the virtues, minimizing the faults" would increase the stream in service, as a spring feeds a river. It was, said the Cayce source, time to begin. For there was a sense in which the present age, despite the promises of God and the way shown by the Elder Brother, was still "a darkened and unregenerate world," in which " the laborers are few." The need and opportunity were great, for the tribulations foretold by Christ of old were coming upon humankind, and the end of an epoch upon earth was being shaped. As love was a reality, a living force, so great was the harm from its absence, the darkness from its eclipse. There was in very fact, in the hearts and experience of men, an "outer darkness" from which even God would not save them forever. So human loneliness and bigotry, sickness and ignorance, hunger and torture were the business of every individual who saw them—"today, now."

Loving and Healing

In the uncertain state of knowledge about healing through prayer, can it be claimed that love may be decisive in freeing that flow of healing?

A psychic who had known much suffering stood looking down at the swollen legs of an old woman. The woman was merry and vital, despite her stumplike legs; she had just served a bountiful meal to the writer and others visiting her home in the country, where the psychic had gone for a rest.

He was weary inside. His efforts to find a niche in modern American society had never quite borne fruit. Two marriages had failed. Men of prominence in business, education, government, entertainment, and the military had come and gone in his life, each promising him aid in developing a foundation for research on abilities such as his, and each in time disappearing. Perhaps the fault was his. Why try any longer? Perhaps he should limit himself to stage and television appearances, and give readings now and then for the rich. He stared at the legs of the old woman seated in front of him and thought his own dark thoughts of how unlovely life can be.

But the old woman teased him. She bantered with him, surprised him, badgered him, pleased him. She was as sly as a child, as supportive as a nurse. The fullness of woman was in her, and she knew it. Cripple or not, she had known how to love and fight with husband, sons, employees; many a man had found he could not hide from her, when she set out to break his dark moods.

The psychic laughed, laughed full and free. Then he looked again at his hostess, and something moved within him. "I just said that to myself," he told the writer later, "I like that old woman; I really do." His heart went out to her, and he felt a prompting he had not felt for years. "I can fix your legs for you," he said. She joked, "What is wrong with my legs? Don't you appreciate my legs?" But she could see he was as serious as he was suddenly free and happy.

He stripped off his coat and bent over her. Others in the room gathered, and speech stopped. All had been stimulated by his messages, his readings, his counsel at one time or another. But nobody there had seen him attempt a healing; he had always said it was too hard, took too much out of him. Now he was evidently praying. Then he began to move his hands. He never touched the legs, which were propped on a footstool; he only ran his hands a few inches above them, in the air, as though stroking away the swollen tissue.

Those who watched expected that the woman might feel a bit better, for she had mentioned how her legs, swollen to unsightly shape for years, often pained her. But nobody was prepared for what happened. For stroke by stroke, the swelling was decreased. It was unbelievable, and the writer remembers saying to himself that it couldn't be done, that it was some sort of animated cartoon he was watching rather than real life.

The psychic was perspiring heavily; the back of his shirt was wet. His face was firm and concentrated but not contorted; he seemed just deeply at work at a job he knew he could do. In a few moments he had finished, and the woman looked at her legs unbelievingly. They were completely normal and shapely. She tried to joke, but she was weak with amazement. The psychic told her exactly how she would have to sleep at night, to keep the legs from swelling again, and what treatments she would have to follow for about two months, to permanently improve the limbs. Then he paced the floor to "cool off," as he often had to do after intense concentration.

Was it hypnosis, the woman's body obeying her own mind under the power of suggestion from the psychic? Was it a force actually going out from the fingers and hands of the psychic to touch and change the very cells of those legs? Or had the real force been there in the laughter and love in the old woman, which unlocked the heart and soul of the psychic and let his own love come through in a burst of helpful energy? At least one who was there thought of the love and trust once in the heart of a sick woman, who only wanted to "touch the hem of the garment" of Jesus in a crowd. But he had felt a force go from him, and he had sought her out, even in the crowd. Was He, too, refreshed by the love she gave Him, that day long ago?

EDGAR CAYCE ON

Religion, Spirituality, and Psychic Experience

By Harmon H. Bro, Ph.D.

Edgar Cayce saw psychic experiences as being related to the spiritual and soul nature of humankind. In fact, the Cayce readings state that psychic ability is a natural by-product of soul growth. For that reason, anyone interested in personal spirituality, religion or psychic phenomena will find this book extremely valuable.

Written by an individual who knew Edgar Cayce personally and had the opportunity to repeatedly see how people's lives where changed by the Cayce work, Harmon Bro draws upon hundreds of Cayce readings on spiritual laws, soul growth and personal trans-formation. Highlighted against basic religious and spiritual principles, the varieties of psychic phenomena demonstrated by Edgar Cayce suddenly come into much clearer perspective. Throughout the discussion, Harmon correlates spiritual laws with examples of psychic phenomena exhibited by Edgar Cayce and others.

People of all faiths should find this information helpful, hopeful and revealing, for it suggests that the nature of the soul is one with potentials and abilities far beyond the physical body.

 **HARMON H. BRO, Ph.D.,** was a psycho-therapist, an educator, a writer, an ordained minister and an inspirational lecturer. He first came to Virginia Beach in 1943 as a young minister, just graduated from the University of Chicago Divinity School. For more than a year, he lived and worked in Edgar Cayce's home and witnessed several hundred readings. That experience enabled him to come to know Cayce's life and work better than most individuals who have written about the Cayce legacy. Eventually, Harmon made Edgar Cayce the topic of his doctoral dissertation and would write several books about the Cayce information, including this one, *Edgar Cayce on Religion, Spirituality, and Psychic Experience.*

Edgar Cayce's A.R.E.

What Is A.R.E.?

The Association for Research and Enlightenment, Inc., (A.R.E.®) was founded in 1931 to research and make available information on psychic development, dreams, holistic health, meditation, and life after death. As an open–membership research organization, the A.R.E. continues to study and publish such information, to initiate research, and to promote conferences, distance learning, and regional events. Edgar Cayce, the most documented psychic of our time, was the moving force in the establishment of A.R.E.

Who Was Edgar Cayce?

Edgar Cayce (1877–1945) was born on a farm near Hopkinsville, Ky. He was an average individual in most respects. Yet, throughout his life, he manifested one of the most remarkable psychic talents of all time. As a young man, he found that he was able to enter into a self–induced trance state, which enabled him to place his mind in contact with an unlimited source of information. While asleep, he could answer questions or give accurate discourses on any topic. These discourses, more than 14,000 in number, were transcribed as he spoke and are called "readings."

Given the name and location of an individual anywhere in the world, he could correctly describe a person's condition and outline a regimen of treatment. The consistent accuracy of his diagnoses and the effectiveness of the treatments he prescribed made him a medical phenomenon, and he came to be called the "father of holistic medicine."

Eventually, the scope of Cayce's readings expanded to include such subjects as world religions, philosophy, psychology, parapsychology, dreams, history, the missing years of Jesus, ancient civilizations, soul growth, psychic development, prophecy, and reincarnation.

A.R.E. Membership

People from all walks of life have discovered meaningful and life–transforming insights through membership in A.R.E. To learn more about Edgar Cayce's A.R.E. and how membership in the A.R.E. can enhance your life, visit our Web site at EdgarCayce.org, or call us toll-free at 800–333-4499.

> **Edgar Cayce's A.R.E.**
> **215 67th Street**
> **Virginia Beach, VA 23451–2061**

EDGARCAYCE.ORG